RELEASED

Social Work and Health Care Policy

As available resources continue to shrink while public needs and expectations remain high, social work professionals in the health care field in the 1980s are beginning to encounter organizational, professional, and personal challenges that seriously affect their ability to meet client needs. This book, which is designed to orient the professional social worker to the policy perimeters that underlie these challenges, presents a detailed examination of the practice, organization, and framing of policies that determine the nature and quality of health care delivery. First identifying problem issues and commenting on social work values, task roles, and policy planning, the book provides discussion of specific policy program areas by leading health policy experts with social work or public health backgrounds.

Social Work and Health Care Policy

Edited by

DOMAN LUM

ALLANHELD, OSMUN PUBLISHERS

ALLANHELD, OSMUN & CO. PUBLISHERS, INC.

Published in the United States of America in 1982
by Allanheld, Osmun & Co. Publishers, Inc.
(A Division of Littlefield, Adams & Company)
81 Adams Drive, Totowa, New Jersey 07512

Library of Congress Cataloging in Publishing Data
Main entry under title:

Social work and health care policy.

   Includes bibliographical references and index.
   1. Medical policy—United States—Congresses.
2. Medical social work—United States—Congresses.
I. Lum, Doman, 1938-   . [DNLM: 1. Social work.
2. Health policy—United States.   3. Insurance, Health—
United States.
RA395.A3S697   362.1'0425'0973   81-68308
ISBN 0-86598-065-9   AACR2
ISBN 0-86598-071-3 (pbk.)

82 83 84 / 10 9 8 7 6 5 4 3 2 1
Printed in the United States of America

To my wife Joyce

my children Lori, Jonathan, Amy, and Matthew

The faculty, staff, and students of
The School of Social Work
California State University, Sacramento

who have been learning resources for this book

CONTENTS

TABLES AND FIGURES

FOREWORD

A social work professional in the field of health care will encounter a number of issues of an organizational, professional, and personal nature that will seriously affect his or her ability to meet client needs of the 1980s. Professor Lum and his associates have provided a helpful volume designed to orient the professional social worker to the policy perimeters that underlie these challenges. *Social Work and Health Care Policy* presents information relevant to the practice, organization, and framing of policies that determine the nature and quality of health care delivery.

The first, and perhaps the most painful, challenge with which the social worker will be dealing in the 1980s is the discrepancy between the available resources and public expectations. This country has been on the verge of some form of national health insurance for more than a decade. Yet this insurance has not arrived, and in a stable or recessionary economy a comprehensive program of health care for all Americans is less likely to arrive. In the 1960s Americans assumed that our seemingly unlimited resources coupled with American ingenuity could solve any problem. Today we find our resources limited. The fuel resources on which we have come to depend are controlled by external forces. Human resources seem harder and harder to marshal for the common good as each individual group seeks its own best interest. Our ability as a nation to gather the financial resources necessary to provide adequate health care coverage to all Americans has come into serious question. What proposals do exist for expanding health care coverage focus on increasingly narrow, although critical, aspects of the financing of health care delivery.

In expanding that boundary between delivery system and client system, the social worker, whether he or she is a planner, an administrator, or a direct service worker, will encounter that conflict between rising expectations and limited resources.

Similarly, the question of who shall be served is one in which the social work profession plays a critical role. New technology has provided us with additional resources for the treatment of serious illnesses, and our citizens are increasingly aware of the potential effect of that technology upon the health care delivery system, whether it means microsurgery to restore a severed limb, heart surgery to restore a productive life, or various therapies aimed at treating degenerative diseases. At the same time, health care policy determines what services will be available to which groups and at what cost. Once again, the social worker is often the professional who stands at the boundary, both poignantly aware of the need that presents itself and constrained by the access perimeters of the current delivery system. An understanding of social policy as it affects the delivery of health care, of the policy development process, and of the role that professionals can play in determining policy at the macro and organizational levels is essential for the social worker if he or she is to carry out a professionally responsible role.

Another situation encountered by the social worker in the health care delivery system, and one to which this volume seems particularly addressed, is the concurrent marginality and centrality of the professional social worker's role in the health care field. The primary task of many institutions is often one in which the social worker plays the central technological role: counseling in a counseling agency, providing emergency supports to a family in a family service agency, etc. This is not so clearly the case in many aspects of the health care delivery system. The health care team, as it is viewed by both consumers and other professionals, consists principally of the physician, the nurse, and perhaps a few other technologists. Professional social work has often stood at the edge of the health care delivery system while providing resources and support for families to enter the system, to fully utilize the resources available within that health care delivery system, and to make the necessary adjustments after health crises in returning to normal social, personal, and family functioning. The core technologies have often been seen as resting with other professions, particularly medicine. This marginality has often made it difficult for social workers to be recognized for the central and critical roles they play in the entire health care process. An ability to articulate the issues that affect the delivery of health care at the local level can be a significant tool for the professional social worker in helping to establish the role of social work in health care policy and practice.

The delivery of health care is becoming recognizably more interdisciplinary, interorganizational, and multi-funded. The social work profession has made a significant contribution toward the creation of a system of delivery in health care — or perhaps at times the false illusion of such a system. As professionals take on more and more leadership responsibility in the delivery of physical and mental health services, the understanding of delivery systems and their interface, the effect of policy on care delivery, and the potential for affecting the quality of care through policy-level interventions, the role of the profession of social work will take on increasing importance in shaping the pattern of care delivery. Professor Lum and his associates provide the reader with a challenging critical analysis of policy development and policy implementation in health care as they relate to the social work profession.

Gregory M. St.L. O'Brien

PREFACE

The crisis in health care has reached grave proportions for millions of Americans who suffer from serious and catastrophic illness, desperation and panic, and the mounting cost of medical care. Such a case was graphically illustrated several years ago when Herbert Gibbaney of Grass Valley, California, offered to sell the cornea of his eye in a local newspaper for $35,000 to pay for medical bills for his wife, Jean. The Gibbaneys' health had deteriorated during the previous two years. Mr. Gibbaney suffered a severe heart attack while he owned and operated a cocktail lounge in Reseda, California. Mrs. Gibbaney ran the business for a while, but soon had to quit. Moreover, it was discovered that Mrs. Gibbaney had several tumors that caused the deterioration of her jaw, requiring a bone and steel replacement.

After moving to a house that once had been a milk shed on a two-and-a-half-acre site, Mrs. Gibbaney was advised that the operation would have to be repeated because the first one had not healed properly. Another complication ensued when Mr. Gibbaney was applying for temporary county welfare assistance and had a second heart attack. Furthermore, following his first heart attack, his health insurance was canceled, but, at 58 and 54 years respectively, Herbert and Jean Gibbaney were too young to qualify for Medicare. Another bind was that a physician declared him totally disabled, which made it difficult for Herbert Gibbaney to find a full-time job.

Living on a $210-per-month Social Security check and a part-time job cleaning up a restaurant for $2 per hour, Gibbaney had been unable to meet his basic living needs. He had spent in excess of $20,000 on his wife's first operation and estimated that the second would cost the same. At the same time, he admitted that he was too stubborn to ask for food stamps from the welfare department.

As a result of widespread publicity, Jean Gibbaney was treated for the deterioration of her jaw by a team of physicians through the Pioneer Community Hospital of Placerville, California, who donated their services. Unfortunately, three weeks later it was disclosed that Jean Gibbaney had cancer of the colon with extensive abdominal spread. Although surgery and chemotherapy were performed and hundreds of letters poured in to the couple from across the country, offering prayers, love, and donations, Mrs. Gibbaney died from her illness less than a month after her story was revealed in the newspapers.

Social workers in health and welfare settings can point to similar, although not perhaps so graphic, case experiences of clients who are caught in medical, financial, and emotional binds. While it is imperative that social workers provide immediate intervention for these persons, their plights reflect the magnitude of health policy and program dilemmas. Health care has captured national attention as a crucial social problem. Concerned with adequate coverage of health services, Americans are willing to accept increased taxes and government intervention in this area, according to a nationwide survey conducted by Pat Caddel, President Carter's national pollster, several years ago. Such a sounding of public interest reflects the growing concern among health consumers for programs and services that will meet their health needs.

Recently the National Association of Social Workers set forth a comprehensive public policy statement on national health for this decade. Social workers in health care recognize the strengths and limitations of the health system in its impact on the lives and health status of Americans. Their practice encompasses relationships between the health system and the social service, educational, and income maintenance. The development of a national health policy requires recognition of its relationship to other social and economic policies. These policies must view each person as a whole being who needs development, sustenance, and productivity and must recognize the fulfillment of individual potential as an expression of the collective responsibility of society. Health, social, and economic national policies must affirm that (1) each person should have a minimum material standard of healthful living and opportunities for educational and social self-fulfillment; (2) each person should be assured equitable access to education, training, employment, housing, transportation, and all public services without regard to race, religion, sex, age, or ethnic status; (3) each person should have available educational and social services, based on the allocation of adequate resources, to support good health and well-being; (4) each person should be protected from commercial encouragement of personal life-styles that are unhealthy, self-destructive, or wasteful of human potential.

Along with these value beliefs, social work is aware of rising health costs that impose the potential for economic catastrophe for a family as well as diverting resources from other human services. Many persons have not received health care because of socioeconomic and geographic inaccessibility. Preventive care, treatment of acute illnesses, and long-term care are obvious areas of need.

The NASW has articulated a policy statement embodying essential principles for national health care. Such a program must cover the entire resident population, insure uniform services for all groups, and provide equal access without separate categories, arrangements, or services. It should offer comprehensive services that maintain optimum health, prevent illness and disability, ameliorate the effects of unavoidable functional incapacities, and provide supportive long-term and terminal care. The primary emphasis must be on prevention of illness and dysfunction and the promotion of health. Health services must be seen in terms of medical, psychological, and social components.

From an organizational and management standpoint, a national framework for policy formulation, funding, and program accountability must allow for decentralized community planning and management and consumer involvement and participation. Delivery systems should reflect variability to meet local needs, continuity and linkage in levels of care, opportunity for choice of plans by consumers, professional provider input (including qualified social workers) into planning and service delivery, and individual and family service needs. The federal government must establish organizational and fiscal standards and assure accountability at the national, state, and local levels. The participation of health care personnel and consumers should be sought in the development of these criteria.

A national health care program must be publicly funded through progressive taxation for long-term stability. The NASW does not advocate partial payment or differential funding for groups. There must be fair and equitable income payment for professional personnel (including qualified social workers) based on cost-funding methods and standards. The payment mechanism should also provide incentives that foster illness-prevention programs and improved delivery systems. Subcontracting should be utilized when services, such as social work, are not available. Cost containment through public regulation is urged to curtail unnecessary expansion, duplication of equipment, and cumbersome procedures. Negotiable rates of reimbursement between providers, payers, and officials should be encouraged. There is particular support for cost-saving integrated health delivery systems such as Health Maintenance Organizations (HMOs).

Standards for professional competence must be set by the professions with consumer and peer review. The purpose of accountability is to improve professional competence, recognize and protect consumer rights, improve the delivery system, and eliminate incompetent and unethical performance. Likewise, attention should be given to health personnel education, training, licensure, and certification. The NASW advocates the development of primary care providers, a variety of educational programs with emphasis on training minorities and women, and separate financing and program assessment. National policy should strive for uniform national licensure and certification standards with regular periodic updating of requirements.

Health-related research and planning are also given attention in this policy statement. Provisions for the discovery of new knowledge and the creation of new technology are vital for improving the health of the American people. Among the major research areas are basic biomedical, psychosocial, and clinical technology; human behavior exploration integrating healthy physical, psychological, and social adaptation; epidemiological research to identify populations at risk; and health management, organization, and technology. National health planning should strive toward developing an adequate, integrated, and efficient health care system, a health-sustaining society and healthy personal life-styles, coordination of services, and resource and manpower distribution to underserved areas and minority groups.

Lastly, a national health policy must advance principles that protect products, services, and human environments. It should develop appropriate education, social support, and life-styles that promote and maintain optimum health (*NASW News*, vol. 25, no. 1, January 1980).

It is significant that this encompassing national health policy statement by the National Association of Social Workers touches on the various themes of this book. In large part, the majority of these components are covered in depth through the introductory and program area sections of this volume.

The focus of this book is on social work and health care policy. The social work mandate in health care is to enhance and improve client social functioning through maximizing physical and social health. Social workers invariably confront health policy and program regulations that affect the lives of their health care clients. Berkman (1978) reported that out of thirteen knowledge-base and program needs, seven areas related to health policy themes: health policy, legislative and regulatory measures, financing of health care as it affects client utilization patterns, intraprofessional and interprofessional collaboration and team practice, legal-ethical issues important to consider in delivery of health care, consultation within the framework of multidisciplinary practice, and consumerism. Therefore it seems appropriate to draw together various educators, administrators, and policy planners who have interest and expertise in social policy issues related to health care. Relevant health policy themes are addressed with program emphasis and implications for social workers.

This book is divided into three parts. Part I provides a basic foundation to health policy from a social work perspective. The definition and problem issues of health policy that form the basis for major programmatic interaction in health care are set forth. Social values and task roles pertaining to social work's contribution in health policy are considered as social workers participate in micro and macro policy situations. A policymaking planning framework is provided that brings together theory and action with health program applications. By the end of the first section, the reader has the essential background to examine more specific program areas with an understanding of problem issues, values, roles, and policy planning.

Beginning with this point of reference for the interaction between social work and health care policy, Part II draws upon the insights and perspectives of leading health policy experts with social work or public health backgrounds. The intent is to update current and selective health policy issues and to reframe them as we begin the decade of the 1980s. While basic health policy history and themes are developing, there is a need to restate strategy approaches to cope with recurring problems. Starting with a panoramic survey of national health policy structure and issues for the 1980s, successive chapters focus on predominant themes in Medicaid, Health Maintenance Organizations, national health planning and resources development, primary health care, long-term care, cost containment, national and state health insurance, and future trends in health policy. Basic history, current analysis, and future directions pertaining to these policy program areas are given, with the anticipation of social work involvement in health policy on local, state, and national levels.

Part III summarizes the various social work and health care policy themes that have recurred in the book. When a single volume has multiple authors, diversity of perspective, style, and emphasis inevitably arise. Each author interprets the parts of the health-care-policy elephant from his or her vantage. At the same time, common themes related to policy programs, critical problems, action roles, and unresolved issues are likely to emerge in the process. This editor is aware of these diverse and similar strands and seeks to bring them together in a systematic fashion. It is hoped that readers of this book will assume the unfinished policy agenda touched on as we cope with the health care problems of this new decade.

As a social work educator, I have had the opportunity to grapple with health policy analysis and program issues. It has been my good fortune to participate in the formation and implementation of a problem-oriented social work and health care curriculum during my years on the faculty of the School of Social Work at California State University, Sacramento. While the CSUS Social Work Health Model is in the process of dynamic development based on faculty and student interaction, I believe that graduates of the health concentration are prepared to enter professional positions related to social work and health as well as to pursue further degrees in public health and public administration. My teaching forced me to search out the literature in these areas, create course outlines with the recognition that more schools of social work have similar offerings, and engage in dialogue with my health concentration colleagues on mutual teaching concerns.

After teaching a health delivery and policy course for five consecutive years without an adequate text, I was aware of the need for an appropriate resource that would link social work with health policy. With the completion of this project, I wish to acknowledge a host of persons who have been helpful in the development of my social work and health care expertise: Jerrold M. Michael, Dean of the University of Hawaii School of Public Health, and the late Herbert H. Aptekar, former Dean of the University of Hawaii School of Social Work, who launched me on my second career in social work and health care delivery and were helpful resources in evaluating my vocational potentials; Arthur Blum, Professor of Social Welfare at Case Western Reserve University, and Gregory M. St. L. O'Brien, Academic Vice-President, University of South Florida, who were stimulating teachers and who provided me with the conceptual and substantive tools to apply to the social work and health care areas; Jesse McClure, former Dean of the School of Social Work, California State University, Sacramento, who invited me to join the faculty and who maintained interest in my teaching, writing, and well-being; John Erlich and Louise Foley, faculty and staff members of the School of Social Work and the Institute for Human Service Management, California State University, Sacramento, who offered valuable criticism and feedback on earlier versions of this book; Nancy Pheil and Marilyn Sue Wentzel, student assistants who spent countless hours typing chapter drafts and working on the references; Maureen McCaustland, social work student, who provided a critical perspective as a reader-consumer to various chapters; Therese Malouf and Autria Egnew, who assisted with the typing and reproduction of earlier versions of the manuscript; my wife, Joyce, and my children, Lori, Jonathan, Amy, and Matthew, who provided the time and understanding for me to pursue the course of this project; and the faculty, staff, and students of the School of Social Work, California State University, Sacramento, who provided a climate for growth and development. Above all, I am deeply grateful to the contributors of this volume, who represent the finest social work and public health experts in health policy across the United States and who willingly participated in this writing venture.

Doman Lum
Sacramento, California

REFERENCES

Berkman, B. "Knowledge base and program needs for effective social work practice in health: a review of the literature." Paper commissioned by the Society for Hospital Social Work Directors of the American Hospital Association. 1978.

PART ONE:

Introduction to Health Care Policy

1

PROBLEM CONTEXT OF HEALTH CARE POLICY

Doman Lum

Health care policy in the 1980s faces an uncertain future marked by an upward-spiraling inflation, an economy moving toward recession, and an austere political climate. As a result, health policy is in a holding pattern with no new major health program implementations (for example, national health insurance) on the horizon.

Present health policy stems from legislative programs passed during the middle 1960s and early 1970s. Medicaid and Medicare, landmark health coverage programs for the poor and elderly, were part of Titles 18 and 19 of the 1965 Social Security Amendments. Health Maintenance Organizations offering a prepaid group practice alternative to a fee-for-service system were funded in 1973. Health Systems Agencies appeared as a result of the 1974 National Health Planning and Resources Development Act. This legislation combined Regional Medical Programs and Comprehensive Health Planning Centers established in 1966. These representative programs established a precedent for future national health structure consisting of coverage for wide populations, group comprehensive practice, and regional planning efforts. To a large extent, when national health insurance becomes an actuality, these elements will be incorporated on a large scale.

In the meantime, a series of health policy statements was issued by the Department of Health, Education, and Welfare. The intent was to integrate these programs into the mainstream of American health policy and to interpret them to the public and private health sectors.

Among the major 1970–76 health policy statements were *Toward a Comprehensive Health Policy for the 1970's,* HEW, May 1971; *Toward a Systematic Analysis of Health Care in the United States, A Report to the Congress,* HEW, HSMHA (Health Services and Mental Health Administration), October 1972; *Forward Plan for Health: FY 1976–80,* HEW, June 1974; and *Forward Plan for Health: FY 1978–82,* HEW, August 1976. Emerging from these policy plans were the identification of health goals, concise analysis of particular delivery programs, specific federal programs, and preparation for national health insurance.

Accompanying these policy blueprints were a number of policy strategies. For example, there was reliance on "reprivatization," in which

3

government utilized the private sector for the purchase of health services, and on pluralism, in which program incentives were used to encourage marketplace competition among health care organizations (Wilson and Myers, 1972). In the interval, health policy economics were refined with the purpose of clarifying price and expenditure differences in medical costs and reassessing supply and demand to medical care price (Fein, 1975). Health service research was applied to national policy needs in terms of management and location of resources, coordination and planning of health services, and theory and methodology development of health policy.

There was an effort to regulate hospital rates by a fixed-growth-increase policy (which would establish a fixed growth 9% per annum increase cap on hospital rates in the USA). The hospital industry vigorously opposed this policy, preferring a voluntary-cost-constraint approach to hospital rates. As a result, there was a reappraisal of available economic goods and resources and political power and influence in the promotion of national health care. A prime example of this was the Carter Administration proposal on national health insurance based on a phasing-in process depending on economic forecasts and political support. But neither cost-containment legislation with mandatory controls in hospital rates nor a national health insurance program has materialized in Congress.

With the rise of the Reagan Administration has come a shift in the roles of the public and private health sectors. There has been an effort toward deregulation of existing health programs (e.g., Health Systems Agencies), as well as toward curbing federal grants for health care delivery systems (e.g., Health Maintenance Organizations). Medicare and Medicaid will probably be revised into a single system of service with coverage for those poor and elderly who cannot afford health care. Uniform employer-employee health plans will have an incentive to select prepaid plans at lower rates and cash rebates for other benefits. The private health sector will have a variety of competitive health plan services for consumers. The emphasis, then, will be on cost-effective programs with adequate, uniform coverage, minimum government regulatory guidelines, and marketplace competition for consumer choice.

One might question, then, the need for a book on health care policy, particularly from a social work perspective, at this time. Perhaps this is an appropriate opportunity to assess present and future directions in health policy as they affect target population groups in need of adequate health care. Moreover, social workers in health care provide particular health-related services such as Medicare and Medicaid and are gatekeepers of a responsive and sensitive health care system for individual and societal needs. With such an investment, social work has a task and program role to play as health policy is shaped for millions of people. Prigmore and Atherton point out that social workers can effect policy change through joint action with interest groups and can shape much of the operational policymaking decisions of agencies (Prigmore and Atherton, 1979). Thus it is important for us to lay a health policy foundation from the social work perspective, explore specific health program policy areas, and raise further arenas of investigation for health policy to pursue in this decade.

DEFINITION OF HEALTH POLICY

What is health policy? Several authorities have attempted to answer this question. Miller believes that health policy is "an understanding of the way society distributes its political power and its economic resources in order to serve the health of its people" (Miller, 1975, p. 1330), Cooper, in his 1976 *Forward Plan for Health* statement, considers national health policy to be a government tactical health plan to help improve the health of the American people through assuring access to high-quality health care at reasonable cost and preventing illness, disease, and accidents (U.S. Department of Health, Education, and Welfare, *Forward Plan for Health: FY 1978–82*).

For our purposes, health policy is the body of stated goals, directions, and guidelines that govern the implementation of programs, activities, and the efforts related to public and/or private health organizations. Accordingly, health policy is an appropriate role for government in consultation with health providers and consumers to achieve desirable social purposes in health care. Among these major health concerns are financial, geographic, and social access for every American to comprehensive health care. Health services should maintain high-quality care, be provided by the public sector, and offer consumers choice among a number of health plans (Enthoven, 1978).

Any definition of health policy must recognize several aspects of policy:

1. *Public policies,* or those policies developed by governmental bodies and officials that are generally purposive or goal-oriented action, courses or pattern of action;
2. *Policy demands,* or those demands or claims made upon public officials by other actors in the political system for action or inaction on a problem;
3. *Policy decisions,* or public official decisions that authorize or give direction and content to public policy actions;
4. *Policy statements,* or the formal expressions or articulations of public policy that indicate the intentions and goals of government and action to realize them;
5. *Policy outputs,* or tangible manifestations of what a government actually does as distinguished from what it says it is going to do;
6. *Policy outcomes,* or the intended or unintended consequences for society from action or inaction by government. (Anderson, 1975)

These dynamics must be considered in an appraisal of health policy. When there is little demand for a change in policy, public policies, statements, and decisions seem to remain in a steady state and policy outcomes consequently are not altered. However, when there is public pressure for policy change, significant repercussions are felt in the health policy decision-making structure.

HEALTH POLICY ISSUES

In order to build momentum for health policy change, we must identify the major issues confronting us. From our perspective, health policy issues are of three major types. Policy entry issues address the entrance barriers to health care that bar various health consumer target groups. Policy service issues occur at the point where treatment and care are given to the patient. Policy monitoring issues reflect the need for external and internal checks and balances over the health system. This section explains various dimensions of these policy issue clusters.

POLICY ENTRY ISSUES

Policy entry issues address such questions as: Where can an individual go for medical care? How much will it cost? What kind of medical coverage is available under his/her particular health plan? These entry-level areas focus specifically on accessibility, medical cost, geographic maldistribution, and other related issues. In particular, social work is concerned with socioeconomic barriers that exclude certain disadvantaged persons and create a discriminatory health care system. Several entry issues are relevant at this point.

ACCESSIBILITY. The issue of accessibility focuses on economic and organizational barriers to health care. From the economic standpoint, an individual's level of income and health insurance coverage dictates the extent of medical services available. At the same time, the degree of organizational accessibility or inaccessibility may create such problems as distant locations of health facilities, the inconvenience of transportation, long waiting periods, and the unavailability of primary care providers in certain geographical areas. Thus, socioeconomic barriers affect the range of available treatment, continuity of care, and deductibles and coinsurance, which discriminate against the poor.

Do disadvantaged people have access to health care? Lu Ann Aday reports that the number of low-income poor seeking short-term physician care has increased. However, the poor may still be at a disadvantage relative to their chronic need for care. According to Aday, between 1963 and 1970, poverty-level people averaged more physician contact per year than moderate-income people. The real point is that the poor used health services at a lower rate than the nonpoor. It is noteworthy that the rate of middle-income-consumer accessibility to physician care declined because of the lack of voluntary private insurance coverage. But public-insured poor without private insurance coverage and a regular source of care suffered the greatest decline. Any discussion of accessibility must recognize these distinctions between rate usage and care coverage (Aday, 1975).

In order to clarify issues of accessibility, Aday and Anderson suggest the following subvariables:

1. the health policy goal of improving access to care through financing, education, manpower, and reorganization programs;

2. accessible arrangements with delivery system resources and organization;

3. different population-at-risk characteristics (e.g., age, economic status, place of residence) affecting the degree of accessibility;

4. the level and pattern of service utilization in a given area;

5. consumer satisfaction with providers in the medical care system.

Health policy decision makers must grapple with these areas as they formulate programs to provide available, obtainable, and comprehensive services (Aday and Anderson, 1975).

MEDICAL COST. The cost of an average hospital stay tripled from $311 (1965) to $1,017 (1975). Similarly, the medical-care-services component of the consumer price index rose 10.3 percent in 1975. During the same year there was a rise in hospital services (13 percent), physician fees (11.8 percent), and drugs and prescriptions (7.4 percent), and total health expenditures under the gross national product increased to 8.3 percent (Council on Wage and Price Stability, 1976).

In order to cope with medical costs, a number of cost control measures have been proposed. Cost containment was the cornerstone of short-range health policy goals in the Carter Administration. H.R. 6575, 95th Congress, contained a hospital-cost-containment program that would have established a 9 percent control rate increase. It was estimated that this would produce an annual savings of $2 billion, which could be transferred to funding new social programs. However, after heavy pressure from medical and hospital lobbying groups, a voluntary approach that allowed hospitals to reduce their operating cost in the aggregate by 2 percent annually for a two-year period was chosen. Other cost-saving proposals have included cutting administration costs of state government health programs in order to provide more community health services (Freedmen, 1975); providing incentive reimbursements to achieve responsible cost control by hospitals themselves (McCarthy, 1975); and settling limits on Medicare hospital charges and physician fees (Council on Wage and Price Stability, 1976).

Several questions regarding medical costs remain unanswered. Can we pinpoint the causes of increased hospital expenses? In an analysis of factors associated with hospital costs, Anderson and May concluded that no single factor is responsible, that any solution will be extremely complex, and that hopes for a painless panacea remain unrealized (Anderson and May, 1972). Do rising costs imply inadequate coverage of the poor and near-poor as well as insufficient outpatient coverage for moderate-income people? Can ambulatory care programs receive sufficient support? Or is there a need for the development of alternative ambulatory care? Blendon believes that medical cost policy must consider cutbacks on nonessential health services, program shifts to cope with hiring freezes, slow and deliberate growth, and careful program evaluation (Blendon, 1976). Certainly these trends are clearly seen in current fiscal health cost control measures.

GEOGRAPHIC MALDISTRIBUTION. Health policy entry is severely affected by the geographic maldistribution of health personnel. Schonfeld, Heston, and Falk reported that at least 133 physicians per 100,000 were necessary to give good primary care. This ratio excluded other services such as dental care, mental health facilities, obstetrics, or routine physical exams for adults (Schonfeld, Heston, and Falk, 1972). The distribution of physicians ranged from 83 per 100,000 in Mississippi to 238 per 100,000 in New

York. Or from another statistical standpoint, there were 173 physicians per 100,000 in urban areas and 80 per 100,000 in rural areas. The maldistribution profile is even more specific in terms of geographic clustering. There were more physicians per capita in the Northeast and West than in the South and the North Central states, and more in coastal regions than in inland areas (Lave, Lave, and Leinhardt, 1975).

Health policies regarding maldistribution have been associated with manpower selection and allocation. For instance, physicians tend to practice near their place of rearing or medical training. They prefer group practice with proximity to urban centers, colleagues, and supporting medical facilities. In light of these findings, spatial distribution policies for physicians have been advocated. Some of the major proposals are the selection of candidates with rural backgrounds for medical schools, the location of new medical schools in nonurban settings, and the establishment of rural group practices. In a national redistribution health policy, medical school graduates might be required to fulfill broad social and professional obligations:

1. a three-year service in rural and inner-city health settings as part of a national service corps in lieu of military service;
2. a rural and inner-city community medicine training phase for all medical interns and residents that would be necessary for board certification;
3. economic incentives in the form of federal education subsidies to medical schools for rural and inner-city medicine programs.

These policy guidelines could emerge from the office of the Health and Human Services Secretary with input from medical school deans, county medical society presidents, and other related parties. Local, state, and federal representatives could establish regional needs and priorities to cope with specific issues related to geographic maldistribution.

Festering beneath the maldistribution problem are social, economic, and political class discrimination and personal professional preferences of medical personnel. How to respect democratic free enterprise and freedom of movement for physicians and still maintain consistent and adequate medical service maintenance on a regional basis is an unanswered question.

POLICY SERVICE ISSUES

Policy service issues speak to the range of health manpower available to staff medical service treatment programs, the extent of preventive and primary care, and the maintenance of quality of care. These service issues form the basis of patient care contact with treatment providers and are at the core of health policy outcomes.

HEALTH MANPOWER. Health manpower is essential to the provision of services. In recent years, there has been a concerted effort to train primary care physicians as well as allied and ancillary health personnel. The intention has been to balance the population's need and demand for medical services and the current supply of physicians (Lave, Lave, and Leinhardt, 1975). At the same time, the emergence of the nurse practitioner and the physician's assistant (Dobmeyer, Sondereggen, and Lowin, 1975) have broadened the range of available health manpower for rural and urban practice.

With the passage of the 1976 Health Professions Education Assistance Act, funds were provided for the education and training of health and allied health professionals and the revision of the National Health Service Corps Program. The aim of the legislation is to improve manpower for urban and rural health services, particularly primary care practitioners. Training funds were provided to educate a variety of health professionals, including health and hospital administrators and health policy analysis and planning personnel.

The question remains whether these manpower program efforts will shift the balance from medical specialization to a variety of medical and allied health practitioners. It is hoped that the federal government will initiate future manpower policy efforts to provide manpower for medically underserved areas.

PRIMARY CARE SERVICES. Primary care functions as an entry, screening, and routing point for the rest of the personal health services. It offers a range of basic health services to preserve health, prevent disease, and care for common illnesses and disabilities. It provides stabilizing human support for patients and families involved in health crises. It also assumes responsibility for continuing management and coordinating personal health services throughout the care process (Parker, 1974). In its broadest sense, primary care encompasses clinical intervention, human support, patient education, community medicine and outreach, transportation, child care, translation, referral, and coordination. It is the first line of defense and a screen to protect hospital specialist services.

Policy incentives need to support primary care programs involving health promotion, disease detection, and self-care. Primary care personnel could instruct patients on the impact of life-style on health, blood pressure testing, breast checks, self-modification of behavior, stress management, and other areas. Primary care is a crucial policy area to insure early detection, treatment, and care; social and behavioral assessment; preventive health; and family planning, nutrition, and other health education areas.

QUALITY OF CARE. Of prime concern among policy service issues is maintaining a standard of care responsive to the medical needs and services satisfaction of health consumers. Criteria for assessing the operation of a health system must be developed. Among the possible criteria are: (1) facilities, equipment, administrative organization, and professional personnel structure; (2) information on the way the system functions (e.g., activities of health professionals in the patient management process); (3) end results (improved health and satisfaction, declaration of health imbalance); (4) medical records of cases (rating medical management of a case by two independent raters); and (5) degree of consumer compliance to follow physician's recommendation.

Crucial to the quality-of-care issue is the type of physician practicing in a medical setting. A University of Michigan quality-of-care survey was conducted on 3,316 hospital discharges by 506 physicians in 16 diagnostic categories from 22 nongovernment short-term general hospitals in Hawaii. The researchers found that medical education and training were the critical factors. Better care was given by medical specialists rather than general practitioners; physicians with longer internships and residencies; physicians who were diplomats or fellows; graduates of medical schools emphasizing teaching and research rather than solely practice; physicians between their sixth and fifteenth years of practice; practitioners in large group practices rather than solo practices; and institutions that controlled physician behavior carefully through medical staff organization (Rhee, 1976).

There are several policy implications for quality of care from this research. Obviously, federal program and funding incentives should be given to coordinated group practices that recruit and retain medical personnel corresponding to the University of Michigan profile. Continuing education of medical physicians could use the general guidelines of the study for ongoing training. Similar research in various geographical regions of the United States may identify different quality-of-care patterns with respect to physicians' backgrounds.

Currently, Professional Standards Review Organizations (PSROs) are in charge of peer review to insure quality of care among physicians. There is a movement to include health consumers in the quality-of-care evaluation process (Helt and Pelikan, 1975). A policy direction might be to increase public involvement in quality of care. The appointment of health consumer representatives on PSRO boards, public disclosure of quality-of-care reviews, and other efforts to enlarge quality-to-care feedback are worthwhile policy directions to consider in this area.

POLICY MONITORING ISSUES

While there has been internal peer review monitoring of medical procedures and practices among physicians, two major external forms of health care policy monitoring are more significant: government regulation procedures governing health programs and consumer participation and involvement in local health agency policy and planning. This section briefly summarizes major issues in both areas.

GOVERNMENT REGULATIONS. Medical practice and organized health care developed historically from a private free-enterprise tradition in the United States. Physicians were medical entrepreneurs loosely related to separate and autonomous hospitals. In light of this history, any major policy move ment toward a nationalization of the health industry is probably unrealistic. Powerful medical and hospital lobbies wage public relations campaigns and are heavy financial contributors to legislators to insure the status of the present health system structure.

In the last fifteen years, government has assumed an active role to insure that adequate care and health protection are granted to all Americans. Health care as an essential public commodity has been declared to be a right. However, the policy debate has involved the diverse views of how to balance government regulation and free-market competition in the health care field. The degree of government regulation in health care is a political issue; opposing groups decry the overinvolvement and intrusion of government and pursue active federal intervention. A number of dynamics influence regulation outcomes on a given policy issue: government bureaucratic politics; interest-group action by those affected by the regulations; the impact of the proposed legislation upon target groups, facilities, and cost measures; and the attitude of the health consumer public.

Assuming that there are increasing government regulations, Krause cites four regulatory choices: incremented consumer protection regulations, centralized federal regulations, nationalization of selected health services, and nationalization of the entire social and economic sector including the human services (Krause, 1975). Certainly we have not reached a critical point where we are ready to nationalize hospital facilities or the entire health industry. Rather, federal and state government has gradually moved into public areas of health concern and brought incremented change based on modification of current health policy while relying on reimbursed private health sector programs.

CONSUMER PARTICIPATION. Although consumer participation has been mandated in the 1973 Health Maintenance Organization Act and the 1974 National Health Planning and Resources Development Act, a sense of ambiguity remains about consumers in health organizations. What are the goal directions for consumers that distinguish them as a major influence in organizational policy? What are the specific roles for consumers on health-related boards? What is the extent of control of consumer representation on a given policymaking body? These questions still plague consumer involvement. Should the basic approach be in the direction of consumer involvement in health education for the general public? (Mushkin, 1974; Wang et al., 1975; Cornacchia, 1976; Gartner and Riesmann, 1976; Haag, 1976). Or should it be the political structural change of the health care system through policy and planning boards (Stratmann et al., 1975; Harrelson and Donovan, 1975; Metsch and Veney, 1976; Christensen and Wertheimer, 1976; Annas, 1975)? What can be done about mandating consumer participation without defining appropriate authority and roles for consumers (Harrelson and Donovan, 1975; O'Brien, 1975)? Should the planning and control of health care be in the hands of members of the medical profession, consumers, or a mix between medical professionals and consumers? (Stratmann et al., 1975) Should consumers who sit on boards represent the community served or be middle-class people who are selected by the health organization receiving funding? These substantive procedural questions have yet to be faced. Certainly the theory advocated and the practice executed in health care consumer participation has been legislatively mandated but the mechanics of implementing the policy has evoked a multiplicity of unanswered questions.

In particular, consumer participation is mandated and accepted as a stipulation for federal funds by participating health institutions. Yet the role of the consumer, criteria for selection, and degree of consumer representation and input on policy development remain unclear and a source of conflict. Short of elaborating on these specifics in federal regulations, there is a need to bridge consumer-participation gaps. It will be necessary to change providers' attitudes toward consumers, train and educate consumers to make sound judgments in health care policies and practices, and define roles and relations between consumers and providers (Metsch and Veney, 1976).

CONCLUSION

We have sought to address the status of health care policy as we begin the 1980s. Although the prospect for significant health policy changes appears nil, it is appropriate for us to appraise present and future trends in health care. A policy definition and problem issues were formulated in order to orient the reader to the health policy field. Policy entry issues speak to the continuing need to minimize access, cost, and maldistribution barriers. Policy service issues identify policy development for expanded health manpower, preventive and primary care efforts, and broader base for determining quality of care. Finally, policy monitoring issues reiterate the function of government regulation and consumer participation to evoke a public perspective.

In the next chapter, we turn our attention to social values and task roles in health policy in light of the problem situation.

REFERENCES

Aday, L. 1975. Economic and non-economic barriers to the use of needed medical services. *Medical Care* 13:447–56.

———, and Anderson, R. 1975. *Access to medical care.* Ann Arbor: Health Administration Press.

Anderson, J. E. 1975. *Public policy-making.* New York: Praeger.

Anderson, R., and May, J. J. 1972. Factors associated with the increasing costs of hospital care. *Annals of the American Academy of Political and Social Science* 399:62–72.

Annas, G. J. 1975. *The rights of hospital patients: the basic ACLU guide to a hospital patient's rights.* New York: Avon.

Blendon, R. J. 1976. The reform of ambulatory care: a financial paradox. *Medical Care* 14:526–34.

Christensen, D. B., and Wertheimer, A. J. 1976. Consumer action in health care. *Public Health Reports* 91:406–11.

Cornacchia, H. J. 1976. *Consumer health.* Saint Louis: Mosby.

Council on Wage and Price Stability, Executive Office of the President. April 1976. *The problem of rising health care,* staff report.

Dobmeyer, T. W.; Sondereggen, L. L.; and Lowin, A. 1975. A report of 1972 survey of physician's assistant training programs. *Medical Care* 13:294–307.

Enthoven, A. 1978. Consumer-choice health plan. *New England Journal of Medicine* 298:650–58, 709–20.

Fein, R. 1975. Some health policy issues: one economist's view. *Public Health Reports* 90:387-92.

Forward plan for health: FY 1978-82. 1976. Washington, D.C.: U.S. Department of Health, Education, and Welfare. Public Health Service.

Freedman, B. 1975. Cost of fragmentation of state government operated health services. *Inquiry* 12:216-27.

Gartner, A., and Riessman, F. 1976. Self-help models and consumer intensive health practice. *American Journal of Public Health* 66:783-86.

Haag, J. H. 1976. *Consumer health: products and services.* Philadelphia: Lea and Febiger.

Harrelson, E. F., and Donovan, K. M. 1975. Consumer responsibility in a prepaid group health plan. *American Journal of Public Health* 65:1077-86.

Helt, E. H., and Pelikan, J. A. 1975. Quality medical care's answer to Madison Avenue. *American Journal of Public Health* 65:284-90.

Krause, E. A. 1975. The political context of health service regulation. *International Journal of Health Services* 5:593-607.

Lave, J. R.; Lave, L. B.; and Leinhardt, S. 1975. Medical manpower models: need, demand and supply. *Inquiry* 12:97-125.

McCarthy, C. 1975. Incentive reimbursement as an impetus to cost containment. *Inquiry* 12:320-29.

Metsch, J. M., and Veney, J. E. 1976. Consumer participation and social accountability. *Medical Care* 14:283-93.

Miller, A. C. 1975. Issues of health policy: local government and the public health. *American Journal of Public Health* 65:1330-34.

Mushkin, S. J., ed. 1974. *Consumer incentives for health care.* New York: Prodist.

O'Brien, D. J. 1975. *Neighborhood organization and interest-group processes.* Princeton, N.J.: Princeton University Press.

Parker, A. E. 1974. The dimensions of primary care: blueprints for change. In S. Andreopoulos, ed., *Primary care: where medicine fails.* New York: John Wiley.

Prigmore, C. S., and Atherton, C. R. 1979. *Social welfare policy: analysis and formulation.* Lexington, Mass.: Heath.

Rhee, S. O. 1976. Factors determining the quality of physician performance in patient care. *Medical Care* 14:733-50.

Schonfeld, H. K.; Heston, J. F.; and Falk, I. S. 1972. Numbers of physicians required for primary medical care. *New England Journal of Medicine* 286:571-76.

Stratmann, W. C.; Block, J. A.; Brown, S. D.; and Rozzi, M. V. 1975. A study of consumer attitudes about health care: the control, cost, and financing of health services. *Medical Care* 13:659-68.

Wang, V. L.; Reiter, H.; Lentz, G. A.; and Whaples, G. C. 1975. An approach to consumer-patient activation in health maintenance. *Public Health Reports* 90: 449-54.

Wilson, V. E., and Myers, B. A. 1972. Health care policy issues in the 1970s. *Health Services Reports* 87:879-85.

2

SOCIAL VALUES AND TASK ROLES IN HEALTH POLICY

Doman Lum

In the preceding chapter a number of policy issues were presented as a starting point for investigation. Problem identification in health policy leads to the formulation of social values and task roles, which can serve as guidelines for policy action. Values influence how policy problems are framed and interpreted and what policy goals are formulated. Task roles delineate potential policy areas for functions and assignments.

Workers in community medicine, health policy and planning, nursing, and social work have increasingly recognized the importance of individual and community well-being and functioning. In particular, social work has been concerned with how health policy programs affect the function and dysfunction of people in the health care system.

As a professional discipline, social work offers a value perspective that advocates the well-being of persons coping with social problems. Necessary to the selection of a policy choice are the identification of values and the development of value criteria. According to Rokeach, a *value* is a belief that a mode of conduct or end state is preferable to an opposite or converse one (Rokeach, 1973). Building value criteria is the objective of this chapter. It requires making choices that are consistent with social work values and useful in the development of health policy. Along with a discussion of social values is the need to identify task roles in health policy. Social workers have functioned in behavior-change, consultation, advocacy, policy-planning, and administrative roles. Within the policy dimension, social workers perform policy-analysis, formulation, and program–planning functions with community and social task roles. In the second half of this chapter, various policy-related roles for social workers are given as a means of expanding health policy dimensions.

VALUE CRITERIA FOR HEALTH POLICY

Establishing value criteria for health policy involves the delineation of choice principles. Prigmore and Atherton list social work values and societal values as part of their policy analysis and formulation framework (Prigmore and Atherton, 1979). In this section, we will identify a set of values which are compatible with social work and which are applicable to health policy value criteria.

THE PROVISION OF ADEQUATE HEALTH CARE RESOURCES. The development of material and life-sustaining resources, goods, and services is of primary concern for health policy. The task of government is to assure that persons have access to qualified health plans that include adequate inpatient and outpatient services. This goal presupposes the existence of sufficient hospital facilities, medical and allied health manpower, equipment and material, and service coverage.

THE INDIVIDUAL RIGHT TO HEALTH SERVICES. Distributive justice requires that we promote equity in health care treatment consonant with the dignity of the human person. This health policy value opposes professional practices and institutional arrangements that are repressive to poor persons and subservient to vested profit-making interests. Its intent is to maximize the health care of the least advantaged with fairness and equal opportunity.

THE HUMANIZATION OF THE HEALTH CARE SYSTEM. According to this humanistic value, patients are unique and whole persons inherently worthy of provider care and concern. Shindell, Salloway, and Oberembt raise four human-oriented questions which support this policy value: What is the concern that bring this person in contact with the health care system? What is the impact of the person, his health concerns, and his disease upon his family? What community resources are available to deal with the specific concerns of the patient and the problems? What can be done to anticipate and to prevent future problems? (Shindell, Salloway, and Oberembt, 1976). Social concern for patients in the health system points to a humanization effort.

THE RESPONSIBILITY OF THE INDIVIDUAL FOR HIS/HER HEALTH MAINTENANCE. This policy value involves health promotion. Anne R. and Herman M. Somers state that responsibility for personal health rests with the individual—not with the government, physicians, hospitals, or third-party financing programs. Meaningful health policy programs should increase the individual's sense of responsibility for his/her own health. Concurrently, however, there must also be policy programs that insure environmental protection and health information about body care and health maintenance resources. (Somers and Somers, 1977).

THE FOCUS ON THE PERSON AND HIS/HER ENVIRONMENTAL SYSTEM. This policy value recognizes the importance of the interaction between the individual's health and community/environmental factors. Crises and stress have an effect on the physical, mental, and emotional condition of a person. Health policy in this area emphasizes primary prevention, treatment employing natural and professional support systems, and other psychosocial health measures.

These policy values speak about a health system that has adequate resources, universal access, human-centered focus, and a psychosocial perspective. In turn, a person interacts with the various health providers and assumes responsibility for his/her health maintenance.

While many health policymakers and service providers may subscribe to these values, a primary question remains: How does one integrate these values into policy decision making and program formulation and implementation? In the next section of this chapter, we will formulate various policy task roles for social workers who are involved in health policy situations.

HEALTH POLICY TASK ROLES

Social work arose during the middle nineteenth century from a social reform movement that sought to improve the welfare of deprived and oppressed groups. Individuals and families under stress were assisted by friendly home visitors who provided practical and individualized services (Bartlett, 1970). The history of early social welfare witnessed social reformers crusading against the appalling conditions of the almshouses where the homeless poor resided. At the turn of the century in England, Charles Loch, secretary of the London Charity Organization Society, worked with physicians and referred patients from his organization to hospitals and clinics. Hospital almoners reviewed applicants to hospital clinics that offered free treatment.

Modern social work in health care retains its social and health care contact with people. However, it has broadened its role to include various dimensions of health policy. Bracht describes four social work and health care objectives: (1) the enhancement of the problem-solving capacities of people with regard to the social aspects of illness, disability, and recovery in comprehensive health care programs; (2) the increase of accessibility into the health system; (3) the promotion of effective and humane health systems; and (4) the analysis and improvement of social policy and program development as they pertain to health care (Bracht, 1978). These task mandates are illustrated in the various work settings of health care social workers. Out of 40,000 social workers employed in health care, over 16,500 administer various aspects of the Medicare program in hospitals, 2,700 are employed in extended care facilities, and 2,600 are in the Veterans Administration Hospital System. These workers are involved in contact with patients with socially related medical problems, Medicare and Medicaid application and procedure, long-term and home health care programs, and other service delivery matters. Policy formulation, program regulations and specifications, and policy changes affect how social workers interpret regulations and relate them to their health patient-clients.

It is interesting to note that the World Health Organization International Collaborative Study on Medical Care Utilization views health care as an essential social service (Kohn and White, 1976). Traditionally, social services have been entrusted to the social work profession, which has an investment in the social aspects of health care. Elsewhere Blum argues that health and medical care are moving toward issues related to social policy and social planning rather than medicine and the biological sciences (Blum,

1976). Social work education with health care emphasis generally offers social policy, planning, and administration courses in a health problem context. Thus social work and health care services and policy are merging together as important components of the human services.

TASK ROLE AREAS

We have established a case for social workers in health care policy in light of social work and health related objectives, work settings, and social trends in the health field. Among the appropriate roles for social workers in health policy are:

MICRO-LEVEL POLICY PARTICIPANTS IN HOSPITALS AND HEALTH ORGANIZATIONS. Social workers represent a vital voice in organizational management and policy planning within a hospital health system. They participate on various standing committees that affect the policy operations of the hospital. Nacman is particularly aware of the need for policy participation on this level. He cites a number of changes in hospitals: (1) organizational change due to institutional survival; (2) the impact of external pressure groups upon hospitals with respect to patient rights and efficient operations; and (3) the state of flux existing in the internal power structure of the hospital (Nacman, 1975–76). These dynamic trends are the ingredients for gradual and major changes in hospital health care. Policy making committees and groups often respond to external and internal changes.

Hospital administrators are particularly sensitive to the need for communication between the hospital and the community. Social workers in hospitals need to build professional credibility and trust with hospital administrators, medical staff, and other personnel. Social workers are adept with skills in community outreach, analysis of patient target populations, and group process. They are natural choices to organize and coordinate a community consumer advisory board for a hospital. This communication vehicle serves as a filter for community input into the policy committee body of a health organization. It is a means of dealing with the issues of institutional survival, pressure groups, and internal power raised earlier in this section.

POLICY ADVOCATES FOR SPECIAL HEALTH CONSTITUENT GROUPS. Social workers play a wider policy role in society as social advocates for particular health constituencies.

Among these target groups are the economically deprived and minorities in metropolitan inner cities and other medically underserved areas. Poor and minority people make fewer visits to physicians; most of their medical care is received at hospital clinics and emergency services. They have high hospital admissions for longer stays because of chronic, untreated conditions. Their health care is piecemeal and fragmented. As a result, they have high mortality, morbidity, disability, and impairment rates.

The elderly often cope with feelings of not being wanted or needed, which contribute to mental health problems. They may be geographically isolated in deteriorating inner-city neighborhoods, far from public transportation routes, undernourished, and nonambulatory. Minority elderly, particularlynon-English-speaking and recent immigrants, have further language and acculturation problems besides the usual dilemmas of old age.

The women's health movement in the United States has also identified health issues related to alternative treatment and operation-related decision making, alternative forms of childbirth, discrimination against women workers in the health field, and other themes. Poor and minority women with unwanted pregnancies are especially caught in the middle of public abortion policies and related legislation limiting abortions under Medicaid.

These target constituents are affected by health policy decisions made on the legislative level, translated into public regulations, and integrated in local public health settings. As service providers, social workers are in contact with these population groups. How service policies are understood, interpreted, and administered are often the responsibilities of social workers in health agencies. Social advocacy is securing the widest range of health services for the client under the limits of policy regulations. In many instances it means advocating an exception to the stated policy or organizing to change regulations that are harmful to the well-being of clients.

MACRO-LEVEL POLICY RESOURCES IN THE LEGISLATIVE ARENA. Social work graduate education is preparing professional social workers to assume macro-level policy positions. Perretz reported that 37 schools of social work offered courses on health and medical care systems while forty had policy-method curriculum emphasizing health and social work (Perretz, 1976). These classes cover federal/state policy, legislative political process, Medicare/Medicaid, Health Maintenance Organizations, health planning, cost containment, national health insurance, and other policy program areas. A 1974 joint National Institute of Mental Health/Council on Social Work Education study revealed that out of 16,590 full-time social work students, nearly 6,000 were in health and mental health field placements.

As a result, social workers are in policy-level positions as legislative administrative aides, legislative researchers, and directors of state commissions and in administrative branches of health and welfare departments. As legislative policy resource persons, they are responsible for legislative bill research, information background, formulation, tracking, and following. As administrative staff on a major subcommittee, social work resource persons write legislative reports in selective areas, prepare for numerous subcommittee hearings, perform behind-the-scenes work for key legislators on the subcommittee, and train and supervise interns assigned to the subcommittee.

In many instances, policy legislation introduced and passed in state legislatures has been framed preliminarily by persons with a social work background. Social workers have been a vital link in translating policy into legislation that affects the lives of millions who are health and human services recipients. These health-related bills embody social values and provisions that, it is hoped, will prove beneficial to the neediest in society.

PARTICIPANTS IN POLICY POSITION STATEMENT. Professional interest groups on the national and state levels generally take policy positions on major issues concerning themselves. In the field of social work, the National Association of Social Workers and the Society of Hospital Social Work Directors of the American Hospital Association have been in the forefront of health-related policy position stances for the profession. An example was the 1977 position paper on national health insurance for state level NASW chapter and committee discussion, staff, and legislative committee hearings.

In 1975 and 1977 the Delegate Assembly of the National Association of Social Workers adopted a policy statement on health that was updated in 1980. Thompson R. Fulton wrote a 1977 policy position paper entitled "National Health Insurance: An Overview of the Major Issues for Social Work." The Fulton study is a policy analysis of the background, policy dynamics, and major components of national health insurance. It advocates universal and comprehensive health care available at reasonable cost to everyone in the United States with minimized financial, racial, clinic, sexual, and geographic barriers. Financing should be progressive in terms of taxes, premiums, and patient direct payments. There must be no separate plan for the poor. The role of federal government is to assure high-quality care at reasonable cost, equitable access without barriers, and accountability for expended funds. Better methods of payments to health providers must be devised, tested, and proved reasonably effective. State governments should not assume national health insurance responsibilities other than participation in health planning and resource development. Numerous social work policy roles are defined, such as policy analyst, consultant, and planner; health systems agency board member; health or mental health clinic administrator; and other holistic and human need perspectives. The private health care industry is recognized as service providers and insurers of voluntary coverage supplementary to the national health insurance program. Consumer participation provision is made in policy development and administration on national, regional, state, and local levels. Funding is recommended for resource development and distribution and for health care planning and research. Finally, a specific and detailed phase-in strategy is outlined (Fulton, 1977).

These eleven courses of action were complete with discussion of issues under each major theme. This policy analysis position paper represents an information and policy document for educating social workers as well as organizing for political action. It reminds us that issues must be laid out, examined, and debated before there is consensus on political organizing and action in the health arena with a social concerns perspective. Social workers in health care must assume this policy task role as they identify other major health care issues.

POLICY ASSESSMENT CRITICS OF CURRENT HEALTH LEGISLATIVE PROGRAMS. A perspective on current health legislative programs is crucial if social workers in health care policy are to assume creative leadership, offer innovative suggestions, and participate in health policy change. Related to this is the monitoring of health service programs and the identification of political and social intervention points to improve existing health care operations.

A major concern is the overhauling of Medicare and Medicaid legislative policy. As a part of the 1965 Social Security Amendments, Title 18 established the Medicare program for persons age 65 and over, while Title 19 provided Medicaid for low-income persons with health needs. Medicare was based on income redistribution for the elderly from prior Social Security contributions by the beneficiary. It administered a uniform set of benefits — incremental coverage of hospital and outpatient care after an initial fixed payment with deductibles and copayments. Medicare policies are centralized by the federal government. In contrast, Medicaid was built on the welfare model of transfer of payments. Medicaid recipients must declare economic need and are subject to varying health service benefits from state to state. States voluntarily elected to participate in the program and established their own medical assistance eligibility criteria.

The result was a two-tier treatment for the elderly and the poor. Medicare was bestowed on the elderly because they had earned these rights based on their years of gainful employment. Medicaid recipients were victims of their economic condition, and they were subjected to eligibility, service, and cost-control restrictions (Newman, 1972; Stevens and Stevens, 1974).

After a decade and a half of a double-standard system, it is time to revise health care legislation for the elderly and the poor. Medicare and Medicaid have been given ample time for learning and shaping a prototype for national health coverage. Medical cost, physician participation, and reimbursement procedures remain major problems. Short of the passage of national health insurance, the federal government should guarantee uniform, equitable, and comprehensive health services for the poor and the elderly. State variation in benefits should cease along with the means test for Medicaid eligibility.

A related program, Health Maintenance Organizations, was enacted in 1973, partly as a cost-control and saving mechanism to contain the rampant health cost of Medicare and Medicaid. As an alternative to fee-for-service, prepaid group practice offers a structural rearrangement that provides comprehensive health services on a monthly or quarterly fixed rate. Utilization and cost evaluation studies favor HMO economies of cost or demonstrate comparable cost to other service alternatives (Perkoff, Kahn, and Mackie, 1974; Freeborn et al., 1977; Berki, 1977). The intent of the 1973 HMO Act was to demonstrate, on an experimental basis, the validity of the prepaid group concept on a national scale. A seven-year period has passed for the evaluation of its operation, particularly service delivery and cost-saving effectiveness.

We believe that there should be funding for the future expansion of the HMO delivery system. Initial development results may indicate that a particular HMO model (e.g., the Kaiser-Permanente prepaid group practice) has fulfilled the goals of the legislation. Further appropriations may be contingent on the expansion of selected HMO types. In this sense, the development of the HMO network is a major component in health delivery. As

McNeil and Schlenker observed: "The most massive intervention in the health care marketplace yet attempted appears imminent in the form of national health insurance. This intervention presents tremendous potential for either improving or crippling effective competition in health care delivery. The uniform application to all health care insurers and providers of many of the provisions now applied solely to HMO's under the HMO Act would do much to promote effective and beneficial competition" (McNeil and Schlenker, 1975, p. 224).

Another step toward a public approach to coordinated health planning on a regional level has been the National Health Planning and Resources Development Act of 1974. This law combined the former roles of Regional Medical Programs and Comprehensive Health Planning Centers. Local Health Systems Agencies now review federally funded applications for area health programs and regional planning of health services. State Health Planning and Development Agencies formulate state health plans, conduct state health planning activities, and review existing and new institutional health services. State Health Coordinating Councils with a consumer majority advise the state agency in state health planning functions and review budgets and applications of Health Systems Agencies. Finally, the National Council for Health Policy develops National Health Planning Policy guidelines based on national health priorities in P.L. 93-641.

In brief, the 1974 legislation is a major step toward shaping local consensus on health policy and planning. The results are informed health system choices and coordinated health care within a given area. Health Systems Agencies should be maintained to provide strong regional authority for coordinated health planning. These planning bodies are in a strategic position to effect uniform and balanced distribution of services.

CONCLUSION

We have identified a set of social values for health policy: adequate health resources, humanistic health care, self-responsibility for health maintenance, and psychosocial perspective. These values, congruent with the social work profession, were translated into task roles in health policy. Among the task areas were policy participation in health organizational settings, policy advocacy for health constituent groups, legislative program policy, policy position statements for interest groups, and current health legislative program assessment. With these value and role perspectives in mind, we turn to the specifics of the policymaking process in health care. Here values and tasks are translated into concrete health policy program outcomes.

REFERENCES

Bartlett, H. M. 1970. *Some aspects of social casework in a medical setting*. Chicago: American Association of Medical Social Workers.

Berki, S. E. 1977. Enrollment choice in a multi-HMO setting: the roles of health risk, financial vulnerability, and access to care. *Medical Care* 15:95–114.

Blum, H. L. 1976. *Expanding health care horizons from a general systems concept of health to a national health policy.* Oakland, Calif.: Third Party Associates.

Bracht, N. F. 1978. *Social work in health care: a guide to professional practice.* New York: Haworth.

Freeborn, D. K.; Pope, C. R.; Davis, M. A.; and Mullooly, J. P. 1977. Health status, socioeconomic status, and utilization of outpatient services for members of a prepaid group practice. *Medical Care* 15:115–28.

Fulton, T. R. 1977. *National health insurance: an overview of the major issues for social work.* Mimeographed paper, 1–73.

Kohn, R., and White, K. L., eds. *Health care: an international study.* London: Oxford University. 1975.

McNeil, R., Jr., and Schlenker, R. E. 1975. HMOS competition and government. *Milbank Memorial Fund Quarterly* 53:195–224.

Nacman, M. 1975–76. A systems approach to the provision of social work services in health settings, part two. *Social Work in Health Care* 1:133–43.

Newman, H. N. 1972. Medicine and Medicaid. *Annals of the American Academy of Political and Social Science* 399:114–24.

Perkoff, G. T.; Kahn, L.; and Haas, P. J. 1976. The effects of an experimental prepaid group practice on medical care utilization and costs. *Medical Care* 14:432–49.

Perkoff, G. T.; Kahn, L.; and Mackie, A. 1974. Medical care utilization in an experimental prepaid group practice model in a university medical center. *Medical Care* 12:471–85.

Perretz, E. A. 1976. Social work education for the field of health: a report of findings from a survey of curricula. *Social Work in Health Care* 1:357–65.

Pineault, R. 1976. The effect of prepaid group practice on physicians' utilization behavior. *Medical Care* 14:121–36.

Prigmore, C., and Atherton, C. R. 1979. *Social welfare policy: analysis and formulation.* Lexington, Mass.: Heath.

Rokeach, M. 1973. *The nature of human values.* New York: Free Press.

Shindell, S.; Salloway, J. C.; and Oberembt, C. M. 1976. *A coursebook in health care delivery.* New York: Appleton-Century-Crofts.

Somers, A. R., and Somers, H. M. 1977. A proposed framework for health and health care policies. *Inquiry* 14:115–70.

Stevens, R., and Stevens, R. 1974. *Welfare medicine in America: a case study of Medicaid.* New York: Free Press.

3

HEALTH POLICYMAKING
FRAMEWORK

Doman Lum

We have set forth a range of policy problem issues, value criteria, and task roles as a basis for the health policy area. Our present aim is to build on this framework. A number of policymaking characteristics are crucial to understanding the social dimensions of health policy. First, a policy framework should be prospective rather than retrospective. Many works of policy analysis concentrate on developmental history and current policy program without any understanding of the present policy situation or recommendation for the future. Policymaking requires a forward-looking approach that raises the horizons of policymakers and recipients.

Furthermore, a policy and legislative program linkage must be established that traces the initial policy position to the final legislative program version. What was the original proposal? What were the crucial forces and events that affected and modified the policy? Was the policy program outcome congruent with the original position? What future proposals are required to fulfill the intent of policy goals or objectives? Or have these goals been reshaped by the introduction of later political, social, or economic factors?

A policy framework should also focus on social change. What social effects do the policy and resulting legislative program have on a particular target population or critical area? What are the roles of effective social change agents in a particular policy area?

Moreover, a policy goal should be assessed in terms of its achievement within a given time period. For example, to what extent can a particular policy goal be achieved in the next five to ten years? What specific legislative programs are necessary to implement the goal? What are the given circumstances and conditions that would make fulfillment possible?

Health policy is articulated through public policy positions that are translated into legislative programs. Presidential and congressional leadership in health care, public and private interest groups, and the political and economic situation influence and affect health legislative outcome. Federal health legislation embodies goal priorities, program policies, and regulations that set forth the intent of the law. Accompanying funding incentives usually induce the participation of the private health sector and compliance with the terms of the legislative program. As a result, application proposals are written on the local level and sent for review, approval, and funding at the national level. State departments of health are liaisons between federal officials and local health participants and assist with the implementation of national health programs on regional, county, and local levels. Implicit to these principles is the need to order these procedures.

The following generic framework is a guide to policymaking that systematizes policy planning principles. It presupposes that present health programs require periodic reassessment and that health policy goals and priorities must be reframed based on current needs and situational problems.

CONTEXTUAL SITUATION

Policy is not created and formed in a vacuum. It is, rather, shaped by a contextual situation consisting of interactional events, actors, and institutional settings. Together they influence the course and context of a policy program. The situational environment is a major influence on policymaking. From a systems perspective, public policy is a response of a political system to demands from the environment. Inputs to the system consist of demands from key individuals and groups that affect the political system and call for action to satisfy their needs and interests. Public policy is the result of group struggle or the equilibrium between the influence of groups and compromises balancing out divergent interests. Groups with influence move policy. Community organization skills in social work are based on the assumption that group influence can affect policy directions.

Related to environmental group demand is an understanding of decision-making centers. We are talking about actors in policymaking with power to make legal and sanctioned decisions. On a micro level, decision-making powers are vested in an executive officer or board of trustees in an organization. From a macro perspective, the power and influence of the executive set the course and content for policy directives and legislative program proposals. Legislators conduct hearings, consider varying viewpoints, and vote on legislative programs, which are rejected or enacted into law. Courts and judges render legal decisions through their interpretation of policy legislation and related issues. These centers for decision making are separate entities, but they utilize persuasion and negotiation, formal and informal cooperation, adjustment and adaptation, and other tactical strategies. They are the policy actors who participate in the process and who are affected by political realities that impinge upon policy decisions. The behavior patterns of these actors are played out over a time period in a policy issue.

These forces are basic to an understanding of the political development leading up to a policy position under investigation. It is important, then, to trace how a particular policy originated and the evolution of major events and ideas. Grumm focuses on factors such as "analysis of the behavior of the authorities; or of the cohesion of authorities in professing the policies; or one could examine the legislative history of a policy, read the hearings and debates and try to determine the basic reasons why the policy was adopted and what compromises had been made along the way" (Grumm, 1975, pp. 442, 443).

Health care policy is a steady state as we begin the 1980s. There is no public furor over universal and comprehensive health care with massive Washington, D.C., marches or public takeover of community hospitals; no physicians or public health officials are held at gunpoint by irate health consumers. Rather, health policy has moved incrementally to stem the rising cost of Medicaid and Medicare through revised regulations, accountability monitoring, and an alternative group practice pilot program. Likewise, hospital costs have been dealt with by regional planning and the threat of an imposed federal mandatory ceiling. National health insurance has been shelved by a fluctuating economy and an uncertain political climate. In the meantime, we are fine-tuning the existing health care system through health prevention and promotion programs, quality-of-care assurance, and support for academic and research medical institutions (*Forward Plan for Health: FY 1978-82*, 1976). The crucial question is: Can we mobilize sufficient momentum to create demand from the environment that will affect the decision-making centers for significant health policy movement?

PROBLEM STATEMENT

In chapter 1, various policy problems were identified as recurring themes in health policy. A particular policy problem must be of sufficient importance to move people to action. Problems must be brought to public awareness. They must have a broad consciousness-raising effect on the majority of the population. Publicizing problem issues is a strategy to get the problem(s) on local, regional, and national agendas. When a particular set of events or conditions of a significant magnitude occurs around a major health issue, there is a probability for policy action (Anderson, 1975).

Arising from its climate is the need to narrow the problem down to a concise and manageable statement. Pinpointing the institutions, events, persons, and forces that contribute to the problem sharpens the focus. The specific policy problem statement is essential at this point.

Since the advent of Medicaid and Medicare, the primary health policy problem has been rising medical costs. In 1965, national health expenditures were $38.9 billion, but by 1975, they were almost $118.5 billion. Major contributors to the rise in costs were inflation, increased utilization of services, quality-of-care improvements, and new developments in medical equipment, drugs, and treatment methods (*Forward Plan for Health: FY 1978-82*, 1976).

Recent attention has also been devoted to the problem of accessibility to health services. Major research and policy studies appeared (Aday and Anderson, 1975; Lewis, Fein, and Mechanic, 1976). Casting the spotlight on accessibility highlighted social barriers rather than economic and fiscal ones; it also reinforced the need to deal with social values related to financial equity, adequacy of resources, and manpower/facilities redistribution.

ALTERNATIVE FORMULATIONS

Once the policy problem has been determined, the task is to formulate a range of policy alternatives to cope with the problem. Policy alternatives are designed to plot a number of courses of action. Who are the actors involved in the policy formulation process? On a micro level, it may be a staff, consultant, director, or coalition. At the macro, particularly the national, level, the President and his chief advisers have been the major source of developing policy proposals.

Recommendations and consultations are sought among the appropriate cabinet department secretaries and their staffs, key members of Congress, influential members of Senate and House subcommittees, and leading national authorities. Congress itself generates its own policy alternatives. Through congressional hearings and investigations as well as final reports, policy position papers are written and used to formulate major legislation. Special interest groups influence policy formulation through contact, persuasion, and public hearing testimony. These groups work with members of Congress and the President's staff to draft and enact legislation favorable to their position. A variety of proposals compete for support among decision-making bodies and influential members.

Behind the concept of policy alternative formulations is the belief that policy is the choice about future events. A prospective view of policy formulation stresses critical choices based on forecasting. As Brewer explains: "The central questions are, who is currently making choices about the problems under consideration? How are those choices made? And under what circumstances might they be improved?" (Brewer and Brunner, 1975, p. 442). Likewise, the choice of goals and situational constraints often limit the range of policy alternatives available. Brewer and Brunner state: "Without public policy alternatives, there can be no choice of solutions. Without goals, there exists no basis for ordering or choosing among possible alternatives. Characterizations of past events and possible future events in terms of goals are necessary to estimate the significance of a given problem with respect to others. Lacking such an estimate, the allocation of attention to the problem may be diversionary. Information about conditioning factors is necessary to estimate the future consequences of alternative courses of action. Without warranted knowledge of conditioning factors, policy is likely to be inefficient at best and counter-productive or utopian at worst" (Brewer and Brunner, 1975, pp. 3, 4).

The Tactical Plan of the Public Health Service for 1978–82 revolves around the goal of improving the health of Americans and the objectives of accessibility to high-quality care at reasonable cost along with illness, disease, and accident prevention. Policy priorities, clearly selected from the range of alternatives, are the strengthening of federal policymaking, priority setting, and implementation; cost containment featuring resource allocation, utilization reorientation and education, malpractice litigation reform, and technology application; prevention of improving disease and illness; quality of care; and strengthening medical institutions, research, manpower, and services.

A major conditioning factor surrounding these areas is curbing cost escalation. Translated, this means controlling cost and increasing the return on the federal health dollar by improving quality (*Forward Plan for Health: FY 1978–82*, 1976). Questions concerning whether these aims are needed or capable of being implemented are secondary to the economic cost factor. That is, policy directives coping with health care cost and rendering the "best return for the least money" are priorities in today's health care. These choices represent a pragmatic and efficient approach of dealing with the current health care structural system.

PROGRAM SELECTION AND DESIGN

The movement from policy alternative formulation to policy program selection involves selecting a policy position which does not satisfy an optimal condition. Policy program selection generally leans toward a middle or central position. Related to this rule of thumb is the actual degree of change or departure from existing policy programming. Dror terms this issue "incrementalism versus innovation" (Dror, 1971). That is, to what degree is there gradual and congruent or significant and marked change from previous policy? Incremental change involves minor adjustment to present policy, while innovative change results in unpredictable consequences. Related to the degree of innovation is the question of political feasibility regarding a policy program selection. Can the policy proposal win support and approval although it may not be an inclusive solution to the problem? What compromises, bargaining, and agreements can be made without jeopardizing the intent of the policy program? Reaching an acceptable agreement or adjusting differences are involved in this process.

Policy program selection and design must also include a social-change dimension. During the last fifteen years, major health policy programs that have brought social change to health care have been designed and passed. The elderly and the poor have received comprehensive health coverage. Prepaid group practices have been established as alternatives to fee-for-service arrangements. Regional health planning agencies have sought to coordinate health services, facilities, and providers. Consumers have made policy inputs on Health Maintenance Organizations and Health Systems Agencies boards.

Based on the national health policy goal priorities, policy program selection and design have reflected the partial fulfillment of these aims. For example, the priority of cost containment is met through a series of incremented policy adjustments: a resource allocation system, reimbursement policy changes, and improved health service utilization. There is major reliance on Health Systems Agencies, which monitor local and state health care resources and services as part of the 1974 National Health Planning and Resources Development Act. Medicare reimbursement policy changes propose use of ambulatory services and other economical efficiency measures. The Professional Standards Review Organization program reduces inappropriate use of health services through a review of short-stay, long-term, and ambulatory care. Health policymakers have utilized these various legislative programs to contain the cost of care.

PROGRAM IMPLEMENTATION

Policy program implementation involves political and legal administrative action that results in the application of a particular policy design to a situation. Current political, social, and economic forces affect how a policy program is implemented. Monetary inflation, rising medical costs, and limited funding resources are factors that contribute to an austerity approach to health program implementation. The tempo of implementation, in other words, is determined by the rate of allocation and deployment of funding, manpower, and power.

A new set of participants is involved in program implementation. In health care, state and county departments implement the regulations of certain federal health programs. In other instances, health legislation mandates an independent body to administer the policies and programs of an act. The Department of Health and Human Services monitors and oversees policy regulations as programs are translated into services. To a certain extent, effective implementation is dependent on the degree of political support from decision makers and interest groups. Policy advocates of particular programs are strategic to the implementation stage. Anderson observes: "agency policy-making and implementation activities will reflect the interests supported by the dominant elements within its constituency, whether they are hostile or supportive" (Anderson, 1975, p. 111). Strong leadership is necessary in program monitoring, administration, and interpretation. How will information necessary to implement the program be communicated to agencies? What are the administrative roles for implementation in terms of coordinating, staffing, supervising, budgeting, and supplying essential sections of a program? What are the terms of compliance for interpreting the rules and regulations affecting the involved organizations, target populations, and service areas?

PROGRAM EVALUATION

Policy program evaluation involves an assessment of particular goals and their effects upon a problem or target group. In order for program evaluation to be conducted, policy program goals must be investigated to determine whether they have been attained. Related to goal attainment is the assessment of program effects upon a problem area or population target group. Goal attainment involves determining program objectives and their achievement, while program effects are associated with external problem or person-related outcomes. In many cases, there is sufficient overlap between achieving program objectives and program effects as they relate to particular problems or target populations.

The evaluation process may uncover intended or unintended program consequences. If there are effects other than those anticipated, the evaluator attempts to determine the cause. Did these consequences support or detract from the stated program intent? Among the range of problem consequences are inadequate resources allocated for a program area, lack of policy enforcement weakening impact of the program, incompatible and contradictory program goals, an insoluble problem unresponsive to the program, changing aspects of the problem requiring goal revisions, and other impediments (Anderson, 1975).

Progam evaluation is used as feedback for policy decision makers and program managers to assess the validity of a policy program. At times, evaluation reports are employed to support political decisions on a program. Political feasibility may be a concern for selecting policy program continuation. However, relevant data on program evaluation are essential to an objective appraisal of effectiveness.

NATIONAL HEALTH INSURANCE: A POLICYMAKING CASE STUDY

The history of national health insurance is a prime example of the policymaking phases described in this chapter. The context for universal health care in the United States arose from a 1935-38 national study and conference for incremental medical coverage through federal grants-in-aid to states. In 1939 Senator Wagner of New York introduced the first congressional bill for a national health program (S. 1620), which was opposed by organized medicine. More moderate proposals were made for a limited coverage and voluntary medical care program based on federal aid to states. During the 1940s, the Wagner-Murray-Dingell national health insurance bills were proposed without enactment. Yet, concurrently, precedents for federal involvement were established in public assistance, unemployment compensation, public health, and Old Age and Survivors Insurance programs. As a result of the Commission on the Health Needs of the Nation Report (1952), a new tactical strategy emerged focusing on national health insurance for the elderly and the disadvantaged. If universal coverage could be legislated for these two groups, there would be a precedent for eventually broadening the scope of the program to cover all Americans. From 1952 to 1965 variations of national medical coverage for the aged and the indigent were introduced, along with legislation for subsidized state insurance plans and federal subsidies to private insurance carriers (Falk, 1973). The initial breakthrough occurred in 1966 with the passage of the Medicare Bill, P.L. 89-97. The partialized coverage strategy was accomplished, but the universal coverage goal has not been achieved.

Universal health coverage is based on the long-standing need for comprehensive and equitable health care for all Americans. It is, however, clouded by a mood of austerity on new government programs. Due to economic constraints imposed on the federal budget, there is uncertainty over whether the country can economically and politically afford a massive or even modest national health insurance program. Keintz declared: "Much of this debate, in fact, has occurred over a long period of time, and while the nature of the forum and the content has altered—the culmination to its present status merely reflects the critical concerns in terms of political and economic goals and consequences" (Keintz, 1976, p. 1). National health insurance is a political and economic issue. The political task is to consolidate the varied NHI legislative versions and to build consensus between the administration and key members of Congress. Such a rapprochement is unlikely after the ideological rift between Carter and Kennedy over national health insurance and the subsequent 1980 Presidential campaign for the Democratic nomination. Congressional passage of national health insurance is unlikely before the mid-or-late eighties. The economic aspect of this problem is dependent on inflation, recession, and a balanced budget.

In short, a tight-money situation prohibits the introduction of national health insurance. Even a plan allowing for a national health system transition in stages (the phasing-in strategy of the Carter Administration) based on the existing flow of federal revenue is remote because of the present economic situation.

National health insurance alternatives have been analyzed based on legislative proposals from the 92nd to the 94th Congress (Berki, 1972; Huang and Shum, 1974; Austin, 1975; Davis, 1975; Keintz, 1976). Alternative versions vary according to coverage, cost, financing, and the roles of the government, private insurance companies, and consumers (Davis, 1975). Several NHI authorities have argued for an equitable plan characterized by accessibility, cost limits, and avoidance of financial hardship (Davis, 1975; Keintz, 1976; Enthoven, 1978). An assessment of the Canadian national health insurance system has even been made, drawing implications for the United States (Andreopoulos, 1975). Yet, to the dismay of government officials and the American public, no final version of universal health insurance has been passed into law and implemented in this country. Political differences over legislative versions and economic/fiscal constraints have not been resolved. National health insurance program action has been suspended for the moment.

SUMMARY

A policymaking framework for health care has been outlined in this chapter. A progressive policy planning process was given: contextual situation, problem statement, alternative formulations, program selection and design, program implementation, and program evaluation. Policy planning principles with health care examples were advanced in each section. Finally, an assessment of national health insurance was presented as a case study of policymaking that is still in process.

So far, we have given a broad overview of health policy problem issues, social values, and task roles related to health policymaking procedures. In subsequent chapters, contributors have been asked to focus on specific policy program areas, analyzing current trends and offering implications for social work and health care. Beginning with an overview of health policy for this decade, Medicaid, Health Maintenance Organizations, and National Health Planning and Resources Development are assessed as major policy programs. Next, primary and long-term care services are examined. Finally, an effort is made to evaluate cost containment, national and state health insurance, and future trends in health policy.

REFERENCES

Aday, L., and Anderson, R. 1975. *Access to medical care.* Ann Arbor: Health Administration.

Anderson, J. E. 1975 *Public policy-making.* New York: Praeger.

Andreopoulos, S. 1975. *National health insurance: can we learn from Canada?* New York: Wiley.

Austin, C. J. 1975. *The politics of national health insurance: an interdisciplinary research study.* San Antonio: Trinity University.

Berki, S. E. 1972. National health insurance: an idea whose time has come? *Annals of the American Academy of Political and Social Science* 399:125–44.

Brewer, G. D., and Brunner, R. D. 1975. *Political development and change: a policy approach.* New York: Free Press.

Davis, K. 1975. *National health insurance: benefits, costs and consequences.* Washington, D.C.: Brookings Institution.

Dror, Y. 1971. *Design for policy sciences.* New York: American Elsevier.

Enthoven, A. 1978. Consumer-choice health plan. *New England Journal of Medicine* 298:650–58, 709–20.

Falk, I. S. 1973. Medical care in the USA 1932–1972: problems, proposals and programs from the Committee on the Costs of Medical Care to the Committee for National Health Insurance. *Milbank Memorial Fund Quarterly* 51:1–32.

Forward plan for health: FY 1978–82. 1976. Washington, D.C.: Department of Health, Education, and Welfare. Public Health Service.

Grumm, J. G. 1975. The analysis of policy impact. In F. I. Greenstein and N. W. Polsby, eds., *Policies and policymaking.* Reading, Mass.: Addison-Wesley.

Huang, L. F., and Shum, E. W. 1974. *Assessment and evaluation of the impact of archetypal national health insurance plans on U.S. health manpower requirements.* Washington, D.C.: Department of Health, Education, and Welfare, Health Resources Administration.

Keintz, R. M. 1976. *National health insurance and income distribution.* Lexington, Mass.: Lexington.

Lewis, C. E.; Fein, R.; and Mechanic, D. 1976. *A right to health.* New York: Wiley.

PART TWO:

Health Policy Program Areas

4

NATIONAL HEALTH POLICY

Herbert H. Hyman

National health policy is generally made by Congress and implemented by federal executive departments and state and local governments. The issue that will be considered in this chapter is whether a national health policy exists and, if so, what implications it holds for social work. The first part of the chapter will explore the nature and types of health policies currently being formulated and implemented in the United States. The second part will show the effects these policies have on the practice of social work.

MICRO AND MACRO HEALTH POLICY

There are two types of health policy at the national level. I use the term "macro policy" to refer to those broad issues enunciated by national decision makers, including the President and his principal health policymaker, the Secretary of Health and Human Services; the chairpersons of congressional committees dealing with health issues; and the spokespersons for the national professional health associations such as Blue Cross, the American Medical Association, and the American Public Health Association. These national leaders generally concern themselves with global trends and issues in health. Currently, the emphases of macro policy are on constraining the rapid increases in health expenditures, improving the quality of care, and providing greater access to health care for undeserved population. These very broad statements of policy set the framework within which microhealth policies are made.

Micro health policies can be likened to the tactics used by military leaders to carry out major strategies. Thus, within the strategy to contain costs, the executive department and Congress have fashioned a number of tactics to implement this macro policy. Among these are certificate-of-need legislation to reduce duplication of unnecessary health facilities and programs, Professional Standards Review Organizations (PSROs) to reduce unnecessarily long hospital stays and improve the quality of hospital care, and Health Maintenance Organizations (HMOs) to substitute early, primary treatment of patients (with some focus on health prevention and health education) for acute treatment in hospitals. Each of these health programs represents a micro health policy designed to effect the overall macro health policy of cost containment. In a sense, micro policies are programmatic innovations designed to achieve macro policies. All health policies are reactions to health care crises that demand solutions. In the 1960s, Medicaid and Medicare were reactions to the fact that poor and elderly were unable to pay for health care. In the 1970s, cost-containment policy is a response to the rapid rise of health care costs.

Once the macro health issues have been clearly identified, new health programs are initiated to cope with the crisis. Keeping the distinction between macro and micro health policies in mind, it then becomes possible to differentiate between the major significant policies forming around disruptions in the health care delivery system at any one time and the minor health tactics designed to alleviate these stresses.

Furthermore, macro and micro health policies are always evolving. The success of one major policy may inspire a second major policy intended either to reinforce or counteract the original. For example, a macro policy to increase knowledge of health issues through research and demonstration resulted in the development of the National Institutes for Health (NIH). The success of this research and the many new medical technologies that emanated from it led to the development of a health manpower policy designed to overcome the shortages of physicians, researchers, and technologists needed to carry out and maintain the medical procedures that had been fostered by health research. The major commitment to health research also led to a major "counteractive" health policy: the drive to regionalize high-cost medical technologies in order to check the unnecessary proliferation of such technologies that resulted from competition among individual health institutions. Thus, one macro health policy led to two others: one that fostered growth of health manpower and the other that attempted to curb the costs resulting from the duplication and expansion of high-cost medical technologies.

The secondary effects of major policies sometimes had negative consequences that generated further policy problems that were often complex. For example, many of the medical innovations spurred by NIH research and federal funding were often assimilated into the mainstream of medical practice before they were thoroughly tested and shown to have benefits that offset potential risks and justified their high cost to the patient. To check this danger, the Food and Drug Administration (FDA) was given by Congress authority to develop standards and procedures for determining the benefits and safety of newly developed drugs, equipment, and procedures (Banta, 1978). These amendments to the Food and Drug Act came about because of controversies that arose over the safety and efficacy of such procedures as mammography, radical mastectomy, hyperbaric oxygen treatment for cognitive deficits of the elderly, and the use of saccharin.

Micro health policies can also generate a secondary set of policies that either reinforce or check the activities of the original policy. In carrying out the broad goal of cost containment, micro policies took two divergent routes. One stressed rationalized use of health care services through development of comprehensive health plans; the other emphasized restrictive use of health resources through regulation. In the first instance, the long-term health systems plans mandated by the National Health Planning and Resources Development Act of 1974 have uncovered numerous populations with unmet needs for health and mental health services. As a result of the regulatory approach, state certificate-of-need laws and national health planning guidelines have combined to set limits on the use of scarce and high-cost medical services. As a consequence, many regions in the United States have been declared to be overbedded based on these regulations. There have thus been situations where certificate-of-need regulations have denied proposals for increases in hospital bed capacity in spite of the fact that many of these requests were made to implement high-priority goals of the health systems plans to meet the needs of underserved populations. Thus, two micro policies — one with a focus on the most efficient use of scarce resources through rational planning, the other with a focus on limiting the development of new resources — may well come into conflict in spite of the fact that both were intended to further a single macro health policy.

This discussion should indicate how complex the enunciation and implementation of macro and micro health policy can become. This complexity, along with a failure to distinguish between major policy emphases and the tactics used to implement them, have caused a number of health decision makers to assert that there is no national health policy. Rather, they see a series of health policies with little rhyme or reason to them. They identify the irrationalities and conflicts in health policies while making no distinction between major or minor policies. However, with the advent of comprehensive health planning through Health Systems Agencies, it is possible to identify major health policies on which both community and national decision makers in Congress, the executive branch, and the national voluntary health professional associations can agree. The issue on which they disagree is the means, or micro health policies, to be used to achieve the ends, or macro health policies. The differences over means are often interpreted as a conflict about ends. To this writer, it would seem that there is substantial agreement that at least the following can be considered to have been the major health policies of the 1970s:

1. cost containment;
2. access of the disadvantaged to health/mental health services;
3. improved quality of care;
4. regionalization of health/mental health services;
5. rationality in the planning and use of services;
6. increased need to provide ambulatory, community-based services.

Even as the greatest amount of national attention is being to these policy issues, a number of other macro health policies, still in their early stages of recognition and acceptance, are likely to emerge as the major policies of the 1980s. Among them are:

1. reducing environmental pollution;
2. increasing the individual's personal responsibility for his/her own well-being through health education;
3. reawakening of a concern for prevention of those factors which promote poor health and disease;

4. greater involvement of community support and social services systems;

5. completion through an incremental process of a national health insurance program.

The emergence of the major health policies of the 1980s does not mean that the policies of the 1970s will disappear. Rather, these priorities have been accepted as an integral part of our national health policy, just as many of the policies of the 1960s have been accepted and have continued to be implemented and improved in the 1970s. Among major health policies of the 1960s that have become accepted in the 1970s are:

1. comprehensive health planning as improved by the National Health Planning and Resources Development Act of 1974;

2. mental health/retardation, as improved by the 1963 Community Mental Health Act into four separate components dealing with mental health, drug abuse, alcoholism and developmental disabilities, and the many acts and amendments that followed;

3. paying for health care of the poor and elderly through Medicaid and Medicare while setting the stage for incremental movement toward a national health insurance program;

4. focusing on control of heart disease, cancer, and stroke, the major killers of our population;

5. increasing the supply of health/mental health manpower and emphasis on bringing physicians' assistants and other physician extenders into the health labor force;

6. beginning focus on community-based health/mental health services with special focus on the health needs of urban minorities;

7. increasing the role of consumers as decision makers in planning and implementing health/mental health services.

All of these major health policies of the 1960s have been fully accepted in the 1970s. The major legislation that authorized these policies has been significantly altered by congressional action in the 1970s. Based on evaluation of these beginning programs, Congress's collective judgment has amended the original laws or substituted laws with greater clarity and specificity in carrying out the intent of the original laws. Thus, the initial general mandate for consumer participation in health/mental health planning formulated in 1966 led to a more refined specification of how that participation should be effected by setting geographical, linguistic, income, racial, and other requirements for consumer representation in the 1974 National Health Planning and Resources Development Act. With respect to mental health policy, the Mental Health Act of 1963 has been divided into separate acts for each of the four major components identified in the original act. Though each mental disorder was given separate attention with its own law, congressional judgment mandated their administrative integration through the creation of the Alcohol, Drug Abuse, and Mental Health Administration (ADAMHA) as a major arm of the Public Health Service. In like manner, all of the major initiatives of the 1960s have or are still undergoing refinement in the 1970s. None of them had an easy time getting started or being accepted by the prevailing health and mental health forces at the time. Only when seen in the perspective of hindsight can it be noted that the radical new policies of one decade become the conservative accepted policies of the next. When any decade is critically examined, there are usually no more than a handful of issues that are so pervasive and significant in their impact on the nation's health that they result in the development of macro health policies that become the major policies for that decade.

In the discussion that follows, it is essential to keep in mind the distinction between macro and micro health policies. Implications for social work can be analyzed and understood only in the context of micro health policy because such policy is specific, concrete, and usually connected to federally funded programs.

CONCEPTUAL FRAMEWORK: THE MEDICAL MODEL

It is one thing to identify macro and micro health policy, and quite another to articulate the conceptual and other determinants of what those policies are and how they will be carried out. The medical model has been traditionally used in determining the resources needed to provide adequate and high-quality care in the United States. This model is based on the assumption that diagnosis and treatment are provided only after a person becomes ill. It is derived from focusing on those illnesses and diseases caused by attacks by viral or other agents on our bodies. Consequently, drugs, surgical procedures, and rest are generally prescribed to counteract these attacks. According to the medical model, it is the physician, specially trained and backed by a body of data based on research findings supported by NIH and others, who makes the decisions about what treatment is needed. The physician is the decision maker and the leader of a team of support personnel who carry out his/her orders. Most funds spent on health care have gone to providing direct services and research support to treat people at the time they are physically ill.

However, there are those who have recognized that enormous changes have taken place in the last 50 years. They assert that there has been a major shift from dealing with infectious, acute illnesses to chronic illnesses (Knowles, 1975, p. 25). Further, they hold that changes in human longevity have stemmed from sources other than medical care, primarily from improvements in public hygiene (sanitation, housing) and improved standards of living (Fuchs in Knowles, 1975, p. 19, and McKeown in Knowles, 1975, p. 35). McKeown, in fact, asserts that therapy and immunization have had less to do with the population's health status than an increase in the food supply, a reduction in exposure to water-and food-borne diseases, and the capacity to control population growth (McKeown in Knowles, 1975, p. 35).

What this means is that the medical model cannot by itself deal with the most pressing health problems facing us today: the chronic physical and mental illnesses such as heart conditions, cancer, alcoholism, mental illness, autism, or arthritis. Except for the diagnosis and treatment of diseases, physicians have a very small role in influencing the factors that are the causes of the many chronic diseases. As Fuchs has stated: "The relative unimportance of the physician in health and his great importance with respect to cost . . . lead us . . . to the folly of trying to meet the problem of access by training more M.D. specialists" (Fuchs, 1974, p. 6).

Consistent with McKeown's findings, Lalonde, Blum, and others have identified four significant determinants of health. These are generally classified as life-style, environment, human biology, and health care delivery system (Lalonde, 1974; Blum, 1974). The first three "nonmedical" determinants have more to do with lowering our mortality rates from leading causes of death (diseases of the heart, malignant neoplasms, cerebrovascular diseases, cirrhosis of the liver, influenza and pneumonia, motor vehicle accidents, homicide, and suicide) than does the delivery of medical care services. Such factors as speed on the highway, alcoholism, lack of physical exercise, poor nutrition, smoking, and lack of safety in the work environment are among the major causes of chronic ailments, and the medical model is not designed to intervene on this level (*Health, United States,* 1978).

This means that if improvements are to be made in our health status, they must come from influencing the nonmedical determinants of health. Breslow and Belloc noted that following seven simple rules would result in an average of 11 years of longer life for a person 45 years of age (Somers, 1976, p. 6). They refer to *life-style* habits, such as not smoking, limiting alcoholic intake, exercising, and proper eating habits. None of these has anything to do with intervention through medical care. The impact must be made on individuals through health education and promotion services. In addition, air and noise pollution in the factory, unsafe highways and poorly engineered automobiles, water contaminants from poor sewage and drainage, and improper storage of toxic waste materials all represent *environmental* dangers that lead to disease and illness. Their improvement requires collective action through voluntary compliance and/or regulation to curb environmental health hazards. Again, until individuals actually become sick, the medical model has no role in reducing these chronic illnesses. *Genetic* disorders such as PKU, hemophilia, sickle-cell anemia, Tay-Sachs disease, or Down's syndrome can usually be detected through screening and genetic counseling, given to prevent and/or treat these conditions in their earliest stages or to deal with the question of abortion (*Health, United States,* 1978, chap. 2). While physicians do play a role in diagnosing these conditions, other professionals, especially social workers, nutritionists, and genetic counselors, play a primary role.

Thus, it is no longer enough to rely on medical intervention to improve a population's health status. Other professionals and social activists are required if any impact is to be made on chronic health problems. Many of them, including highway engineers, social workers, health educators, legislators, environmentalists, and corporate boards of directors, have little or no connection with medicine, but their actions or inactions will have more impact on the state of our nation's health than will physicians' activities.

Yet, of the federal and state tax dollars spent on health care in 1978, about 6 percent went for such public health activities. About 9 percent has been allocated for the environment (*Health, United States,* 1978, p. 390). Almost all the rest was channeled into medical care and research related to biomedical conditions. In other words, governmental hindsights reflect an inverted order of priorities if compared to what public health experts consider to be the main determinants of health and how public funds ought to be expended to meet those needs. For this reason, the Lalonde model is a useful concept for analyzing current health care budgets.

THE FEDERAL GOVERNMENT'S HEALTH BUDGET

A government's budget generally reflects both its current priorities and an indication of what will be the probable future priorities in the field of health. Based on the proposed 1980 budget for the Department of Health and Human Services, the amounts of funding shown in Table 4.1 have been recommended for the four determinants of health.

It should be stated that these figures are only approximate. Without a detailed breakdown of each of the programs within the large headings of the four major determinants of health, it is not possible to know precisely what allocations are actually intended for one determinant rather than another. Yet it is clear that the overwhelming sum of 85 percent of the funds goes for the medical care system. The smallest amount, less than 1 percent, goes for style of life, which requires educating the public to recognize and take responsibility for preventing the major causes of mortality. Regardless of their accuracy, what these figures reveal is the overwhelming disparity in allocations for medical care delivery system compared to the other major determinants of health.

While this general funding disparity is the main point highlighted by Fuchs, Lalonde, and others, it is not the entire story. For within these allocations are hidden bits of information that clearly identify current trends and foretell emerging future trends in macro health policies. The same issue of *The Nation's Health* (March 1979) reveals three macro health policies emphasized in the federal budget — cost containment, prevention, and accessibility of services to the disadvantaged.

Cost Containment

The most important cost-containment tactic is the proposed cost reduction in Medicare/Medicaid budgets resulting from a variety of efforts, the most important of which is placing a 9.7 percent ceiling on the cost reimbursement from the federal government for these programs. Only 1 percent of that increase is for new health services. The rest is to cover the cost of anticipated inflation. The imposition of a ceiling puts great pressure on hospital administrators and physicians to become cost-conscious and to devise means for reducing costs. In addition, substantial savings are expected from such efforts as reducing inefficiency in hospital services, lowering medical malpractice rates, reducing fraud and error, and changing the

Table 4.1   1980 Health Budget

Determinants of health	Dollars (billions—items)	Dollars (billions—total)	Percentage
A. Human biology (genetics)		3.21	6
National Institutes for Health	3.2		
Center for Disease Control			
(genetic services)	.01		
B. Environment		5.2	9
CDC: rat control, lead-based			
paint, occupational safety and			
health, buildings, and facilities	.09		
Environmental Protection Agency			
operations for air, water quality,			
solid waste, pesticide, etc.	1.3		
Construction grants	3.8		
C. Style of Life		.18	0.03
Family planning	0.15		
Health education	0.03		
D. Medical Care		47.90	84.7
Medicare/Medicaid	44.00		
Health Resources Administration	.50		
Office of Asst. Secretary for Health	.30		
Alcoholism, drug abuse, and			
mental health	1.10		
Health Services Administration	2.0		
Total		$56.49	100.00

Source: The Nation's Health, March 1979.

insurance coverage of working aged. A second tactic in the Department of Health and Human Services budget calls for a major reduction in man-power training costs in health and minor reductions in mental health. In both cases, the emphasis is on a better redistribution of manpower based on the premise that the current supply is adequate, but poorly distributed. Most of the shortfalls are located in the rural and inner-city communities. Social workers would be among those severely affected by the proposed cut-backs in manpower funds. A third cost-containment tactic is the develop-ment of a new program to pay for costs associated with closing or convert-ing unneeded medical facilities. Past studies have shown that the greatest savings are achieved when entire hospitals, rather than individual buildings or wings of facilities, are closed down.

Thus, with those budget proposals, the executive branch has continued the efforts started in previous administrations to bring the rampant costs of medical care under control. The carte blanche policy of the 1960s and early 1970s, which permitted higher costs for medical care services to go un-challenged, is no longer being tolerated. Now, programming is targeted for particular populations, along with an effort to reduce duplication and the cost of care. These tactics, among others, represent the micro health policies currently employed by the executive branch to achieve its macro health policy of containing costs.

Access to Care of Disadvantaged and Underserved

A little over one billion dollars has been allocated to assist the poor, rural, and inner-city minority populations in gaining access to care. The major tactics cited in the budget for implementing this macro policy goal are the continued provision of funds for maternal and child health programs, com-munity mental health centers, and an increase in the development of com-munity health centers. In addition, the National Health Service Corps has been expanded to help bring an adequate number of physicians and other professionals into underserved areas of the nation. All four programs are aimed at increasing access to quality services.

Prevention Services

Prevention services have also been given a major boost in the proposed Department of Health and Human Services budget. Over $400 million is allocated for these services. Almost all of the Center for Disease Control funds are expended on one or more facet of prevention of illness and disease. Among these programs are those dealing with venereal disease, im-munizations, health education, and occupational safety and health. In ad-dition, some $45 million has been allocated to four different Public Health Service administrations in a coordinated antismoking campaign. An addi-tional $60 million is designed to prevent pregnancies in adolescents. In-asmuch as improved access to services for disadvantaged groups entails some focus on health education and prevention of illness, these policies will also add to the emphasis on prevention.

Compared to expenditures for medical care, few dollars are going into prevention. It can be anticipated that, as results begin to show themselves as reduced mortality and morbidity rates, preventive measures should claim an increasing portion of the health budget. Likewise, it is anticipated that as efforts by the Environmental Protection Agency achieve results in curbing a wide variety of pollutants in the general environment and in the work place, many potential causes of disease will gradually be brought under control. To the extent that NIH-sponsored research uncovers some of the biologic and genetic determinants of disease, the nation's health status can be expected to improve through primary prevention. However, because all of those preventive tactics claim less than 10 percent of the health budget, prevention must be considered an emerging macro health policy that can be expected to mature and to be fully accepted in the 1980s.

Without going into every facet of the federal government's health budget for the first year of the new decade, it becomes clear that a shift in macro health policy is beginning to take place. This shift is subtly evidenced by proposed budget increases and decreases in the tactical programs designed to achieve macro health policies. There is little question that the supporters of maintaining a high expenditure level for medical care services both in Congress and in the national professional medical associations will continue to press for their favorite programs. Alford makes an impressive case for his thesis that the medical care establishment in league with the middle-level executive branches of the Department of Health and Human Services and congressional committees have a need to maintain the gains they have posted in the medical care programs they have championed in the past (Alford, 1975). There is a tendency for Congress, and particularly the House, to substantially modify major cuts recommended by the executive branch's budgetary proposals in the direction of status quo. This tendency places the major burden on the top level of the executive branch to press for proposed new macro health policies if they are to become anything more than token advances. However, as long as the severe fiscal constraints experienced by the federal government in the past decade continue, there is an incentive to shift toward the policies noted in the earlier part of this chapter. In short, it can be expected that these policy changes will take place but that they will be gradual and come in incremental movements.

MICRO HEALTH POLICY

The 1978 edition of *Health, United States* cites as its major health policies: cost containment, prevention, children and youth, mental disorders, long-term care, and quality of medical care. All of these areas encompass one or more of the macro health policies cited above as emerging major issues for the 1980s.

The National Health Planning and Resources Development Act of 1974 identifies ten priorities for improving the health care delivery system while reducing the costs of that care. Seven are concerned with cost-containment approaches such as emphasis on integration of health services, use of physician extenders, encouraging use of HMOs, and development of a uniform cost accounting system. One deals with quality of care through use of PSROs; one, with personal health education; and one, with environmental research and improvement. The twin overall goals articulated in the act are cost containment and improvement of the quality of care. The assumption underlying this potential conflict of goals is that savings generated through containing cost should be used to provide improved care for medically underserved population. However, this author's analysis of the first Health System Plans produced in New York and New Jersey indicates that the scope of unmet need in the health care system is great. The cost of filling them would far outstrip the recommended reductions in health costs (Hyman, 1978). All of this suggests that while Congress and the executive branch may agree on what the major contours of macro health policies are, they will have a difficult time in implementing them.

In this section, two of these macro health policies, cost containment and prevention, will be examined in terms of (1) the micro policy tactics used to achieve them and (2) the implications of these policy tactics on social work.

Cost-Containment Tactics

Six tactics have been tried thus far to contain costs:

1. hospital certificate of need;
2. hospital conversion and closure;
3. mandatory hospital revenue ceilings;
4. restricting the number of physicians;
5. prospective institutional rate setting;
6. utilization review.

All of these tactics except restricting the number of physicians are based on regulatory practices (*Health, United States,* 1978, chap. 1). In implementation they involve the use of health planners, economists, engineers, architects, budget analysts, and accountants. Only in utilization review are medical professionals (physicians, nurses, and social workers) involved in setting standards for length of hospital stay and the use of accepted procedures for the patient's illness. All other strategies attempt to impose limitations of one type or another on medical facilities or how and where medicine is practiced. The certification-of-need process determines whether a medical facility or service is needed. Hospital conversion determines whether a facility ought to be closed or converted to another more important use. Mandatory hospital revenue ceilings such as the Economic Stabilization Program determine the general rate of permissible increase in hospital charges, as does the Carter Administration's proposed in 9 percent "cap." By reducing the federal government's capitation grants for medical professionals, an attempt is made to reduce the number of practitioners produced by medical and other professional schools. Prospective institutional rate review forces a hospital to live with a predetermined maximum on how much it can spend during its fiscal year. Finally, utilization review determines how long patients ought to stay in a hospital and whether the patient should be admitted in the first place. All of these tactics are efforts to reduce costs. However, most have been in existence for several years, and thus far none has appreciably reduced health care costs. The inefficacy of these strategies is not surprising because the forces at work to increase the costs of medical services operate almost independently of them. Inflation, the higher cost of better-trained professional and support staff, the high cost of more sophisticated and complex medical technology, greater demands by the population for medical services, and the payment of hospital operating costs through third-party insurance mechanisms all converge to drive costs higher. Consequently, regulatory efforts that do not deal with these factors will find their intentions at cost containment frustrated.

The cost-containment tactics discussed above have led to other, secondary tactics which may, in the long run, have some impact on costs and great influence on the pattern of the delivery of medical services. Among these are integration of services, use of ambulatory services in place of acute care or inpatient services, and fostering of competition in health care.

Integration of Services

Integration of services involves (1) the interdisciplinary involvement of professionals within an institution and (2) institutional coordination — the sharing or merging of different types of services (health with mental health, social services with home health care, etc.). In both models, the aim is to reduce costs through fostering services that will result in more rapid recovery of the patient (interdisciplinary) or reducing overhead and professional costs by preventing duplication of services (institutional integration). It has long been recognized that physicians and psychiatrists are the team leaders in their areas of domain. Yet within health and mental health institutions there have been increasing attempts by professionals to work as integrated interdisciplinary teams. Several studies have been published that show the results of these efforts (McNamara, 1975–76; Thoma, 1977; Carlton, 1977; Parad, 1976). They all illustrate that, with the "team" approach,

1. diagnosis and treatment of patients is more reliable and effective;
2. treatment of patients is more humane;
3. the patient is more likely to be regarded and dealt with as a whole person; and
4. conflict among professional team members is radically reduced as tensions are recognized and dealt with openly.

These are all positive findings. However, the one important negative finding that could offset potential gains was the relative lack of involvement of the physician or psychiatrist in the team efforts. This lack of investment on the part of traditionally accepted "leader" raises the question of how valid such team efforts can be. It is as though the physician is saying that it's all right for the support staff to go through the motions of working together as long as it does not interfere with the physician's leadership or challenge the doctor's ultimate decision-making authority.

A second negative finding was that, in spite of its good intentions, the team did not truly involve the patients in their own treatment as much as it might have. As one researcher stated: "Another problem is the inability of the model thus far to incorporate the views and considerations of the patients who interface with the team" (Carlton, 1977, p. 71). This implies that the support professionals are more interested in their own coordination than they are in encouraging the autonomy and involvement in patients in matters of their own medical care.

With respect to institutional integration, the American Hospital Association reports that 84 percent of hospitals responding to a survey share in one or more of ten common services such as blood banking, laboratory services, education/training and diagnostic radiology (*Nation's Health,* March 1979, p. 16). This emphasis on sharing is strongly supported by the ten stated priorities of the National Health Planning and Resources Development Act of 1974 and by the 1978 amendments (P.L. 95-622) to the Revenue Sharing Act (mental health section). This sharing takes such forms as psychiatric beds being set aside in general acute care hospitals, mental health clinics being developed in outpatient departments of general hospitals, or nursing homes commingling with psychiatric medical cases. These changes stem not only from a need to reduce the costs of duplication costs and conserve limited resources, but also to provide more comprehensive professional services to patients.

IMPLICATIONS FOR SOCIAL WORK. The integration tactic can have the following potential consequences for social work.

The team approach may well produce a blurring of roles (Parad, 1976, p. 675). Nurses, physicians trained in community medicine, and even secretaries and appointment clerks all believe they have a role in providing social services. Whose role is it to help a patient accept a new diet: social worker? nurse? nutritionist? Who takes a patient's history and how does one separate the social, medical, economic, and special characteristics of that history? Determination of roles, once a major issue in the mental health team approach, has been worked out over time with the core roles sharply defined.

Social workers, who traditionally have supported the idea of clients assuming an integral responsibility for their own treatment, will have to work through potential conflicts with health professionals who have fostered the dependency in patients. As one researcher noted about the team approach: "the model and the system are for the most part totally incompatible" (Carlton, 1977, p. 71). The incompatibility arises because the hierarchical nature of the health care system does not lend itself easily to joint decision making embodied in a team approach. The team approach can readily produce more conflict and adversely affect patient care unless differences in attitudes toward patient roles are resolved.

Ambulatory Services as a Way of Reducing Costs

The second tactic fostered by federal and state authorities is to reduce costs by having more services provided on an ambulatory rather than an inpatient basis. This is evidenced by the federal executive budget's emphasis on developing more neighborhood health and mental health centers despite an atmosphere of fiscal crisis and an austere 1980 budget. Deinstitutionalization is the catchword that symbolizes this movement in mental health (*Health, United States*, 1978, chap. 4).

IMPLICATIONS FOR SOCIAL WORK. In both acute care and mental hospitals it is the social worker who is responsible for making discharge plans that involve special services. Home health services are often needed for the chronically ill, while transitional and community support services are required for discharged patients with chronic psychological disturbances. Both kinds of service are in very short supply, with the result that mental health institutions are often accused of "dumping" their patients on the community without providing appropriate assistance. Acute care hospitals are sometimes accused of keeping patients longer than they should in order to maintain a high occupancy rate, although they, too, are affected by the fact alternative community resources are not available. The burden falls onto the social worker to find makeshift services, which often do little more than maintain the patient at the level of functioning at which he or she left the hospital. Until recently, when the outcries of community residents offended by the bizarre behavior of mentally ill patients drew attention to the problems of discharged patients, state mental institutions made little pretense of even maintaining the patient's level of functioning. In recent years, states have been making budget shifts to provide more services in the community. In spite of these new efforts to increase the supply of community services with federal and state resources, the burden still falls on social workers to arrange makeshift services to meet the complex and unique needs of these discharged patients. Failure is assigned to both social workers and to patients when patient behavior results in antisocial acts that require their return to a hospital setting.

A second phenomenon that is occurring with the shift toward ambulatory services is the loss of professional positions in hospital settings and an increase in their availability in community settings. This change will require social workers, as well as other professionals, to learn to use their skills in a different way to assist the patient population. No longer confined to an authoritarian hospital setting where they are under the control of professional staff, patients have much more freedom to accept or reject professional services when discharged to the community. Social workers will have to learn to accept the discharged patient as a partner in making decisions with respect to his or her own welfare.

Competition in Providing Services

One recent tactic that has been pushed by the federal government is the stimulation of competition among medical providers via support of the Health Maintenance Organization (HMO). In the HMO model, patients prepay for a comprehensive range of services. In the HMO, the physician and other health workers are responsible for keeping patients well by encouraging their early entry into the health system for treatment and prevention. Through a triage system, the "walking well" and "worried well" patients are screened out or given social services. In competition with fee-for-service or group practices, HMOs provide a comprehensive range of services (medical, social, nutrition, laboratory, and education). The burden is thrust on the physician to reduce costs in order to live within the HMO's prescribed budget. In spite of their offering comprehensive services, HMOs have been particularly effective in reducing the number of days their members spend in the hospital without apparent jeopardy to health status (*Nation's Health,* March 1979, p. 16, and *Health, United States,* 1978, pp. 14–15). Congressional interest in competition in the medical marketplace has led to a proposed amendment to the National Health Planning and Resources Development Act of 1974 which would add an 11th priority encouraging competition in the provision of health services with special attention to HMOs.

IMPLICATIONS FOR SOCIAL WORK. The stress on HMOs gives social workers an opportunity to broaden their orientation to the medical model to include patient care concerns associated with a more humanistic, social model of health services. The finding that the attitudes of physicians who work in HMOs are more accepting of other professionals' participation in the diagnosis and treatment of patients than are solo or group practitioners, or hospital-related care, encourages greater participation for social workers (*Health, United States,* 1978, chap. 1). However, on the other side of the coin, there is the pressure on the physician to live within a restrictive HMO budget. In times of budget reductions, physicians may well choose to reduce social services rather than medical services to stay within their budget.

PREVENTION: MICRO HEALTH POLICY TACTICS

The current interest and emphasis on prevention is based on the recognition of the limitations of medical care to improve the nation's health status. The greatest improvements in life expectancy occurred in the United States between 1900 and 1950. Thereafter, and in spite of vast sums spent on research and treatment, life expectancy increased by only 3.6 years (*Health, United States,* 1978, p. 174). Consequently, the shift in focus of health services has been toward primary prevention (preventing a disease from occurring) and secondary prevention (detecting a disease before it is acute).

Preventive programs would touch on all four of the determinants of health status identified by Lalonde. Preventable health problems stemming from *life-style* include smoking, alcohol and drug abuse, overeating, motor vehicle accidents, homicide, suicide, physical inactivity, and some infectious diseases (venereal diseases, viral infections); *environmental* preventable diseases include pollution of food, air, and water diseases and injuries of the work place (lead and mercury poisoning, cancer, injuries, and some degenerative diseases), product safety (food-related illness from food contamination), and injuries and deaths related to medical devices and diagnostic products (defects in products such as cardiac pacemakers, oxygen delivery systems, and contaminated or superpotent drugs); and *genetically* preventable diseases and deaths include mental retardation, sickle-cell anemia, Tay-Sachs disease, cleft lip, and club foot. It has been estimated that of the two million deaths annually, one in eight could be prevented by timely medical intervention, many more with intervention in the person's life-style or working environment (*Health, United States,* 1978, p. 21). Furthermore, Fuchs points out that "increases in life expectancy . . . [have] been the result . . . of reductions in death rates at *early* ages, not [of] lengthening of the normal life span" (Fuchs, 1974, p. 40; emphasis is the author's).

There are a number of approaches to deal with this wide variety of preventable health problems:

1. legislation/enforcement/regulation;
2. behavior change;
3. incentives;
4. research;
5. modifying the environment;
6. health maintenance; and
7. health education.

The primary influence on *life-style* determinants would be through behavior change, maintenance options in the short run, and research in the long run. Programs dealing with *genetic* determinants would focus on health education and maintenance for the short run and research and legislation in the long run. Those affecting *environmental* determinants would focus on health education and incentives in the short run and legislation, incentives, and research in the long run (*Forward Plan for Health,* 1975, "Prevention" chapter).

Congress has enacted a great many bills dealing with most of the preventable diseases. The major federal administrations with a mandate for prevention are the Environmental Protection Agency, the Center for Disease Control, the Health Services Administration, the Food and Drug Administration, and the National Institutes for Health. The EPA is primarily concerned with regulation, maintenance, and research of all facets of environmental pollution. The Center for Disease Control provides funds for an array of programs concerned with venereal disease, communicable diseases, and lead poisoning. Approaches vary for these programs, but the main ones are health education, maintenance efforts, modification of the environment, and some behavior change. The Health Services Administration focuses on hypertension, family planning, genetic counseling, and black lung services. Again, health maintenance, behavior change, and health education are the means. The Food and Drug Administration has a wide variety of programs dealing with the safety and efficacy of medical technology (drugs, devices, and medical procedures). Through research and regulation and enforcement, the National Institutes of Health focus on the major chronic health problems of the nation such as heart disease, cancer, hypertension, and arthritis, with research and demonstration of the effects of research findings being their primary activities. Finally, the Alcohol, Drug Abuse, and Mental Health Administration (ADAMHA) has recently turned its attention to the prevention of mental disorders. Its major approaches are behavior modification, research, health maintenance, and health education.

IMPLICATIONS FOR SOCIAL WORK. In implementing preventive programs, social workers have obligations and opportunities to involve themselves in social actions that lead to legislative change and enforcement, behavior change in clients, some research into the causes of life-style changes, and some modification of an individual's environment. Since social workers recognize and respect the client's responsibility for his/her own well-being, their approaches require the client's active participation involvement in the social worker's efforts to change the harmful aspects of his life-style. In addition, the social worker has a major role to serve as a liaison or "ombudsperson" in assisting the client to negotiate the fragmented social service system.

With respect to *social action,* there are any number of issues that require social workers to intervene and promote legislative and/or enforcement changes. The 1977 Delegate Assembly of the National Association of Social Workers voted to support policy changes respecting senior citizens, deinstitutionalization of the mentally disabled, families and children, gay issues, juvenile delinquency, adult crime, and racism (*NASW News,* July 1977). Almost all of these issues involve the health and mental well-being of one or more target populations. Specific changes are recommended for the elderly regarding health care, mental health, long-term care, and social and other supportive services. Eight points of policy are recommended for deinstitutionalization of the mentally disabled. Health and mental health services are recommended for minority groups who lack access because of location of facilities or lack of funds. These are only a few of the issues with which social workers must be involved. In league with environmentalists, they should also be supportive of efforts to improve the environment, and especially the work place, where one industry study found 40 percent of workers manifesting symptoms of mental health problems (*Health, United States,* 1978, p. 34). With respect to the mental health professions, Brown noted that they "were unable to avoid . . . the fact that individual pathologies were linked to social pathologies, and that one could not be eased without correcting the other" (Brown, 1977, p. 475). Thus, whether the problem is a health or mental health problem, social workers must be involved in both areas.

Regarding *behavior change in clients,* social workers have a major role. This pertains especially to persons whose life-style includes drinking, drug abuse, obesity, or homicidal or suicidal attempts. Whether working with nutritionists, psychiatrists, or police enforcement officers, social workers can be of major importance in assisting clients to change their behavior and in supporting clients' families to encourage and sustain them in their new behavior. It is well recognized that changing such habits, which are often lifelong, is frustrating and difficult both for the social worker and for clients and their families. There is a need for additional *research* to test new methods of behavior modification, and social workers should take a part, either in directing such research or in providing the data required by other researchers.

Social workers also have a role in *changing a client's environment.* This may mean moving a poor family with a large number of small children to an apartment free of lead-based paint, assisting a poor mother to obtain proper nutrition and medical attention for her pregnancy, or helping a client change to a job more appropriate to his or her skills.

It will normally be expected that most of these approaches will involve social workers with either secondary or tertiary prevention modalities. Except for altering the social environment through legislation or enforcement (primary prevention), social workers—like physicians—have usually intervened only after the symptoms have been identified.

POLICIES OF THE REAGAN ADMINISTRATION

A recent dramatic shift in federal policy has occurred that requires even more urgent social action by social workers. Essentially, the Reagan Administration plans to carry out three major policies:

1. shift the burden of providing services from the federal to the state and local levels of government;
2. reduce the amount of federal expenditures for social and health services; and
3. package categorical health programs with similar outcomes into health block grants.

The overall objectives of these major policy shifts are to stimulate the expansion of the American economy and to increase the number of jobs available in order to reduce unemployment and the welfare rolls. A so-called safety net of basic health and welfare services is to be made available to insure that no person or family falls below a minimal standard of living. These shifts have some very important implications for health services.

First, they shift the arena for the resolution of major health issues from the federal to the state and local levels. This means that instead of concentrating programatic and funding resources on one point at the federal level, they will be dissipated in 50 states and countless other local and county jurisdictions.

Second, these policies will result in fewer health services for the poor and near poor.

Third, in the quest for a more robust economy, federal environmental regulations will be weakened, resulting in higher health risks from increased pollution.

Fourth, efficiency in providing care will be more important than the effectiveness of this care in treating or preventing health problems.

These policies will force the states to decide which health services to provide for citizens while putting pressure on them to be as efficient as possible in the use of the federal block grants. With flexibility in the allocation of block grant funds, states may opt for home health services instead of nursing home or extended hospital stays, may stimulate use of ambulatory services rather than hospital services, may utilize lower-cost but appropriate medical personnel such as physicians' assistants rather than physicians, and may regionalize high-cost medical services rather than encouraging duplication of services.

The cornerstone, however, of the Reagan Administration's drive to reduce costs is to foster competition in the medical field. A number of bills have been introduced that would require employers to offer their employees three or more alternative health plans. This would have the effect of shifting the responsibility for selecting a health plan that best suits their needs from the employer and union negotiators directly to the employees. Similar choices would be given to the poor and elderly under federally funded medical programs such as Medicaid and Medicare. These bills would provide incentives to physicians and medical organizations including hospitals, insurance companies, foundations, and unions to develop their own equivalent of an HMO. Although it has not been conclusively proven, federal policymakers strongly believe that HMOs do reduce hospital utilization significantly without doing any harm to the health status of patients. These bills would stimulate the creation of competing HMOs, each trying to attract a larger clientele by providing a more comprehensive scope of services at a lower cost than its competitors. The HMOs in turn would be expected to put pressure on hospitals to reduce their charges in return for a guaranteed number of patient days. It is anticipated that, in time, the whole nation would be blanketed with one type or another of prepaid, comprehensive health plans that would provide a series of mandated basic services. Should this occur, national health insurance would no longer be needed because a prepaid network of health services would be established as a viable substitute. In essence, the Reagan Administration is striving to convert a quasi-regulated medical industry into a corporate, competitive model that is influenced by the vagaries and needs of the market as represented by individual buyers of service. At this time, no one knows whether the government can loosen the strong controls exerted by physicians and their associations in order to make this competitive model work. Those who have studied and advocated this model most deeply estimate that it would take 15 to 20 years for it to involve as much as 40 percent of the population in the United States (Enthoven, 1980, and Ellwood et al., 1981).

While such a program would have an immense influence on medical care in the United States, its main impact would be on how medical care services are structured and the resulting changes in the roles and influence of consumers and medical providers. This program would weaken the close patient-physician relationship and diminish the autonomy and independence of the physician. More important, consumers would gain influence at the expense of providers. For these and other reasons, one cannot envision physicians, hospitals, unions, and employers giving up the immense power, prestige, and influence they now collectively wield to the "invisible hand of the market" and consumer choice without an all-out struggle.

None of these changes, however, will in any way change the importance of the major health issues that will need to be resolved in the 1980s. Environmental pollution problems will undoubtedly become worse as the Reagan Administration reduces its surveillance of and regulatory controls over industry. Also, reductions in public health funds will retard the goal of creating a comprehensive community support and social services system. On the other hand, the increase in provider competition for patients should lead to progress on three other issues: increasing the individual's responsibility for his/her own health, fostering greater concern for preventing conditions that affect a person's health, and developing a network of HMO-type health plans as an alternative to national health insurance.

In all of these goals, social workers have an important social-action role to play. It would seem that they are most directly affected by the reductions in federal support for social services system. On one hand, they must develop a strategy for determining how the smaller share of public health funds will be spent. This requires using their planning skills to set priorities among competing interests. On the other hand, it is necessary for them to take an active role in setting forth ways and means for replacing the lost federal funding. For this, they will have to use their community-organization and public-relations skills.

Just as physicians and hospitals will be put in the position of competing for consumer favor, social workers will likewise be required to attract clients to their services. Clients will be assessing the social workers' skills, their results, and how they deliver services. As a member of the medical provider team, they will come under the same scrutiny as any other professional service offered in the institution. Competition should have the salutary effect of improving the social workers' technical skills, their efficiency in providing service, and their effectiveness in helping their clients.

It can be seen from this discussion of the micro health policy tactics to achieve cost-containment and prevention changes, as well as the new direction of the Reagan Administration policies, that social workers do have a major role to play. However, they must choose where and for what types of policies they are by tradition, education, and practice most competent to intervene. The shift from an emphasis on the medical model to a broader social/environmental/behavioral model requires changes in their traditional pattern of practice. The real question is whether the profession of social work can make the shift from casework practice to taking greater initiative in meeting the social action challenges posed by the Reagan Administration.

SUMMARY

National health policy has been shown to be complex and to be operating at two levels, the macro and micro. Each decade produces its own major health policies that deal with significant health problems. For the 1970s, such policies have been cost containment, access by the disadvantaged to health/mental health services, improved quality of care, and planned regionalization of services. As the 1970s came to a close, the contours of the major policies for the 1980s began to emerge. Reducing environmental pollution, establishing preventive services, encouraging the individual to take greater responsibility for his/her well-being, and the incremental completion of a national health insurance program or health service network appear to be the major issues.

Lalonde's four determinants to health were used as the basis for examining both the allocation of the proposed 1980 federal health budget and the micro health policy tactics used to implement them. The analysis revealed that a gross imbalance exists in the distribution of budget allocations among the four determinants involved in improving health status. Very little change has taken place in the life expectancy indicators over the last 30 years in spite of the fact that 85 percent of the budget is expended on medical care services. A shift in allocation is consequently recommended in order to focus expenditures on the health determinants dealing with life-style, environment, and human biology.

Examples of micro health policies were identified for the two macro health policies of cost containment and prevention. Implications for social work in implementation tactics were noted, and a partial shift in emphasis was recommended from its current focus on behavior modification to social action to modify the environment through legislative or enforcement strategies. While the Reagan Administration policies will not change the major health issues requiring resolution, they will hinder the achievement of some of these goals while promoting the success of others.

REFERENCES

Alford, R. R. 1975. *Health care politics.* Chicago: University of Chicago.

Banta, D. 1978. *Assessing the efficiency and safety of medical technologies.* Washington, D.C.: U.S. Congress, Office of Technology Assessment.

Bloom, B. L., and Parad, H. J. 1976. Interdisciplinary training and interdisciplinary functioning. *American Journal of Orthopsychiatry* 46:669–77.

Blum, H. L. 1974. *Planning for health.* New York: Human Sciences.

Brody, S. J. 1976. Common ground: social work and health care. *Health and Social Work* 1:17–31.

Brown, B. S. 1977. Conflict and detente between social issues and clinical practice. *American Journal of Orthopsychiatry* 47:466–75.

Cambridge Research Institute. 1975. *Trends affecting the U.S. health care system.* Washington, D.C.: Department of Health, Education, and Welfare, Health Resources Administration.

Carlton, W. 1977. The health team training model: a teaching-learning approach in community health. *Health Education Monographs* 5:62–74.

Ellwood, P. M.; Malcolm, J. K.; and McDonald, J. 1981. *Competition: medicine's creeping revolution.* Excelsior, Minn.: InterStudy.

Enthoven, A. C. *Health plan.* 1980. Reading, Mass.: Addison-Wesley.

Finney, R. D.; Pessin, R. P.; and Matheis, L. P. 1976. Prospects for social workers in health planning. *Health and Social Work* 1:8–26.

Forward plan for health: FY 1977–81. 1975. Washington, D.C.: Department of Health, Education, and Welfare, Public Health Service.

Fuchs, V. R. 1974. *Who shall live?* New York: Basic Books.

Ginzberg, E. *The limits of health reform.* 1977. New York: Basic Books.

Health, United States. 1978. Rockville, Maryland: Department of Health, Education, and Welfare, Health Resources Administration.

Humanization of health care: a statement of scope and credo of social work in health care. 1975. *Social Work in Health Care* 1:5–6.

Hyman, H. H. 1978. Most important regional and state hsp/aip objectives. Department of Health, Education and Welfare, Regional Office Two, Division of Health Planning and Resources Development. Mimeographed paper.

Kane, R. L. 1978. Societal values and modern medicine: how do we measure costs and benefits? *Journal of Community Health* 4:97–103.

Knowles, J. H. 1975. *Conference on future directions in health care: the dimensions of medicine.* New York: Rockefeller Foundation, The Blue Cross Association and Health Policy Program, University of California, San Francisco.

Lalonde, M. 1974. A new perspective on the health of Canadians. Ottawa: Health and Welfare Directorate.

McKinney, E. A. 1976. Health care crisis—for whom? *Health and Social Work* 1:103-16.

McNamara, J. J. 1975-76. Social work designs a humanistic program to enhance patient care. *Social Work in Health Care* 1:145-54.

NASW news. July 1977. National Association of Social Workers.

Nation's health, the. March 1979. American Public Health Association.

Parad, H. J.; Resnik, H.L.P.; and Parad, L. G., eds. 1976. *Emergency and disaster management.* Bowie, Md.: Charles.

Somers, A. R., ed. 1976. *Promoting health.* Germantown, Md.: Aspen Systems.

Thoma, M. A. 1977. The effects of a cultural awareness program on the delivery of health care. *Health and Social Work* 2:124-36.

Wershow, H. J. 1977. Setting priorities in health services. *Health and Social Work* 2:7-24.

Westerman, J. H.; Spano, R. M.; and Keyes, M. A. 1976. Public accountability, quality assurance and social work. *Social Work in Health Care* 2:33-42.

5

MEDICAID

Stephen M. Davidson

Medicaid was the result of a compromise engineered in 1965 by Representative Wilbur D. Mills to secure the passage of Medicare, the national health insurance program for the aged. As Title 19 of the Social Security Act, it had two principal purposes: (1) to make needed medical services financially accessible to eligible poor people who otherwise would be unable to afford them; and (2) to encourage the utilization of those services in "the mainstream of American medicine" (i.e., in the private office-based sector, which serves the majority of Americans).

The goals were to be achieved through a greatly expanded system of payments to providers of medical services for care rendered to individuals who qualified either as recipients of public assistance or, in those states which chose to cover them, as "medically needy." The latter were people who would qualify for public assistance except that their incomes were somewhat higher than those specified for cash grants. The program is financed jointly by the federal and state governments and administered by the states, under regulations established by the federal government. In FY 1976, more than $14 billion was spent for medical services to more than 24.5 million people (Health Care Financing Administration, 1978a, table 1).

Evidence is accumulating that growing numbers of physicians, who are the gatekeepers to the American medical care system, have become disaffected with the program and either are limiting their participation in it or are withdrawing altogether. A California study revealed that in 1974 approximately 40 percent of physicians there had reduced or intended to reduce their participation (Garner, Liao, and Sharpe, 1979). Kushman found that in 1973 and 1974 the proportion of California physicians making claims for compensation under the state's Medi-Cal program was as low as 56 percent in some areas of the state (Kushman, 1977). The Michigan State Medical Association reported in 1976 that only 68.3 percent of Michigan physicians indicated they would accept new Medicaid patients, a drop from the 1973 figure of 83.5 percent (Garner, Liao, and Sharpe, 1979). A Mississippi study conducted in 1976–77 found that 58 percent of office-based physicians in that state earned $2,000 or more from Medicaid (Garner, Liao, Sharpe, 1979). And, more recently, the president of the Massachusetts Medical Society estimated that "physician participation in

Medicaid during calendar year 1977 fell to 51 percent of the 14,875 physicians licensed in the state" (Massachusetts Medical Society, 1979).

The figures vary with the state, the year, and the measure of participation (e.g., the number of physicians seeing any Medicaid patients, the number seeing new patients, the number submitting claims for services rendered, the proportion of visits paid for by Medicaid, and the dollars paid to each physician by Medicaid). But the common theme is that physicians are limiting their participation in Medicaid programs and that the phenomenon seems to be a national one.

One implication of this fact is that the program goal of assuring care in the mainstream of American medicine is being undermined. Another more controversial one is that escalating program costs may be partially attributable to the limited participation or withdrawal of substantial numbers of physicians.

When private practitioners withdraw from the program, many patients turn to hospital emergency rooms (Davidson, 1978), which furnish care at higher prices than private practitioners. A North Carolina physician related that in a small, rural county in his state "there are five family practitioners . . . and no other primary care doctors. The physicians charge $10 for an office visit. Medicaid pays them $4.80. Because of this, all physicians stopped seeing Medicaid patients last year. Now a few Medicaid patients are seen by nurse practitioners in the county health department, but most go to the Ambulatory Care Unit of [the local] hospital where Medicaid is charged $21.25 per patient visit and pays $17.02 per visit" (Edwards, 1978).

Some states, moreover, have deliberately fostered the use of public health clinics in the provision of Early and Periodic Screening, Diagnosis, and Treatment services to children, instead of private, office-based physicians (Foltz and Brown, 1975), one result of which is higher prices. In Louisiana, for example, it is reported that when the state Division of Health bills the Division of Family Services for a screening examination, the cost is 25 percent to 30 percent more than would be charged by private practitioners (Dunlap, 1978).

The cost of services recommended for children through the age of five when done in his own office was compared by a North Carolina pediatrician with the amount paid for the same services when they were provided by the health department. He showed that, in September 1975, eleven visits to the private doctor's office cost $190 (an average of $17.27), whereas ten visits to the health department cost $270 or $27 per visit (Edwards, 1977).

The cost of the program depends on several factors: the number of eligibles, the number of services provided, the types of care provided, and the sources of that care. To the extent that one source is not available, others will be substituted, sometimes at higher unit costs. Further, if the care in those substitute sites is episodic or of poor quality, it may result in the need for additional services that otherwise would not be necessary. These points, while not yet verified with systematically obtained evidence, are empirical questions that are susceptible to study.[1]

The point for our purposes is that, apart from the extent to which the program's original goal is being achieved, there is reason at least to wonder aloud whether increasing the participation of office-based physicians, particularly those delivering primary care, would help to contain medical care costs. If states with lower levels of physician participation spend more on Medicaid because of the substitution of emergency department care for office-based care or because of the substitution of episodic, sick-call care for continuing, comprehensive care, state officials will want to take steps to increase that participation. Therefore, it is important to understand what factors influence a physician's decisions regarding his participation in Medicaid.

In October 1978, the Health Care Financing Administration, which has responsibility for Medicaid at the federal level, funded a two-year, 13-state study with three goals: (1) to determine the extent of physician participation in Medicaid programs, using several measures of participation; (2) to identify factors associated with participation, some of which may be susceptible to policy intervention; and (3) to investigate the implications of differing rates of participation. The rest of this paper presents findings from the initial phase of that research, which identified some of those factors for testing in the main study. It derives from a review of the limited literature available and from an informal survey of pediatricians. Since this part of the study was an effort to generate ideas, not to test hypotheses, it can be said with certainty only that these factors are influential with some physicians. We cannot yet comment on their relative strength when compared with one another, the proportions of physicians affected by them, or the extent to which their impact is uniform from state to state.

The underlying thesis is that physicians are influenced principally by fiscal considerations and by factors that interfere with their ability to exercise their professional judgment. This does not mean that the physician will not participate unless he gets the exact fee he wants or that he will withdraw if there is *any* attempt to restrict the extent of his discretion in the treatment of patients.[2] On the other hand, these are items that physicians care about. Accordingly, if an administrative decision or policy diverges enough from their wish or expectation, or, more likely, if an accumulation of state actions offends them sufficiently, they are likely to reduce or end their participation in the program, other things being equal.

The appropriate focus for a consideration of these issues is the state, which, although it operates under federal regulations, retains many important decisions. Thus, although some aspects are common to all, each state makes its own decisions—within the limits established by federal rules—regarding who is eligible, the amounts and types of services covered, how claims are paid, and how much money to spend. One of the central facts about Medicaid is the considerable variation among the states on all these dimensions. In the next section, I will discuss decisions regarding each of these major programmatic functions which represent impediments to physician participation in Medicaid.

IMPEDIMENTS TO PHYSICIAN PARTICIPATION
IN MEDICAID

Benefits

States are required to cover seven basic services in their Medicaid programs:

Inpatient hospital services
Outpatient hospital services
Physician services
Laboratory and X-ray services
Nursing home services
Family planning services
Early and Periodic Screening, Diagnosis, and Treatment services for children (EPSDT)

In addition, they have the option of covering virtually any other health service available, including transportation to and from sites of care and home health services.

Variation enters in several ways: while all states must cover the seven services, each may set a maximum amount of each service (e.g., 15 hospital days or 30) and establish the conditions under which they are available; second, each state may limit its program to those seven services or add almost any other health care service to its list; and third, from time to time states, with federal approval, may change certain aspects of their programs. These three factors limit the care received by eligible patients and, equally, the physician's ability to exercise his best clinical judgment in behalf of his patients.

Benefit Limitations

Inpatient hospital services are provided as long as medically necessary or virtually without limitations in some states (Illinois, Louisiana, Massachusetts), but in other states a variety of restrictions are imposed.[3] For example, prior authorization may be required for all hospital admissions (California, Maryland); for stays beyond a certain number of days (12 days in New Hampshire, 15 days in Rhode Island); or for admissions for particular conditions (renal dialysis or kidney transplants in Georgia, all nonemergencies in Hawaii, or cosmetic surgery and surgical transplants in North Carolina). Other states simply set a maximum number of days covered (10 days per admission in Oklahoma, 21 days in Oregon, 90 days for each spell of illness in Ohio, 20 days per fiscal year in Tennessee, 40 days in South Carolina).

Similarly, physician services are subject to a variety of rules. In Colorado, a person is eligible for 12 home and office calls in a calendar year; in Arkansas, it is 18 visits; in Ohio, it is 10 visits per month. Other states have no limitations (North Dakota, Texas, Virginia).

Moreover, immunizations and routine examinations for children who apparently are well, both of which are established aspects of standard pediatric care, are excluded under Medicaid programs in some states (e.g., Kentucky).

One of the seven basic services that must be part of all Medicaid programs is the Early and Periodic Screening, Diagnosis, and Treatment program (EPSDT) for children, which requires states not only to *pay* for the requisite services, but to see to it that they are *provided*. The underlying assumption of EPSDT is that, if health problems are caught early enough—through early and periodic monitoring—appropriate treatment in childhood can prevent more serious problems later on. EPSDT has been beset by problems since its inception (Children's Defense Fund, 1977).

One of the areas of difficulty arises from the fact that some state Medicaid programs do not include the services needed to treat some of the conditions uncovered during screening. As the Children's Defense Fund writes, "States have strongly resisted the expansion of required services in their Medicaid programs" (Children's Defense Fund, 1977, p. 144). The ability to achieve the special intent of this program is thus reduced by policies that either exclude required services altogether (e.g., speech therapy to correct problems found during a speech evaluation; treatment for asthma uncovered during screening; prosthetic devices or orthopedic shoes) or establish restrictions that exclude some children who need treatment (e.g., setting the standard for vision problems at 20/50, thus denying corrective glasses to some children who need them; or allowing only one eye exam or only one pair of glasses in a year, even though some vision problems require more frequent examinations and even though active children may be expected to break their glasses occasionally falling off jungle gyms or during sandlot ball games).

Participating providers of health care services must keep informed about these limitations and the changes in them that affect their ability to treat Medicaid patients. The limitations effectively reduce the practitioner's ability to exercise professional discretion in treating patients. While they are often justified as cost-containment measures, most of the limitations affect relatively small numbers of patients and only limited portions of their care.[4] Finally, many of the limitations are on inexpensive services used by few people whose impact on the total state Medicaid budget must be small.

While these characteristics of the benefit structure probably reduce to some extent the amount of services delivered, they may also contribute to other results that are not desirable. For example, some of the services thereby omitted may be necessary for the optimal treatment of patients, and some of the omissions may result in the use of additional more expensive services later on. While direct evidence is not available on the extent to which these additional results are produced, they do undoubtedly occur in some measure. In addition, it is likely that these features tend to discourage physicians and other professionals from participating in the program and, to that extent, reduce the degree to which the program's goals are achieved (i.e., fewer patients will be served in the mainstream; and if patients are thereby diverted to more expensive sources of care, costs will be increased unnecessarily). The questions to be asked are, "Is the gain in dollars saved large enough and reliable enough to warrant the secondary effects?" And alternatively, "Are there better ways to achieve the primary goals without producing the undesired secondary effects, as well?"

Benefit Changes

States may change their benefit coverage with federal approval. In the nine months between October 1, 1975, and July 1, 1976, 26 states changed at least one aspect of their coverage. Some of the changes represented increases in benefits, and some were reductions, including the following: physician visits for chronic, stable illnesses outside hospitals were limited to one per month in Alabama; in Arkansas recipients were limited to three prescriptions per month;[5] Maryland eliminated payment for hospital inpatient medical-social days (i.e., days without a medical justification, but for which no more appropriate level of care is available); 30-cent copayments on drugs were imposed in Kansas and Mississippi; and a 50-cent copayment, in South Dakota; Massachusetts eliminated hearing aids for adults; Michigan eliminated occupational and speech therapy; Maryland eliminated custom foot supports and all disposable medical supplies except for ostomy supplies and those for permanent urinary incontinence.

In addition, fees were reduced in a number of states: Florida reduced its EPSDT screening fee from $10 to $6.25; New Hampshire reduced payments to nursing facilities from 95 percent to 90 percent of allowable cost.

In some cases, reductions were only temporary. For example, Michigan eliminated physical therapy in long-term care facilities and hearing services and, less than a year later, restored both. Moreover, it eliminated vision services, including eyeglasses and related services, and later restored them as well, though with some limitations. Florida reduced inpatient hospital days from 45 to 30 days per year in January 1976 and restored the maximum to 45 days in July; it limited outpatient hospital services to $50 per year without prior authorization and later raised the amount to $100 with exceptions up to $200. Even some fee reductions were later restored. For example, in Michigan maximum fee screens were reduced by 11 percent for physicians, dentists, and laboratories, were later restored, and still later were reduced by 4 percent. In Vermont, provider fees were cut by 3 percent and four months later were restored.

Eligibility

Eligibility for Medicaid benefits is intimately tied up with the American public welfare system. Recipients of Federal Supplemental Security Income benefits (aged, blind, and disabled) are eligible for Medicaid in their states, though in some states eligibility is not automatic. Recipients of Aid to Families with Dependent Children, a federal/state income maintenance program, are automatically eligible for Medicaid benefits. In addition, in more than half the states, people who meet all the requirements for SSI or

AFDC except that their incomes are slightly too high are eligible for Medicaid benefits because they are considered to be "medically needy."

ELIGIBILITY FOR PUBLIC WELFARE. Most of the eligibility problems regarding Medicaid arise from the welfare system. Since welfare is an income support system, it is by definition a system for people whose incomes fall below standards established by the states.

Eligibility is determined on a monthly basis. That is, a person may receive public assistance in one month, but because he was able to get a temporary part-time job, for example, he may lose his assistance benefits the following month. Superficially, at least, that seems reasonable, given the income maintenance intent of the program, but it has implications that reduce the family's ability to leave welfare permanently (these are beyond the scope of this paper) and that, in addition, affect certain aspects of the medical care they receive.

For example, the on-and-off nature of eligibility reduces the extent to which a patient can establish a relationship with a single "medical home" providing continuous, comprehensive primary care services. During a month of eligibility a patient may see a physician for a condition that the physician needs to check the following month after a course of treatment. But when the patient comes for his return apointment, he may no longer be eligible for Medicaid benefits, yet still be too poor to pay the physician's bill directly. While some physicians will continue to treat such a patient, others understandably will not.

The situation is a particular problem under EPSDT, a long-term program with multiple phases extending over many years. The diagnostic and treatment follow-up from a single screening examination may itself take several months. Keeping in mind that such screenings are intended to occur not only early in a child's life, but periodically as well, it can be seen that short-term eligibility can reduce the effectiveness of the program. The Children's Defense Fund quoted a South Carolina EPSDT official as saying, "Turnover in eligibility of Medicaid recipients is the biggest problem with EPSDT. People become ineligible as many as three times per year. How are we supposed to give them treatment?" (Children's Defense Fund, 1977, 143).

The Congress enacted a provision in the law, effective in January 1974, which required states to extend eligibility for four months to AFDC families who lost it. The Children's Defense Fund found, however, that, while formal state plans have been brought into conformity with the law, actual practice still limits Medicaid eligibility to shorter periods in some states. Furthermore, non-AFDC recipients are not covered by the provision; and children with chronic conditions who need ongoing care continue to be left without coverage.

In addition to problems of temporary eligibility, another issue concerns the coverage of newborns. Since eligibility for Medicaid is an individual affair, each potential recipient must be identified separately. Thus, even though a child's eligibility depends on his family's income and composition, it must be established individually. In some states, therefore, newborns whose eligibility has not been independently determined are not entitled to Medicaid services even though the mother's prenatal care and the baby's delivery *were* covered. Research shows the first month of life to be critical to the survival of the child, yet often benefits will be denied because eligibility has not been established. Some states will permit the mother to register the child prior to birth, but others require that eligibility be established by the mother only after the baby has been born, and then only by the mother's visit to a public assistance office to complete the necessary forms. At a time when state laws require private insurance companies covering other family members to cover a newborn child automatically for the first thirty days of life (American Academy of Pediatrics, 1977), it is anomalous that medical care programs paid for directly by those same state governments do not provide similar coverage.

ELIGIBILITY FOR THE MEDICALLY NEEDY. An additional eligibility problem stems from the fact that 29 states provide benefits to medically needy individuals whose incomes are somewhat above those of public assistance recipients. Those states are permitted to offer a different package to the medically needy than they provide to categorical recipients, and some states have exercised that option. As a result, physicians and other providers in those states must know not only that the patient is eligible for Medicaid benefits, but also the precise nature of his eligibility. For example, Pennsylvania pays for prescribed drugs, dental services, prosthetic devices, and podiatrists' services only to financial aid recipients and not to the medically needy, even though other services are available to both groups. In Maine, clinic services, emergency hospital services, and service in intermediate care institutions are available only to categorical recipients, while other services are available to the medically needy, as well.

These rules, in addition to those limiting covered services, reduce the clinician's freedom to provide what he determines to be needed by his Medicaid patients. In so doing, they increase the burden felt by the provider who is willing to participate in the program. Since the particular restrictions — e.g., limitations on the number of hospital days permitted, on the numbers of physician visits, on specific services such as those provided by podiatrists or chiropractors, or hearing or vision services — often account for relatively little of the Medicaid dollar, one must ask again whether the money saved justifies the secondary effects they produce.

Compensating Providers

The most direct deterrents to providers are related to compensation. They fall into several categories: the rates of pay, the speed with which claims are processed, the predictability with which they are paid, and the simplicity of the forms and procedures used. The following discussion concerns payment for physician services only, but it has relevance to other providers, as well.

RATES OF PAY. The most common complaint about Medicaid is that the states pay providers at low rates. One survey found that 57 percent of responding physicians identified the fee structure as the one aspect of the program they would most like to change (Physician's Management Staff, 1978). In another, 63 percent of physicians in a southern state complained about "low reimbursement" (Garner, Liao, and Sharpe, 1979).

While recognizing the importance of other factors, the authors of two studies attempted to isolate the impact of Medicaid fees on physician participation in the program. Using data from a national survey of physicians, Sloan and his colleagues found that, "holding other factors constant, a statistically significant fee elasticity of Medicaid participation of .70 was found. If the average Medicaid fee schedule in a defined geographic area doubled, the percentage of a phsyician's practice devoted to Medicaid patients would increase about 70 percent" (Sloan, Cromwell, and Mitchell, 1977, p. 18). Examining data from California representing experience over a four-year period, Hadley found remarkably similar results. His analyses "suggest that a 10 percent increase in average revenue per Medicaid patient would increase participation (for the three specialities in the study) by about 7 percent (roughly from .42 to .45) and the number of Medicaid patients per participating physician by about 18 percent (or about ten patients)" (Hadley, 1978, p. 65).

Thirteen states, including the District of Columbia, use the Medicare basis for payment—that is, the 75th percentile of usual, customary, and reasonable charges for a particular service in the area.[6] Other states pay physicians on the basis of reasonable and/or customary charges or fee schedules. Whatever the basis for paying the physicians, dissatisfaction arises from state practices of setting fees at rates below usual charges and of failing to revise them to compensate for increases in the cost of providing services.

The fundamental complaint is that fees are set at low rates and, once set, are not increased. When New York first established its Medicaid program, it paid professional practitioners on the basis of reasonable charges, but shortly afterward shifted to a fee schedule that effectively reduced rates paid for service even then. The result was a decline in utilization of practitioners' services, as planned, but it is not clear how much of the utilization thus eliminated was overutilization and how much represented the reasonable use of services. Those fee schedules have not been revised since the late 1960s. The result is that a pediatrician practicing in New York receives $12.00 for any visit for a new illness and $7.20 for a return visit. Moreover, New York State announced recently that the $12.00 fee could be charged only once in a three-month period for any child regardless of the child's medical condition. As the director of one of New York's county-operated Medicaid programs has written:[7]

Virtually all other classes of providers—hospitals, nursing homes, suppliers of drugs, appliances, etc.—are paid on the basis of rates and prices which are influenced by the prevailing cost of doing business. This results in public and private clinics receiving $40-$80 for a clinic visit for the same service which, if given in the private physician's office, is priced in the State Fee Schedule at $12 if it is the first visit to a pediatrician or, if it is a follow-up or routine office visit, at $7.20.[8]

Similar views are expressed in other states where fees often are less than those in New York. In Maryland, for example, the rate is $7 and makes no distinction between a new visit and a return visit.

One question that might be asked, however, is "What is wrong with $12 for an office visit?" If four are done in an hour, the resulting $48 does not sound bad for an hour's work. Furthermore, the physician may be able to charge his private patients more than $12 and thus raise the hourly figure beyond $48.

Part of the answer concerns the relationship of the gross payment to the cost of operating a modern medical practice. As one Vermont physician has written:

The overhead in our practice group is 64 percent of gross billings and the fee offered by Medicaid is 61 percent of our regular fee. At the same time, our calculations show that the average gross bill of the Medicaid patient for a visit is 7½ percent higher than for a non-Medicaid patient, but the reimbursement is the same (i.e., 61 percent of the fee). The net result is that Medicaid reimburses us 57 percent on the average gross billing for a Medicaid patient, which represents a net loss of seven cents on each dollar charged every time we see a Medicaid patient. . . . Seeing a Medicaid patient costs us $9.13 in overhead expenses, and we were reimbursed $8.00.

A similar statement was received from a physician practicing in the state of Washington. He wrote:

Reimbursement for standard office calls is slightly above the overhead level in those pediatric offices having small staffs. In an office providing more comprehensive service and having a larger support staff, reimbursement will be at less than the overhead level. . . . With the overhead going on minute by minute, and with the pressure from front office staff to see paying patients with problems not requiring this time expenditure, it is a rare physician, in spite of altruism and all other motivation, who does not feel reluctant to continually steal time and money from paying patients in order to provide care for more complicated problems of Medicaid children.

Another part of the answer is related to characteristics of Medicaid patients that distinguish them from other patients, including the amount of services needed. As a Seattle pediatrician wrote:

Medicaid children are far more difficult and time-consuming to care for than other patients, because of the following: (a) language barriers; (b) no home phone to receive the doctor's return call; (c) Medicaid parents report most illnesses after office hours, on weekends, and holidays because that is when they are with their children; (d) Major communication problems arise because adults other than the parents frequently take Medicaid children to the doctor's office.

This testimony is corroborated by a Baltimore physician, who wrote:

The effort and time required for the care of a Medicaid patient is often greater than that for one's regular practice because of: (a) The tendency for many of the patients to ignore the making and keeping of appointments. They either don't show up, placing an additional burden on the physician for retrieval, or they arrive with four children instead of the one for whom the appointment was made; (b) The frequent lack of telephone facilities; (c) The restriction against telephoning prescriptions; (d) The additional and often cumbersome paperwork; (e) The usual delay of the agency in making payment to the physician; (f) The difficulty of securing consultation through the usual channels.

The Vermont physician mentioned earlier indicated that services provided to Medicaid patients in his practice are more expensive on the average than those provided to other patients because "Medicaid patients actually require a disproportionate amount of time and support services as compared with others." In Vermont, however, services provided under EPSDT administered as part of the same Medicaid program are compensated on the basis of usual and customary charges, which "serves to alleviate some of the problem." In Illinois, on the other hand, the opposite is true. Practitioners there are paid more to provide a service under Medicaid than to provide the same service under EPSDT.

Low fees are intended as a means of saving tax dollars. To the extent that they result either in an increase in the amount of services provided or in the diversion of services to more expensive sites of care, however, that intent is defeated. When private practitioners withdraw from the program, many patients turn to hospital emergency rooms (Davidson, 1978), which furnish care at higher prices than private practitioners. The North Carolina experience cited earlier is one example.

OTHER COMPENSATION PROBLEMS. In addition to low fees, providers complain frequently about delays in payment, its unpredictability, and the complexity of the forms required (Garner, Liao, and Sharpe, 1979; Physician's Management Staff, 1978). An Illinois study showed that 26 percent of physicians' and other practitioners' bills paid in May 1974 by the state's Department of Public Aid were more than four months old, and approximately 5 percent were more than one year old (Davidson, 1974). A more recent study in Connecticut showed that 25 percent of bills submitted were rejected the first time they were presented for payment and that the backlog on old claims was more than three months. The authors wrote that staffing in the Connecticut Medical Payments Section was at such a low level that work on the backlog could only be done on an overtime basis, which further aggravated the state's financial position (Connecticut General Assembly, 1976, pp. 83–84).

In some states, particularly those which still rely on considerable hand processing (as opposed to more extensive use of the computer), physicians complain that when they submit a bill, they do not know whether it will be paid or, if so, whether the amount of the payment will be the same as the last similar bill submitted. The computer promises to bring greater reliability as well as improved efficiency to the processing of claims and the management of the complex Medicaid program. It may continue to bring dissatisfaction from providers, too, however, if the forms required are complex, as reports from a number of pediatricians indicate they are. While the need for accountability is understandable, many practitioners believe that the forms require more detail than is usable.

IMPLICATIONS

It appears from the material presented that, regardless of their intent, many of the policies and practices of Medicaid programs have the effect of increasing the providers' burden of participating. Since participation is voluntary, providers are likely to withdraw or curtail their participation as that burden grows. The sources cited above provide ample evidence that, in fact, many physicians have done exactly that.

Medicaid officials are concerned about this tendency, which has been observed throughout the country, in part because it reduces the extent to which the goal of providing care to poor people in the mainstream of American medicine can be achieved. In addition, it is more expensive and less efficient not to rely heavily on primary care practitioners.

Discouraging private physicians from partidcipating results in more referrals of Medicaid patients to emergency department of hospitals, more nonreferred use of those emergency departments, more use of public health department clinics (especially for EPSDT services), and more use and encouragement of high-volume "sick-call" offices.[9] Yet none of these sites should be encouraged as a principal source of ambulatory medical care. Hospital emergency departments are overstaffed and overequipped to provide the routine first-contact care people need most. Moreover, they are geared to respond to discrete episodes of illness and accidents, not to offer comprehensive care with a measure of continuity. Health department clinics — which often are understaffed, established for limited purposes, and operated for less than even 40 hours per week — are also ill equipped to provide primary medical care. And the high-volume, storefront sick-call practices found principally in low-income inner-city areas, while perhaps capable of being primary care providers, typically furnish care as episodic as that found in emergency departments.

In addition to these reasons for not wanting to encourage the use of these sources of routine care, the fact is that costs in each are higher than those found in typical private practices — whether of the solo, small group, or comprehensive clinic variety — as a number of examples provided above affirm (David and Schoen, 1978, p. 206). Thus, greater use of private practitioners should reduce Medicaid expenditures.

None of this denies the assertion that, as a nation, we do not have enough private practitioners or comprehensive care clinics in the right places to treat all poor people. On the other hand, any strategy to increase the numbers of primary care practitioners in inner cities and among other concentrations of poor people must include reasonable means of compensating those practitioners for their services.[10] A Medicaid program that discourages them will not contribute to increasing the availability of services. While a sound Medicaid program is not sufficient by itself to attract additional services to inner-city or underserved rural areas, it is unlikely that any deliberate strategy to increase the amount of services available in such locations can succeed without it.

Officials charged with spending public funds must be concerned about the amounts of money spent and the appropriateness and quality of the services purchased. Accountability is an appropriate and necessary part of the game. The need for accountability, concern about overspending, and worry about quality, however, do not require that Medicaid officials view all providers with suspicion and therefore act to restrict their opportunity to perform as responsible professionals.

A more successful approach would begin with the assumption that clients and providers alike are reasonably honest and want to use or furnish services appropriately. It would concentrate energies in developing the elements of a strategy to create "incentives so that public goals become private interest" (Schultze, 1977, p. 6); that is, so that practitioners would benefit directly from accomplishing the program's purposes. It would begin by attempting to simplify the program in ways like those suggested below. It would build accountability into the system by retrospective examination of the utilization and service provision patterns of samples of clients and providers. The more common "command and control" approach cannot work because the medical care arena is too complex, and medical services depend too much on the practitioner's art as well as his knowledge.

RECOMMENDATIONS

To increase the rates of participation among primary care physicians, policymakers must address the factors that, singly and in combination, discourage physicians from treating patients whose care is paid for by Medicaid. Among those reasons are limitations on covered services, arbitrary and rigid definitions of services, short-term and unstable eligibility, frequent changes in program characteristics, cumbersome claims payment forms and procedures, unpredictable payment, low rates of compensation, burdensome accountability forms and procedures, and brusque, disinterested public employees.

Some of these contributing problems may be overcome with a program based on the assumption that most clients, providers, and government officials are honest and reasonable and interested in building a program that makes needed services available to people who otherwise cannot pay for them. The following specific recommendations, which start from that premise, may help:

Benefits

1. Require that a broad range of services be covered to maximize the practitioner's ability to treat patients at the most appropriate, least costly level of care. The physician should not be discouraged by the range or amount of services covered from exercising his best fiscally responsible professional judgment as to the services needed by a particular patient.

2. Adopt standards that require that medical services needed to treat conditions discovered during EPSDT screening be covered regardless of restrictions in a state's Medicaid program. Screening implies treatment, and special efforts should be made to see to it that reasonable expectation is not frustrated.

Eligibility

1. Once an eligible individual has used covered medical services, he should retain eligibility for services for a stated period or as long as is necessary to complete the treatment for the condition for which care was sought.

2. Care for newborns should be paid for whenever the mother is eligible herself or when older children in the family are eligible on the presumption that the new child, too, will be eligible.

3. Special attention should be given to pregnant teenagers because many states do not consider them to be eligible for public assistance until after the birth of a child. Where this practice is followed, it has acted as a deterrent to the receipt of adequate prenatal care, which can reduce the high rates of obstetric complications during pregnancy and delivery and higher rates of premature delivery and low-weight births.

4. The function of paying the provider for services rendered to newborns should be separated from the function of determining the financial responsibility of other parties (e.g., the child's father or an insurance carrier). If the services were rendered in good faith, they should be paid for, and efforts to recover those funds from another source should proceed independently.

Compensation

1. When providers are paid on a fee-for-service basis, the fee should be closely related to the provider's costs. To pay less discourages providers from participating in the program and results in increased use of higher-cost hospital emergency departments.

2. Experiments should be conducted with other means of paying providers, including capitation. These methods, by encouraging restraint in the provision of services (especially hospitalization), can reduce expenditures for services without compromising quality. Yet more research is needed, especially regarding the application of these methods to a Medicaid population, before expansion on a large scale should be advocated.

3. Heavy penalties should be imposed on states for failure to pay bills within a reasonable period of time. At the present time, failure to achieve this goal is attributable in large part to the difficulty providers have in submitting "clean" claims (that is, bills that will not be rejected). Therefore, part of this effort must be directed toward alterations in the system that will increase the chances that the claims submitted are, in fact, "clean." Two aspects of that task are simplifying reporting forms and simplifying the eligibility process.

4. The state's basis of payment, rates of payment, and other aspects of the claims payment process should be made clearer to providers so that they will have a better ability to predict the outcome of a claim submitted.

Accountability

1. The need to hold providers of care accountable for the care they furnish to Medicaid patients should be met in ways that do not interfere with the care at the point of delivery. They should begin with a retrospective analysis of claims paid and concentrate on samples of providers who furnish higher-than-normal rates of service. Subsequent analysis of their practices should be as unobtrusive as possible using clear standards developed with medical input. Finally, staff should approach practitioners with courtesy and respect.

Communication

1. Require that all changes in benefits go through a review process with input from affected parties, including practitioners. Changes in the rules would thus be discouraged because they would be more difficult. In addition, the likelihood that those changes which *were* made would have unanticipated side effects would be reduced.

2. Medical advisory committees should be reestablished in each state and should be given clear responsibilities for considering and approving changes in the state plans and for meeting at specified intervals to review the program.

3. Each HCFA Medicaid Regional Office should have at its disposal a physician consultant to provide advice and guidance regarding relations with professionals in the states. He or she should be someone who, on the one hand, is supportive of the program and, on the other, has had experience as a provider of services under it.

For Medicaid to achieve its goals of making medical care financially accessible to poor people in the mainstream of American medicine is a formidable challenge, especially under the condition of fiscal constraint. As long as the medical care system remains basically the private-practice, office-based, fee-for-service mode, the best hope for success is a strategy that promotes that system's best features: imagination, independence, and continuity and comprehensiveness of care. Such an approach has been outlined in the preceding pages. If it is followed, not only will poor people be better served, but taxpayers will save money in the bargain.

Social workers and other interested people can perform two services that will contribute to the ability of Medicaid programs to accomplish the purposes identified at the outset. The first is, in every discussion of the program, to reaffirm the intent of the original legislation—to make needed medical services financially accessible to poor people in the mainstream of American medicine. To a considerable extent, the focus of activity has become instead to contain costs and eliminate fraud and abuse. The former, undeniably important, should be addressed without undermining the program's purposes; the latter is a problem whose substantive implications are not nearly so significant as its public prominence suggests. The need is for a return to the basics.

Second, social workers can help to identify the central substantive issues and to infuse the debate on them with sensible analyses so that decisions can be made with the benefit of greater knowledge. Emotions run high about welfare and about government intervention in the private sector, and so the need for information is perhaps even more important here than on many other public policy issues. The question of physician participation raised in this chapter is a major issue inextricably linked to others (e.g., expenditures, utilization, distribution, and availability of services, quality, methods of paying providers, and others). Further, its importance extends beyond Medicaid to other medical care programs, present and future. Not all of the implications of the recommendations made here are fully known. Studies that will clarify some of them are already under way, and others are needed. Those involving demonstrations of new strategies require complicated, expensive methodologies; but others can be done using public data generated routinely by state and local programs. The first requirement is a clear focus on the real issues, which, at base, remain how to achieve the program's goals more completely and in a cost-conscious manner. Social workers knowledgeable about the program through their work with low-income citizens in hospitals and other settings are in a particularly good position to provide that focus. By doing so, they will help to improve the program and benefit their clients as well.

NOTES

1. The Health Care Financing Administration (HCFA), the agency charged with responsibility for Medicaid at the federal level, has solicited research proposals on the substitution of hospital outpatient and emergency department services for those provided in private physicians' offices.

2. Nor does it mean that he *should* be free to make absolutely any decision he wishes. In addition to professional ethics, a physician should be held accountable for the prudent expenditure of public funds.

3. Data on the characteristics of state Medicaid programs presented in this and subsequent sections were taken from two sources. They are the state-by-state summaries in the *Medicare and Medicaid Reporter* published by the Commerce Clearing House (Chicago, Ill.) and the Institute for Medicaid Management's revised report called *Data on the Medicaid Program: Eligibility, Services, Expenditures, Fiscal Years 1966–1978* (Health Care Financing Administration, Medicaid Bureau, 1978b).

4. Moreover, if often is possible, though tedious, to circumvent the rules. If prior authorization is required, for example, it frequently is possible to write the request for coverage in a way that cannot be denied.

5. This is important not only because some patients may need more than three prescriptions in a month, but also because some pharmacies — partly to compensate for low rates of pay — divide a single prescription in order to collect a double fee. For example, instead of providing the 50 pills ordered by a physician, the pharmacy may claim to have only 30 on hand and require the patient to return later for the other 20, at which time an additional fee can be collected.

6. This practice creates problems in relation to services that are not used by Medicare recipients. Medicare does not have financial profiles on pediatricians, for example.

7. This and subsequent quotations from practitioners are taken from letters from pediatricians who were asked to respond to several questions regarding their experience with Medicaid.

8. It should be pointed out that the two rates may not be entirely comparable. The physician's fee includes primarily, if not exclusively, the examination of the patient, while the clinic fee may include the costs of laboratory work, X-rays, and a much higher overhead, as well. If services provided as a result of a visit to a private physician but billed for separately were added to the physician's fee, obviously the true cost of a visit would be higher. Even though it is not known how much more the cost would be, however, it is likely that it would still be considerably less than the clinic fee.

Moreover, it should also be said that the combination of low fees and the requirement that each service provided be itemized may result in the physician's providing some unnecessary services in order to bring his revenues closer to his costs. Private patients paying higher fees often receive additional services without extra charges. Additional research could measure the effect of these policies on medical practice and on aggregate Medicaid expenses.

9. While these assertions are supported by considerable anecdotal evidence, no systematic studies have yet been done that demonstrate the extent to which they affect Medicaid programs in the aggregate.

10. The particular method of compensation (Gabel and Redisch, 1979) may turn out to be less important to primary care practitioners than their belief that the rate is just and their knowledge that they are treated with respect. Support for this contention is found in the experience of the United Health Care Plan in Seattle (Moore, 1979).

REFERENCES

American Academy of Pediatrics. October 1977. *Newborn health insurance laws.* Evanston, Ill.

Children's Defense Fund. 1977. *EPSDT: does it spell health care for poor children?* Washington, D.C.: Children's Defense Fund.

Commerce Clearing House. 1979. *Medicare and Medicaid reporter.* Chicago.

Connecticut General Assembly, Legislative Program Review and Investigations Committee. September 1976. *Containing Medicaid costs in Connecticut.*

Davidson, S. M. 1974. *Report to the Medicaid investigations committee.* Springfield, Ill.: Illinois Department of Public Aid.

———. 1978. Understanding the growth of emergency department utilization. *Medical Care* 16:122–32.

Davis, K., and Schoen, C. 1978. *Health and the war on poverty: a ten-year appraisal.* Washington, D.C.: Brookings Institution.

Dunlap, W. Personal communication, February 27, 1978.

Edwards, S. Personal communication, February 14, 1977 and April 17, 1978.

Foltz, A. M., and Brown, D. 1975. State response to federal policy: children, EPSDT, and the Medicaid muddle. *Medical Care* 13:630–42.

Gabel, J. R., and Redisch, M. A. 1979. Alternative physician payment methods: incentives, efficiency, and national health insurance. *Milbank Memorial Fund Quarterly* 57:38–59.

Garner, D. D.; Liao, W. C.; and Sharpe, T. R. 1979. Factors affecting physician participation in a state Medicaid program. *Medical Care* 17:43–58.

Hadley, J. 1978. *An econometric analysis of physician participation in the Medicaid program.* Washington, D.C.: Urban Institute.

Health Care Financing Administration, Office of Research. 1978a. *Medicaid state tables, fiscal year 1976.* Washington, D.C.: Department of Health, Education, and Welfare.

Health Care Financing Administration, Medicaid Bureau. 1978b. *Data on the Medicaid program: eligibility services, expenditures, fiscal years 1966–1978.* Washington, D.C.: Department of Health, Education, and Welfare.

Kushman, J. E. 1977. Physician participation in Medicaid. *Western Journal of Agricultural Economics* 2:21–33.

Massachusetts Medical Society. January 1979. *Newsletter,* p. 3.

Moore, S. 1979. Cost coniainment through risk-sharing by primary-care physicians. *New England Journal of Medicine* 300:1359–62.

Physician's Management Staff. November 1978. Is anybody happy with Medicaid? *Physician's Management,* pp. 34–37.

Schultze, C. L. 1977. *The public use of private interest.* Washington, D.C.: Brookings Institution.

Sloan, F.; Cromwell, J.; and Mitchell, J. B. 1977. *A study of administrative costs in physicians' offices and Medicaid participation, final report.* Cambridge, MHss.: Abt Associates.

6

HEALTH MAINTENANCE ORGANIZATIONS

Claudia J. Coulton

As the cost of health care rises, there is a growing interest in health service delivery systems that have the potential for controlling costs while providing high-quality care. Since the early 1960s, the Health Maintenance Organization (HMO) has been recognized as a system that could possibly achieve such a favorable cost-benefit ratio.

A Health Maintenance Organization delivers comprehensive health services to its voluntarily enrolled members who have prepaid a fixed fee for a given period of coverage. The amount of this fee is based on the average cost of serving a member for that time period (i.e., capitation payment). The member is entitled to use basic health services as needed, and the fee is not related to the quantity of services used by the patient. This is in contrast to the predominant fee-for-service health care system, in which patients or their insurers are charged for each service they use.

Several assumptions underlie public policy supporting the growth of HMOs. First, it is assumed that patients in HMOs will experience fewer days of hospitalization, thus lowering health care costs. Since the HMO gets its revenue through a capitation payment, it will strive to avoid using costly inpatient services when not absolutely necessary. In this way it differs from the fee-for-service system, in which the use of hospitals is stimulated since inpatient costs are often more fully reimbursed than ambulatory services.

A second assumption is that HMO patients will receive more ambulatory and preventive services and have better access to primary care. HMOs, desiring to avoid the high cost of illness, are expected to encourage the use of these services that promote early detection and treatment. Because fees are prepaid, patients will have no financial barriers to seeking prompt treatment or preventive services. The guaranteed access to primary care should eliminate unnecessary or duplicative visits to specialists.

A third assumption is that care in an HMO will be of a higher quality with less unnecessary surgery and greater continuity than care obtained through traditional practice arrangements. Quality assurance mechanisms are expected to be stronger in HMOs, and there will be a financial inducement to limit surgery. Ready availability of consultation will contribute to quality, and a common health record and proximity of specialists will facilitate continuity.

A fourth assumption is that costs will be reduced through the effective use of ancillary health professionals. HMOs will find it to their advantage to supplement physicians' services with those of other personnel. This will be made possible by an organizational structure that can efficiently deploy these employees. Economies of scale will be realized.

Within the broad HMO concept there have arisen a variety of health service structures and arrangements some of which may be more effective than others. Furthermore, there seems to be empirical evidence that HMOs have both advantages and disadvantages. Therefore, this chapter will examine the public policy related to HMOs, describe several HMO models, review the evidence regarding the HMOs' impact on health care costs and quality, and identify issues that may need to be addressed in future policy debates.

LEGISLATIVE BASE

Although Health Maintenance Organizations have been in existence since the 1920s, there was no federal legislation governing or supporting their operation until 1973. Prior to the passage of the Health Maintenance Organization Act of 1973 (P.L. 93-222), the major public policy relevant to HMOs was contained in state insurance regulations. The act represents one of the first attempts by the federal government to influence the structure of the health service delivery system.

The primary purpose of the HMO Act is to encourage the growth and development of this type of health care organization. This is to be accomplished through three major inducements. First, agencies may receive grants for feasibility studies and grants or loan guarantees for HMO planning and initial development. Second, qualified HMOs are eligible for loans and loan guarantees for initial operating costs. Third, when an HMO is designated as qualified by the Department of Health and Human Services, employers in the HMO's service area are required to offer it as an option in their employee health benefits program. Thus, the legislation provides incentives for existing HMOs to meet federal standards and for new groups to undertake HMO developmental activities.

In order to be considered qualified, an HMO must comply with many regulations. Some of the standards in the original act were eventually seen as too stringent and were amended in 1976 (P.L. 94-460). For example, the original regulations were difficult for HMOs to meet while remaining competitive with other health insurance (e.g., Blue Cross–Blue Shield). The requirements for dental care and open enrollment were particularly problematic. Dental care was dropped and open enrollment modified as a result of the amendments. However, the most important of these federal requirements govern the HMOs' type of services, the providers, the payment mechanisms, the structure, and quality control.

BASIC AND SUPPLEMENTARY SERVICES. Basic services must be made available to all members as part of the HMO's benefit package. The package must include the following services: physician, outpatient and inpatient, emergency, mental health, family planning, well child and adult examination, eye and ear examination (up to age 18), and immunizations. A variety of supplementary services may also be included in the package of members who contract for them.

PROVIDERS. Services may be delivered by health professionals under several arrangements. The HMO may directly employ salaried professionals or contract with a medical group or an individual practice association. A medical group is defined as several health professionals who practice together and devote over 50 percent of their professional activity to coordinated practice. They must pool their income, from which they collect a salary, and must maintain shared health records. The group must put 35 percent of its efforts into caring for HMO members.

An independent practice association is an entity that has an agreement with individual professionals or groups of professionals to deliver basic health services for some predetermined compensation. Compensation may be in the form of either fee-for-service or capitation arrangements. Joint records and other cooperative activities are encouraged to the extent possible.

PAYMENT MECHANISMS. Basic health benefits are to be financed through a capitation payment that is to be the same for all HMO members regardless of utilization. The amount of the capitation payment must be fixed under a community-wide rating. A nominal copayment may be charged, but it is not to serve as a barrier to service use and cannot exceed 20 percent of the total yearly costs of providing care. Medical groups and individual practice associations must be compensated on a capitation basis.

STRUCTURE. The board of the HMO must be at least one-half consumers, and grievance mechanisms must be available to resolve consumer complaints. Health education, nutrition, and social services should be available to members, and every member should have a designated primary care provider. No more than 75 percent of the membership may come from a medically underserved area, and only 50 percent may be Medicaid or Medicare eligible.

QUALITY CONTROL. HMO services must be subjected to a quality assurance program including peer review and outcome studies. Continuing education should be available to all providers. Compliance with federal regulations will be monitored.

In addition to the HMO Act, several other public policy actions have been supportive of HMO development. Medicare and Medicaid regulations have been modified to make it possible for these two programs to be used for HMO capitation payments. Public health monies have been made available to subsidize enrollment of the medically underserved in some HMOs (Public Health Service Act, 42 U.S.C. 314). Many states have modified insurance regulations that had previously served as barriers to HMOs. Finally, proposed cost-containment measures frequently exempt HMOs from many of the requirements that would be placed on the fee-for-service system.

Thus, public policy seems generally supportive of HMO development through financial assistance, removal of barriers, and enforcement of the HMO as an option in employee health benefit plans. The regulations strongly support the concept of comprehensive health care benefits and capitation payments to the HMO. Although priority has been given to reaching the medically underserved, limits on the proportion of low-income consumers are designed to avoid the situation where any HMOs exclusively serve the poor.

Beyond these basic principles, public policy seems fairly permissive. There is allowance for wide variation in the organizational structure of the HMOs. Providers may work in one large group, in many small groups, or in solo practice. Depending on their work setting, their compensation may be in the form of salaries, capitation payments, or fee-for-service arrangements. Hospital care may be provided directly by the HMO or through contractual arrangements. The requirements for peer review, continuing education consumer involvement, health education, and social services are not specific as to quantity or quality.

Is public policy on HMOs adequate? Should they be supported at a higher or lower level? Are they actually accomplishing what the framers of policy believed they would? Is more regulatory specificity desirable? In order to answer these questions an examination of existing models of HMOs and studies of HMO performance follows.

MODELS

HMOs have been organized in several ways. The three most common models, all of which are permitted under present public policy, are the medical care foundation model, the network model, and the prepaid group practice model (Prussin, 1974). A summary of these models is presented in Table 6.1.

The first type of HMO, the medical care foundation, arranges for health services rather than directly providing them. The consumer pays a fixed fee to the foundation, which contracts with individual or group providers around the community. The providers usually bill the foundation on a fee-for-service basis in accordance with a prenegotiated rate schedule. Providers may agree to lower fees if utilization exceeds certain expectations. This model would be considered an individual practice association in the language of the HMO Act.

The network model is also a form of an individual practice association. It differs from the foundation model in that the HMO contracts with many solo or group primary care providers, to whom it pays a capitation rate. The primary care providers share in the financial risk for hospitalization

Table 6.1 Models of Health Maintenance Organizations

Model	Payments to primary care providers	Payments to specialist providers	Risk for hospitalization	Location of providers	Incentives (possibly affecting costs and quality)
Medical care foundation	Fee-for-service	Fee-for-service	Risk borne by HMO, usually not shared by providers.	Solo or small group practice in many locations.	Fee may be reduced if more than expected quantity of services are provided. Wide choice of providers and locations.
Network	Capitation	Fee-for-service	Risk shared by primary care providers.	Solo or small group practice in many locations.	Reduce hospitalization, avoid use of specialists.
Prepaid Group Practice (PGP)	Capitation	Capitation	Risk shared by multispecialty group. May have own hospital.	Practice together in multispecialty group at one or a few locations.	Reduce hospitalization, use ancillary personnel, prevent illness, share single medical record, use consultation.

because they receive bonuses when there is a surplus in the funds set aside to cover patients' hospitalization.

In the prepaid group (PPG) practice model the physicians are organized in a multi-specialty group that is responsible for providing comprehensive services. The provider group is compensated for the number of members they serve (i.e., capitation) rather than on a fee-for-service basis. Individuals receive a salary and usually share in any "profits." Prepaid group practice is the model that has been studied most thoroughly and the model on which most discussions of HMO advantages are based.

Although programs resembling all of these models are called HMOs, the structural differences seem to have major implications. First, there is an incentive for the provider who is reimbursed on a fee-for-service basis in the foundation model to deliver more services. Since foundation providers do not share the financial risk for hospital care, there is no financial impetus to reduce hospitalization. In the prepaid group practice, the incentive is to enroll more patients but control the quantity and cost of the services they use. Providers working under this model will find it especially beneficial to avoid expensive hospitalization when possible. Like the PPG model, the network model may induce providers to avoid hospital care. However, unlike the PPG model, in which specialist care is also prepaid and provided by the group, providers in the network model usually purchase specialist care on a fee-for-service basis. Thus there is an additional incentive to avoid specialist services.

Some of the other presumed advantages of HMOs are not as likely to be present in the foundation or network models. Informal consultation and on-site peer review are not as available when providers are located in solo practice. A unified health record and the use of ancillary health professionals are not as feasible under some foundation and network arrangements. The patient may have to travel to several locations to get both primary and specialist care, perhaps decreasing continuity and the perception of comprehensiveness.

HMO PERFORMANCE

COSTS AND HOSPITAL UTILIZATION. A preponderance of evidence suggests that HMOs of the prepaid group practice type have lower costs than the traditional health care system. This difference seems, in part, to be a consequence of lower hospital utilization. One of the earliest studies compared members of a labor union enrolled in an HMO with those using the fee-for-service system. For this population the adjusted rate of hospital admissions was 20.5 percent lower for the group enrolled in the HMO, the biggest difference being in female surgical admissions. Since the two groups were similar in pre-enrollment health status, the authors suggested several possible explanations for these results. First, the availability of consultation and diagnostic facilities in the HMO allowed some hospital admissions to be avoided. Second, the physicians' fees were not linked to services rendered in the HMO. Third, traditional insurance plans provided an incentive for hospitalization because more services were covered under those circumstances (Densen, Balamuth, and Shapiro, 1960). Numerous other studies have also reported lower hospital utilization rates for persons enrolled in HMOs (Falk and Sentura, 1960; Klarman, 1963; Gaus, 1976). Conversely, another study found no difference in the number of hospital days between a regular Medicaid group and one enrolled in an HMO (Cherry, 1975).

Gaus, Cooper, and Hirschman (1976) provide some evidence about the differential effects of the several types of HMOs on provider behavior relative to hospitalization. Surgical rates for patients in prepaid group practice plans were half those of a matched control group, while surgical rates for patients in medical care foundations did not differ from their controls. Similarly, hospital utilization for group practice members was two and one-half time less than for their controls. For foundation members, hospital utilization was no different from that of the comparison, fee-for-service group. They did not study any HMOs of the network type.

The cost efficiency of HMOs has been examined in several studies. Greenlick (1972) described the experience at Kaiser-Portland (a prepaid group practice), where the cost per patient per day increased from $13.23 per day in 1950 to $54.80 in 1966, paralleling the national increase. However, the cost of hospitalization per member per year increased from $12.53 in 1950 to only $27.31 in 1966. A fourfold increase in cost per patient per day was thus reflected as a twofold increase in cost per member per year because the use of hospital days per person per year decreased concurrently. According to Greenlick, it is this difference in the rate of increase in cost per day and cost per person per year that accounted for the difference in the cost of hospitalization for the Kaiser-Portland population in relation to the remainder of the community. Stevens (1971) also examined the cost efficiency of Kaiser-Portland and concluded that if the entire health care system achieved its level of efficiency the United States would need 10 percent fewer physicians than existed at the time.

Cost savings have been reported when Medicaid patients have been enrolled in HMOs. The state of Washington reported a 29.8 percent cost savings through the use of HMOs as opposed to the fee-for-service system for AFDC families (Washington Department of Social and Health Services, 1974). Massachusetts found that an HMO was able to provide health services at lower cost than projected Medicaid payments for a comparable period of time (Birnbaum, 1971). The savings were due mainly to elimination of the administrative costs of the vendor system. In Washington, D.C., a 37 percent cost savings was reported for Medicaid enrollees in an HMO (Fuller, Patera, and Kozil, 1975).

Hawaii's experience in contracting with an HMO on behalf of Medicaid recipients has also been reported. Two matched samples were compared, one receiving services through the HMO and the other receiving traditional services. The comparison revealed that the HMO provided more comprehensive services at a lower cost in the rural areas and at a similar cost in the urban areas. There was little difference in overall patient satisfaction between groups (Worth, 1974).

HMOs also seem to compare favorably with neighborhood health centers. In 1965 the Office of Economic Opportunity contracted with four HMOs to provide services to low-income families. A study at one of these facilities compared the utilization of services of the 1,500 OEO families with a random sample of the non-OEO members of the plan. The rate and pattern of utilization was essentially similar except for pediatrics and obstetrics, in which the OEO group's utilization was higher. The cost of providing health services through the HMO was reported to be considerably lower than similar services provided through programs constructed solely for the delivery of health services to the poor (Greenlick et al., 1972; Coburn, 1973).

AMBULATORY CARE. As previously noted, one of the expected benefits of HMOs is that consumers will use more preventive and ambulatory services since the payment barrier has been removed. They will also be encouraged in this behavior by providers who wish to treat illnesses early, before hospitalization is required.

Dutton (1979) compared ambulatory care use between patients belonging to an HMO (i.e., prepaid group practice) and those using the fee-for-service system. She reported that HMO patients made more patient-initiated visits than did those in the traditional system. This difference was largest among the low-income persons in both systems. The fee-for-service patients, on the other hand, had a higher volume of provider-initiated follow-up visits.

German, Skinner, and Shapiro (1976), comparing Medicaid recipients and the near poor, found that the near poor used fewer traditional ambulatory health care services. However, when Medicaid and near-poor HMO members were compared, these differences were greatly reduced. The major postive impact of the HMO seemed to be on those low-income individuals who needed regular care for a chronic condition.

Gaus, Fuller, and Bohannon (1973) found that the volume of ambulatory care for children increased when a Medicaid group was enrolled in an HMO. This was probably indicative of higher use of preventive services. Conversely, Fuller, Patera, and Kozil (1975), studying a similar group, found that ambulatory utilization decreased by 15 percent after HMO enrollment. Similarly, Medicaid recipients in a network-type HMO were observed to underutilize ambulatory services (Hester and Sussman, 1974).

Finally, Gaus, Cooper, and Hirshman (1976) reported no difference in use of preventive services between persons enrolled in an HMO of the foundation type and a matched comparison group. However, they did find patients in a prepaid group practice used fewer preventive services than those in their fee-for-service comparison group.

CONSUMER SATISFACTION. In order to be a viable means of delivering health services, HMOs must be capable of enrolling and satisfying sufficient numbers of consumers. The findings on patients' satisfaction with HMO services seem to be mixed. There is little evidence that patients are less satisfied with HMO services but only sporadic evidence that they are more satisfied. The reason may be that the measurement of patient satisfaction has been difficult and has frequently produced little variability among individuals, making it impossible to detect significant differences.

Pope (1978) compared the satisfaction of patients who remained enrolled in a prepaid group practice with that of recently terminated subscribers. Only 12 percent of the terminees had dropped out because of dissatisfaction. The large majority of patients were generally highly satisfied with accessibility, social and emotional, and technical aspects of care. The major sources of dissatisfaction revolved around delays in getting appointments for nonacute conditions. Patients who did not have a regular physician within the plan were more likely to terminate because of dissatisfaction.

Studies comparing the satisfaction of HMO with fee-for-service consumers have been inconclusive. Tessler and Mechanic (1975) found members of prepaid group practice to be less satisfied with their care than were subscribers of alternative health insurance plans. They reported greater difficulty in obtaining appointments and longer traveling time to sites of care. Studies of Medicaid enrollees in a California medical care foundation found them less satisfied with accessibility than were their fee-for-service counterparts. Roemer and Shonick (1973), on the other hand, found that HMO members were generally more satisfied with care than fee-for-service consumers. Similarly, Fuller, Patera, and Kozil (1975), found patients more satisfied with an HMO than with their previous source of care.

QUALITY OF CARE. Some have argued that HMOs would deliver a higher quality of care than the traditional system. This was anticipated with group practice arrangements in some HMOs, which were expected to contribute to peer review, consultation, and continuity of care. Also, the emphasis on controlling cost through prevention and early treatment was expected to result in better health for consumers.

The evidence regarding the actual impact of HMOs on quality of care is limited. In 1958, Shapiro et al. found a lower rate of prematurity and perinatal mortality among HMO subscribers than among a comparison group. However, this was prior to the advent of Medicaid and many of our maternal and child health services. Similarly, the elderly in a New York HMO had a lower mortality rate than a matched comparison group (Shapiro et al., 1967).

Robertson (1971) found that teachers enrolled in an HMO had fewer days lost from work due to illness than did their colleagues. On the other hand, Gaus, Cooper, and Hirshman (1976) found no difference in health status between HMO enrollees in both a medical care foundation and a prepaid group practice and a comparison group.

The appropriateness of surgery can serve as an indicator of quality of care. Lo Gerfo et al. (1979) compared surgery rates in two types of HMOs. They found a higher rate of unnecessary surgery in a medical care foundation in which providers were reimbursed on a fee-for-service basis. However, when patients with unnecessary surgeries were removed from the study, the prepaid group practice patients continued to have substantially lower surgery rates for selected conditions. The authors suggested that prepaid group practice patients may not have been receiving needed surgeries due to the financial disincentives of the capitation payments.

Based on the above empirical evidence, what can be concluded about HMO performance? First, it seems clear that there are differences between the three main types of HMOs in their effects on costs, hospital utilization, ambulatory care utilization, consumer satisfaction, and quality of care. The majority of prepaid group practice plans studied have been successful in substantially reducing their member's inpatient hospital days, rates of surgery, and overall costs of care. For low-income people they seem to have removed the barriers to using preventive care and seeking early treatment. For the chronically ill, they have resulted in more consistent management of their conditions. The number of provider initiated follow-up visits has also been reduced.

Although there have been relatively few studies of HMOs of the medical care foundation or network type, it seems that the network model has been somewhat successful in reducing hospital days and increasing use of preventive, primary care services. Medical care foundations have not demonstrated their ability to reduce hospital days or surgery rates. Similarly, no foundation effects on ambulatory care utilization have been documented.

Studies of consumer satisfaction are inconclusive. The biggest source of dissatisfaction with HMOs seems to be inaccessibility. However, some studies suggest that consumers are more satisfied with all aspects of HMO care than their previous source of care. This seems particularly true for low-income patients or others who had no regular source of medical care. Since satisfaction is always related to expectations, its interpretation is somewhat ambiguous.

There is little evidence to suggest whether the quality of care is different in HMOs than in the fee-for-service system. The elements believed to contribute to quality, such as consultation, comprehensiveness, continuity, and peer review, are present in higher quantities in prepaid group practice than in the other types of HMOs or in the traditional fee-for-service system. However, whether or not these things affect patients' health status is unclear. It appears that HMOs are most likely to have a positive impact on the health status of previously underserved consumers.

Another way HMOs may be affecting the quality of health care is through their influence on surgery. It seems that patients enrolled in HMOs of the network or prepaid group practice models have less unnecessary surgery than patients using traditional health services. However, while the surgery rates in foundations do not differ much from those in the traditional system, there is an indication that a few potentially beneficial surgeries may not be performed in prepaid group practice. Since there are problems in judging surgical necessity, this hypothesis clearly requires further testing.

POLICY ISSUES

When the HMO act was introduced in 1971, it was expected to produce rapid growth of these organizations and important changes in the health service delivery system. Cost reductions and improved health were anticipated. These expectations have not completely materialized. Several policy issues can be identified as potentially relevant to the future success of the HMO movement.

RATE OF GROWTH. In the early 1970s President Nixon predicted that 40 million people would be served in HMOs by 1976. Others speculated that 20 percent of the U.S. population would be enrolled in HMOs by the 1980s. In reality, growth has not occurred at this expected rate. Before passage of the act, HMO enrollment was estimated at about 6 million persons and currently there are only about 7 million members of HMOs.

Part of this slow HMO development has been attributed to the confusion and excessive demands of the initial regulations. A major problem was the requirement for a broad range of basic services that made it difficult for HMO prices to be competitive with other insurance plans. This situation was improved, particularly when the requirements for dental care and open enrollment were modified in the 1976 amendments. Another barrier to development had been some states' insurance regulations. Many of these have recently been eliminated or superseded by federal legislation.

Since the removal of some of these barriers many more HMOs have been created, although fewer than half have as yet been designated as federally qualified. Receiving this designation is crucial to an HMO's success in recruiting members because employers must offer to employees the option of joining a qualified HMO if one exists in the service area. It is also a prerequisite to receiving planning or operational grants. The amount of such funds available for HMOs has been increased, and the 1978 amendments raised the ceiling on the size of start-up grants.

Thus, it appears that the pace of HMO development will increase somewhat in the future. If even more rapid growth were deemed desirable, several policy changes would be needed. First, an even greater portion of the health care budget could be earmarked for HMO planning and operational grants. Second, the process required to become a qualified HMO could be simplified. Third, since a key factor in HMO development is knowledgeable management, specific funds could be designated for training potential HMO administrators. Finally, although recruitment of physicians has not yet been a major problem it is not clear whether this pattern will continue as the quantity of HMOs increases. Unlike the network and foundation models, prepaid group practice plans require a physician to make major changes in his or her practice arrangements. Since there is beginning evidence to suggest that the greatest advantages are realized in this type of HMO, inducements to engage in prepaid group practice may need to be built into funding for medical education.

COSTS, UTILIZATION, AND QUALITY. The originators of the HMO Act emphasized the need to allow flexibility in organizational structure. They believed that this would allow for healthy competition and stimulate development. However, expectations of reduced costs and improved quality and utilization patterns were based on experience with prepaid group practices.

Now studies are beginning to reveal that the structure of the HMO has major implications for whether these expectations will be realized. Independent practice associations that pay providers on a fee-for-service basis (i.e., the medical care foundation model) may not be equally able to reduce hospital days and costs. Independent practice associations may not be able completely to realize the benefits of readily available consultation, informal peer review, efficient use of ancillary professionals, and the continuity of a unified record.

Where primary care providers in an independent practice association are paid on a capitation rate, there may be a tendency to avoid necessary specialist consultations that would have to be purchased out of this set rate. In multi-specialty prepaid group practice, there may be instances where necessary surgery is not performed.

This suggests that several policy issues may require consideration. First, should public policy continue to allow the present flexibility in organizational structure? If HMOs that reimburse primary care providers on a fee-for-service basis do not achieve most of the HMO benefits, they should not continue to be encouraged to the same extent as other models.

Second, if paying providers a capitation rate increases the risk that necessary services may not be provided, some controls will need to be exerted. This may, in part, occur through stricter enforcement of peer review requirements. Additionally, efforts should be made to develop utilization standards against which the utilization patterns in each HMO could be compared. Where deviations are found, investigations would be made. Such standards would require continuous updating as health care technology changes.

Third, if continuity of care, economies of scale, and use of ancillary professionals are to be achieved in independent practice associations, the requirements for these elements will need to be strengthened. Presently, the regulations suggest but do not require that these components be present in independent practice associations.

THE POOR. A great deal of evidence suggests that the poor can be served at lower cost through HMOs of the prepaid group practice type. The low-income enrollee's utilization patterns usually become more preventive, and, in some cases, satisfaction increases. Unfortunately, there are relatively few state Medicaid contracts with HMOs.

There are several impediments to the enrollment of Medicaid recipients in HMOs (Bartlett, 1979). First, it is difficult to determine a fair capitation rate because there are insufficient data on utilization and health status for this population. Second, state Medicaid monitoring mechanisms are geared to a fee-for-service payment system. New procedures would have to be implemented to insure HMO accountability. Third, the incentive for the Medicaid consumer to join an HMO is not strong. Any cost savings would not affect him directly but would be passed on to the state. The only attraction to the consumer might be the promise of more comprehensive or convenient care. This might be seen as an advantage of a multi-specialty group practice but is unlikely to be a feature of an independent practice association. Fourth, since states cannot release the names of Medicaid recipients, marketing the HMO to this group is difficult. Information must usually be provided during the intake process and may not be given sufficient attention. Fifth, as Medicaid eligibility changes, consumers must disenroll in the HMO. This results in a loss of continuity as well as increasing administrative costs.

Although legislation has recently been introduced to facilitate HMO-Medicaid contracts, it has been defeated. There seems to be some hesitancy to promote contracting that may be partly a reaction to California's disastrous experience in contracting with some HMOs of the independent practice association type. Also, the General Accounting Office (1978) has raised doubts about the abilities of states adequately to monitor HMO contracts.

Several possible steps toward facilitating Medicaid-HMO contracting seem possible. The creation of adequate approaches to monitoring should be supported. Data on utilization patterns should be collected and shared to form the basis for accurate rate setting. Since prepaid group practice plans are most likely to hold some attraction for Medicaid consumers, priority should be given to contracting with this type of HMO.

A final issue requires some discussion. Present regulations require that no more than 50 percent of an HMO's members be Medicare or Medicaid recipients. Some have argued that this may inhibit the development of HMOs in low-income areas (Bartlett, 1979). However, history suggests that services designed solely for the poor become poor services. This regulation should not be changed without assurance that quality of care will be adequately controlled.

NATIONAL HEALTH INSURANCE. Most of the major national health insurance (NHI) plans make some provision for HMOs. Depending on the benefit package provided under NHI, the consumer will have more or less incentive to choose an HMO. Presently, most consumers who join an HMO will avoid paying some out-of-pocket costs for ambulatory care that they would have had to pay under a traditional insurance plan. If such visits were to be fully covered under NHI, this would no longer be a perceived advantage of HMOs. Again, only the prepaid group practice model would hold the attraction of providing comprehensive, multi-specialty service. Since it will be particularly important to build incentives for cost containment into NHI, there must be strong inducements for consumers to join HMOs.

IMPLICATIONS FOR SOCIAL WORKERS

Social workers have an interest in HMOs from a variety of perspectives. As advocates for reform of the health service delivery system, social workers will want to encourage the growth of HMOs. However, they will want to assure that HMOs that do develop are of the type that actually will reduce costs and improve the quality of care. Thus, their policy recommendations should always be based on a careful analysis of the empirical evidence available at the time. These goals will require action directed toward both federal regulations and legislation. Increased funding or changed funding priorities will be mainly a legislative decision. The degree to which existing regulations are tightened or enforced will be primarily controlled by the HMO program in the Department of Health and Human Services.

Social workers also play an active role in state Medicaid programs. However, since there is evidence that many low-income people will be better served in an HMO, social workers will probably want to work toward facilitating Medicaid-HMO contracts. They must simultaneously demand that the Medicaid contracts with HMOs include adequate provisions for monitoring and protection of the consumer.

There are many decisions made within the HMOs themselves that have a major effect on their success and quality. Social workers will have an interest in attempting to influence some of these decisions. For example, in any primary care setting a sizable proportion of physician visits are precipitated by stress and problems in living. People with these types of problems tend to overutilize physician care. Health care costs can be reduced by making available social services to deal adequately with these psychosocial problems, and it will frequently be to the advantage of the HMO to provide such services. Social workers should work with HMO administrators toward recognizing these and other changes that will benefit both the patients and the organization.

One of the most important points that should guide all social work thinking about HMOs is that they are not a single phenomenon. The three HMO models presented here have such different effects that they should be considered quite separately under most circumstances. Regulations may eventually need recognize these differences by including some provisions that apply separately to each HMO type. Social workers should support the development of HMOs, but they should do so critically, with a recognition of both their strengths and their weaknesses.

REFERENCES

Bartlett, L. 1979. HMOs and the poor: problems and possibilities. *Public Welfare* 37:50–53.

Birnbaum, R. 1971. The Harvard community health plan: to provide broad access to quality comprehensive care. *Public Welfare* 29:42–47.

Cherry, J. August 1975. *Hospital utilization of an enrolled Medicaid population.* Paper presented to the meeting of the Joint Statistical Meetings, Atlanta.

Coburn, S. 1973. Health Maintenance Organizations: implications for public assistance recipients. *Public Welfare* 31:28–32.

Densen, P.; Balamuth, E.; and Shapiro, S. 1960. Prepaid medical care and hospital utilization in a dual choice situation. *American Journal of Public Health* 50:1710–26.

Dutton, D. L. 1979. Patterns of ambulatory care in five different delivery systems. *Medical Care* 3:221–42.

Falk, I. S., and Sentura, J. 1960. *Medical care for steelworkers and their families.* Pittsburgh: United Steelworkers of America.

Fuller, N.; Patera, M.; and Kozil, K. November 1975. *Medicaid utilization of services in prepaid group plan.* Paper presented to the meeting of the American Public Health Association, Chicago.

Gaus, C.; Fuller, N.; and Bohannon, C. 1973. *HMO evaluation: utilization before and after enrollment.* Baltimore: Department of Medical Care and Hospitals, Johns Hopkins University and Department of Human Resources, District of Columbia Government.

Gaus, C. R.; Cooper, B. S.; and Hirshman, C. B. 1976. Contrasts in HMO and fee-for-service performance. *Social Security Bulletin* 39:5.

General Accounting Office. 1978. *Can Health Maintenance Organizations be successful?* Washington, D.C.: General Accounting Office.

German, P.; Skinner, E.; and Shapiro, S. 1976. Ambulatory care for chronic conditions in an inner city population. *American Journal of Public Health* 66:660–66.

Greenlick, M. 1972. The impact of prepaid group practice on American medical care: a critical evaluation. *Annals of the American Academy of Political and Social Science* 399:100–13.

Greenlick, M.; Freeborn, D.; Columbo, T.; Prussin, J.; and Seward, E. 1972. Comparing the use of medical care services by a medically indigent and general membership population in a comprehensive prepaid group practice program. *Medical Care* 10:187–200.

Hester, J., and Sussman, E. 1974. Medicaid prepayment: concept and implementation. *Milbank Memorial Fund Quarterly* 52:415–43.

Klarman, H. 1963. The effect of prepaid group practice on hospital use. *Public Health Reports* 17:955–65.

Lo Gerfo, J. P.; Efrid, R. A.; Diehr, P. K.; and Richardson, W. C. 1979. Rates of surgical care in prepaid group practice and the independent setting. *Medical Care* 17:1–10.

Pope, C. R. 1978. Consumer satisfaction in a Health Maintenance Organization. *Journal of Health and Social Behavior* 19:291–303.

Prussin, J. A. 1974. HMOs: organizational and financial models. *Hospital Progress* 55:33–35.

Robertson, R. L. 1971. Economic effects of personal health services: work loss in a public school teacher population. *American Journal of Public Health* 61:30–45.

Roemer, M., and Shonick, W. 1973. HMO performance: the recent evidence. *Milbank Memorial Fund Quarterly* 51:271–317.

Shapiro, S.; Williams, J. J.; Yerby, A. S.; Densen, P. M.; and Rosner, H. 1967. Patterns of medical use by the indigent aged under two systems of medical care. *American Journal of Public Health* 57:784–90.

Stevens, C. 1971. Physician supply and national health care goals. *Industrial Relations* 110:119–244.

Tessler, R., and Mechanic, D. 1975. Consumer satisfaction with prepaid group practice: a comparative study. *Journal of Health and Social Behavior* 16:95–113.

U.S. Department of Health, Education, and Welfare. 1973. *Summary of SRS supported HMO research and development efforts funded under section 1116 of the Social Security Act as amended,* Washington, D.C.: U.S. Government Printing Office.

Washington Department of Social and Health Services. April 1974. *Health Maintenance Organizations: comparison of costs and utilization for group health Medicaid enrollees and other persons certified for Medicaid in Washington State.*

Worth, R. 1974. A comparison of fee-for-service and capitation medicine in a low income group in Honolulu. *Hawaii Medical Journal* 33:91–96.

7

NATIONAL HEALTH PLANNING AND RESOURCES DEVELOPMENT

Charlene Harrington

INTRODUCTION

Congress's most recent legislative effort to establish a system of health planning for the United States—the National Health Planning and Resources Development Act of 1974 (P.L. 93-641), amended in 1979 (P.L. 96-79)—appears slated for phaseout by the Reagan Administration and Congress in 1983. While the health planning system established by the act was a major step toward rational restructuring of the health care delivery system in the United States, the legislative has had a number of serious limitations that have reduced its expected impact on health status and the health care delivery system. Criticism of the program from various political sectors at a time of major cutbacks in federal health and social programs has placed the program on a list for elimination.

The first policy issue addressed in this paper is whether the health planning system should change its priority to improving the health status of the population, rather than its current focus on improving the health care delivery system. In order to improve health status, the planning system would have to emphasize changes in economic, social, and environmental conditions that directly influence health and place less emphasis on the development and restructuring of the health care delivery system.

A second policy issue is the limited scope and authority of the present legislation. The act omits the major health provider group—physicians—from its planning and regulation activities, even though physicians make a majority of decisions over the use of health services. The legislation also does not give the health planning system adequate regulatory controls over health expenditures. Planning, certificate-of-need, and appropriateness reviews are not linked to controls over reimbursement, power of decertification, or authority to close unnecessary services and facilities. And the act fails to provide budgetary or rate-setting authority over health services. While the authority of the planning system over health facilities was greatly expanded beyond that of previous planning legislation, the controls stop short of a comprehensive regulatory approach to health care delivery.

A third set of issues is the organizational and operational problems associated with inadequate funding for the program and the community board structure. These problems have made the planning agencies less stable and have limited their capability of carrying out regulatory activities in an effective fashion.

The major structural problems created by the present health planning legislation could be corrected by strengthening the effectiveness of the planning and regulatory system. Powerful special interests of provider organizations continue to oppose both the planning and the regulatory components of the present system. Consumers have also failed to give strong support to the present planning program. As a result of growing criticism of regulatory approaches, by providers and the public, the Reagan Administration is proposing to phase out the program with its federal regulatory controls in favor of competitive models.

BACKGROUND

P.L. 93-641 provides for a system of planning and regulation of health care services and facilities by establishing a complex organizational structure at the regional, state, and federal levels to implement its provisions. The new approach consolidated and replaced three earlier legislative programs— Hill-Burton, Comprehensive Health Planning (CHP), and Regional Medical Programs (RMP). P.L. 93-641 represents the second attempt to control unnecessary expansion of medical facilities. The first attempt, still used by some states, Section 1122 of P.L. 92-603, allows the U.S. Department of Health and Human Services to withhold Medicare, Medicaid, and Title 5 reimbursement for facility projects determined by the states to be unnecessary (Bauer, 1977; *United States Code,* 1972).

While the concept of health planning developed in the 1930s in the United States, the Hill-Burton Act of 1947 was the first major federal effort to implement the concept. The act provided funds for construction of hospitals and for the establishment of state agencies to survey the needs and establish priorities for the funds. More than $4.4 billion in grant funds and $2 billion in loans were made between 1947 and 1975 (U.S. Institute of Medicine, 1980). The Hill-Burton program was oriented toward the physical planning of hospitals; only in the mid-1960s did it include outpatient facilities and public health centers. In the 1970s, the program came under criticism because of the overbuilding of hospitals and the unnecessary costs caused by underutilized facilities, and it was eventually phased out of existence.

The Regional Medical Program established in 1966 expanded financing for planning, research, training, and demonstration projects primarily in the areas of heart disease, cancer, and stroke. The program received large sums of funds ($505 million) with little public accountability (U.S. Institute of Medicine, 1980). The federal government became more involved with planning when the Comprehensive Health Planning Program (P.L. 89-749) was established in 1966 as an effort to develop a broad-based health planning system. It provided funds, on a matching basis, to establish statewide agencies and local organizations to plan for health services and facilities. The nearly 200 agencies established carried out voluntary planning for the health care delivery system. The program received criticism because its planning efforts were voluntary and lacked enforcement authority. Efforts were undertaken to rewrite the legislation to correct these weaknesses (Atkisson, 1976; Cain and Thornberry, 1977). In 1974, Congress began hearings on the deficiencies of past planning efforts, eventually leading to modifications and reauthorization of the legislation under the National Health Planning and Resources Development Act (P.L. 93-69).

Purposes of P.L. 93-641

The need to restructure the health care delivery system was widely recognized by Congress and served as the basis for the new legislation. The legislation focused on basic deficiencies in the health care delivery system including serious problems of access to health care, quality of care, continuity of care, and the availability of services (Cain, 1978). While the legislation focused on broad defects in the health system with particular respect to low-income groups that have not had access to health care, the primary focus was on health care costs. The dramatic increases in national health expenditures, combined with a seriously malfunctioning health care delivery system, provided the impetus for the legislation in 1974.

The total national investment in health care climbed from $25 billion (5.2 percent of the gross national product) in 1960 to over $212 billion (more than 8.9 percent of the GNP) in 1980 (Gibson, 1980). The increases in health costs, especially for hospitals, have exceeded the general rate of inflation (hospitals reported a 19.7 percent increase from 1979 to 1980; Morris Report, 1981c), so that the government spends increasingly greater proportions of its total resources on health care. Such costs have been translated into dramatic increases for the private sector, through employee health insurance premiums paid by business, industry, and labor. For example, General Motors reported spending more for employee health insurance coverage in 1975 than it did for steel. These increases became a major focus of national attention for policymakers and health planning legislation (Cain and Thornberry, 1977).

The 1974 national health planning legislation envisioned a more effective and equitable health care delivery system at the most reasonable cost possible, with the following objectives (*United States Code*, 1974):

1. improve the health of residents of a health service area;
2. increase accessibility, acceptability, continuity, and quality of health services provided;
3. restrain increases in the cost of providing health services; and
4. prevent unnecessary duplication of health resources.

The underlying assumptions in health planning are that resources are limited in a number of ways. In order to improve the general health status of residents, all segments of the public need to have access to health care services. At the same time, services are costly and methods of restraining or reallocating expenditures are needed. The overall goal of the health planning system is to restructure health services into a rational delivery system to achieve its purposes.

Organizational Structure and Functions

HEALTH SYSTEMS AGENCIES (HSAs). The act provided for dividing the United States into health service areas to create a regional health planning structure. Each health service area has a Health Systems Agency that encompasses 500,000 to three million people, based upon the decision of the governor of each state. A total of 206 HSAs were established, most of which were private nonprofit agencies except for 22 public agencies established by local governments. The agencies are governed by a governing body of at least 30 members, of which a majority (50 percent to 60 percent) must be consumers and the remainder providers (physicians, other health professionals, health care institutions, insurers, health schools, and allied health professionals) (*United States Code,* 1974).

HSAs are required to develop long-range health plans for their communities, as well as annual implementation plans to carry out the objectives for meeting the long-range goals. The agencies are to integrate the national and state health goals with locally perceived needs in developing a plan with which to improve the health of the people in the community. In order to develop their plans, the agencies assemble and analyze data on the status of the areas's health care delivery system, the population, and the health problems (*United States Code,* 1974). HSAs, mandated to cooperate with public and voluntary agencies and other organizations in the community, also provide information and public education about their activities. The agencies also provide technical assistance to individuals and organizations developing projects and programs that the agency determines are necessary to achieve its desired objectives.

The major new component under P.L. 93-641 was giving authority to state government over new capital expenditures for health facilities, and advisory authority for such decisions to Health Systems Agencies. Certificate-of-need (CON) approval requires the determination by the state agency that a proposed capital expenditure project or service change is needed (*United States Code,* 1974). The need determination must be based on the health planning needs of the area. While the laws vary from state to state, CON generally covers hospitals, nursing homes, and other related licensed facilities such as ambulatory facilities and laboratories, over a specified dollar amount for the project (Urban Systems, 1978; Cohodes et al., 1979). States employ a wide mix and variety of standards in reaching decisions under their CON programs, but must consider the federal criteria.

STATE HEALTH PLANNING AND DEVELOPMENT AGENCIES (SHPDAs). Each state was required to establish a State Health Planning and Development Agency and to develop the state health plan, the state medical facilities plan, and other health plans as required by federal statutes and state laws

(*United States Code,* 1974). The law provides that SHPDAs must base their decisions on prior actions, documents, and recommendations of the HSAs. The state must show that its agency has the authority and resources to carry out the health planning and development functions required under federal law, including the CON program, and that appropriate state laws and regulations have been adopted to carry out federal law. The state agencies must also review the appropriateness of facilities and may recommend reimbursement under federal programs for facility services.

STATEWIDE HEALTH COORDINATING COUNCILS (SHCCs). The SHCC, an advisory body to the SHPDA, was designed to ensure that the interests of HSAs, consumers, and providers are heard at the state level. At the same time, the SHCC has veto authority over the health system plans of each HSA and the state agency. P.L. 93-641 prescribes the composition of the SHCC, of which 60 percent must come from HSAs with a consumer majority. The SHCC has the following functions: reviews and approves HSA plans, prepares and revises the state medical facilities plan, reviews HSA applications for planning grants, reviews state plans or applications for federal funding, and reviews HSA annual budgets and funding applications.

U.S. DEPARTMENT OF HEALTH AND HUMAN SERVICES (DHHS). The U.S. Department of Health and Human Services, Health Resources Administration, administers P.L. 93-641, establishing health planning goals and priorities, and regulations for the operation of the entire health planning system. The federal government establishes and monitors performance standards for the HSAs, SHPDAs, and SHCCs and grants the funds for the programs.

Planning Advances

P.L. 93-641 made significant advances over previous planning legislation. The health plans, unlike earlier plans under the CHP Act, are not vague and poorly defined and are geared to implementation (Bauer, 1977). The plans are required to have a broad perspective that addresses prevention of disease and improvement of health-related factors, such as environment and nutrition. But most important, the regional plans have greater authority than the old CHP plans because regulatory mechanisms are assigned to the planning systems. The plans are not based solely on community need, as in the former CHP Act, but must balance cost impact and financial feasibility considerations with access, acceptability, continuity, and quality of care (Bauer, 1977). The authors of P.L. 93-641 specifically sought to avoid some of the earlier pitfalls of health planning by establishing clearer lines of authority, with responsibility and accountability specifically detailed. Broader mandates for implementation were provided, stronger sanctions were authorized, and funding arrangements were improved so that agencies would not be dependent upon contributions from health care providers (Kennedy, 1978).

The health planning amendments to P.L. 93-641 introduced in 1978 and passed in 1979 (P.L. 96-79) corrected additional administrative and pro-gram problems identified by Congress. These included removing the Health Maintenance Organizations from the CON process to prevent bar-riers to their development; assuring the governor of each state a role in finalization of the state health plan to give the governor greater authority; ensuring cooperation between health planning and mental health pro-grams; and reaffirming the requirement for appropriateness review of ex-isting health facilities. The changes made were generally minor, keeping the basic health planning system consistent with P.L. 93-641 (Kennedy, 1978).

POLICY ISSUES

Shifting Priorities to the Improvement of Health Services

One major goal of health planning is to improve the population's health status. P.L. 93-641 requires health planning agencies to develop goals to improve health status, and it states that the measure of success of the pro-gram will be overall improvement in health status indicators. Yet the plan-ning legislation focuses primarily on strategies for making changes in the health care delivery system. Even though the lack of relationship between health status and the health care delivery system was not widely recognized in 1974 when P.L. 93-641 was passed, policymakers have since become in-creasingly aware of the distinctions.

Health status is related to a number of factors including economic, social, and environmental conditions. Health services are probably not a major factor influencing health status of the population. While the im-provement of health services is a legitimate goal, there is little evidence to suggest that the improvements in access, quality, and availability required by P.L. 93-641 will have any direct measurable impact on health status (Reeves, 1977). A recent study by Roemer and Schwartz (1978) indicated that there may even be an inverse relationship between health services and health status. This study showed that during the physicians' strike in Los Angeles, when surgery was not being carried out due to the malpractice situation, the mortality rate of the area declined significantly. The relation-ship between the number of practicing surgeons and the overall mortality rate was found to be inverse in that situation. Cochrane's (1972) work demonstrated the direct relationship between health status and factors other than medical services, such as improvements in birth control, housing, nutrition, and sanitation.

Demographic and environmental factors directly associated with health including poverty and affluence, education, exposure to occupational hazards, general physical environment, housing, air pollution, traffic, noise, stress (population density, sociological stressors, and psychic pressures), behavior, habits, life-style, genetic contributions, maladapta-tion, specific disease conditions, and resistance to disease (Blum, 1976). Blum (1976) points out that, although the effects of scientific medicine can be measured in some cases (such as poliomyelitis vaccine), there is "no particularly convincing evidence that more and more scientific doctoring is associated with better and better health status, nor even with increased survival." While the positive effects of medical care are difficult to measure, so too are the negative effects, known as iatrogenic illnesses — those caused by what the healer does. There are increasing reports on the number of deaths caused by drug reactions, unnecessary surgery, and hospital infections. Although these negative impacts are difficult to document, they must be considered.

The obstacles to shifting from medical intervention strategies to strategies that emphasize improving economic, social, and environmental conditions are overwhelming. The financial constraints on health resources may help encourage a shift from intervention to prevention. Health systems agencies can also influence public support (through information and education on health issues) for prevention strategies. But the health systems agencies alone should not be expected to reorient national health priorities away from health services and toward prevention. In order to have an impact on health status, HSAs must devote greater attention to alternatives to health services. In the past, health planning organizations directed a great deal of resources toward secondary prevention and treatment services for various diseases. Milio (1977) found that only 20 percent of health planning was aimed at improving health status and less than 10 percent at providing preventive services even within the health delivery system.

An ecological approach to health planning for illness prevention is not always popular. Some HSAs that have taken active public positions around environmental hazards, highway safety, abortion, smoking, and other health issues have been criticized by special economic and political interest groups. In response to such disputes between HSAs and special interests, Senator Schweiker (now DHHS Secretary) introduced a congressional amendment to the planning legislation in 1978 to ask HSAs to confine their activity to health planning in the traditional sense, i.e., to focus on the health delivery system (McGraw-Hill, 1978e). Although the proposed amendment did not pass, it is clearly controversial for health planning to attack underlying causes of disease, injury, and death directly. A change in planning priorities toward improving health status would place an emphasis on altering environmental and socioeconomic conditions to promote health. Of particular importance are income maintenance programs for the poor. The energy of planning agencies would be directed in part toward public policy decisions and private sector policies that promote health. Activities related to improving health status could have a greater impact upon the health of citizens than the current priorities established by the planning legislation.

In an era of limited health care funding that tends to limit health prevention activities, there is one alternative health care organizational approach that offers potential for promoting health and preventing illness. This approach is that of Health Maintenance Organizations (HMOs), developed to change the relationship of health services and their financing. HMOs provide comprehensive health care services for specific population groups. They are built upon the principle of prepayment for an enrolled group. Thus the HMO undertakes the financial risks of caring for a specified population. The less expensively the organization can provide services, the greater surplus it realizes; this develops a clear financial incentive for physicians to reduce costs and prevent illness (Luft, 1978). HMOs have been found to provide care to patients less expensively than traditional fee-for-service medicine. This is achieved primarily by impressive reductions in hospitalization rates. Savings are not attributable to increased ambulatory care but rather to a combination of factors: financial incentives not to hospitalize, strong peer review procedures to determine appropriateness of hospitalization, and restriction of bed supply available to physicians (Chassin, 1978; Luft, 1978). This type of organization of health services also serves as a competitor to the fee-for-service system, forcing that sector to make operational changes that result in cost savings. While HMOs can obviously err in providing too little care if there are no regulations or consumer protections, the concept of changing the organization and reimbursement system incentives is clearly sound.

A great potential exists for HMOs to achieve cost savings through health promotion and prevention. HMOs have financial incentives to shift their emphasis to improving health status and the capability of providing health education, health promotion, and prevention activities.

The health planning system can do a great deal to promote HMOs from encouraging public enrollment to special planning for the development of HMOs. By developing special review criteria for HMOs, public accountability can be maintained, and prepaid organizations can be encouraged to expand programs. Public policies to promote HMOs have been supported by Congress (e.g., removing CON requirements from HMOs under P.L. 96-79 (Kennedy, 1978; *United States Code,* 1979)) and by the Reagan Administration, which has proposed removing participation restrictions for Medicaid eligibles (Morris Report, 1981a). HMOs are the basic organizational foundation for competitive health care models advocated for future health policies (Enthoven, 1979).

EXPANSION OF THE SCOPE AND AUTHORITY OF P.L. 93-641

PHYSICIAN REGULATION. One of the most serious limitations of P.L. 93-641 was its failure to include physicians in its planning and regulatory authority. Physicians, who are the major controllers of health care delivery, are autonomous from CON provisions. Yet their decisions determine the type and volume of health services, as well as the location of service and the nature of the care. All are decisions that directly affect the cost of health services. Health planning agencies have no direct control over the number, distribution, or type of physicians available. The health planning system may identify underserved areas and overconcentrations of physicians but has no authority to encourage or discourage physicians in practicing in those areas. Physicians are not regulated in their practice selection. They have the right to restrict their practices to paying patients and to discriminate if they want. Although shortages of primary care physicians exist in many areas, planning agencies have no authority to increase the number of such physicians and restrict the number of specialists.

Physicians dominate hospital decision making and are difficult for hospital administrators and trustees to control because they provide the major revenue source for the facilities. While a hospital board of trustees is legally responsible for hospital administration, hospital physician staff privileges, and the operation of the facility, the physicians on the hospital staff are solely responsible for patient care decisions. Thus, administrators have difficulty imposing limits upon the activities and practices of physician staff members. The power of physicians varies, of course, among hospitals. But it is directly related to whether hospitals are competing for physicians or whether physicians are competing for hospital staff privileges. Where hospital occupancies are low, hospitals have greater difficulty in resisting physicians' demands for expansion of facilities, services, and equipment. It is no accident that physicians are not covered under the planning act. Physicians have developed into a powerful lobbying force in Washington, where they spend more than other special interest groups (Sinclair, 1978; Feldstein, 1980). In addition, regulation of physician practices poses a major administrative problem because of the large numbers of practitioners operating individually and in groups. Before effective regulatory controls over physician activities could be administered, physicians would probably have to be encouraged to work in organized groups rather than independently.

The long-range consequence of excluding physicians from cost-containment controls and regulation while including health facilities was to create a loophole that stimulates activities outside the certificate-of-need process. This has enabled some physicians to expand facilities and services where hospital providers might have been denied. For example, a computed axial tomography (CAT) scanner may cost up to $1 million to install, have an annual operating cost of $300,000 to $500,000, and produce physicians' bills of about $200,000 for interpreting the scans (Fineberg et al., 1977). The CON law has made an effort to reduce unnecessary scanners and to encourage equitable distribution of available scanners. These efforts have been thwarted in some cases by legal loopholes that allow physicians to purchase such equipment without going through CON review. During 1978, the Kennedy Health Planning Amendment (S.2410) would have required all purchases of equipment of $150,000 to undergo CON review regardless of location, even in a physician's office. An opposition amendment (Huddleston-Hatch Amendment), sponsored by the American Medical Association, was defeated in the Senate. However, the House did oppose CON for physicians' offices, which in part prevented passage of the planning legislation in 1978 (McGraw-Hill, 1978c, d, f, g). Until physicians are included under planning and regulatory controls, the current planning system will have no direct impact and little indirect impact upon the behavior and practices of physicians and the costs they generate.

REGULATORY CONTROLS. Although the authors of P.L. 93-641 were oriented toward decertification of excess hospital capacity, the American Hospital Association opposed this concept. Consequently, the law provided only for "appropriateness review." This provides tht an HSA shall make a "review on a periodic basis of all institutional health services offered in the health service area of the agency and shall make recommendations to the SHPDA respecting the appropriateness in the area of such services" (*United States Code,* 1974). Opponents of these activities have urged elimination of the appropriateness review functions on the grounds that agencies are not capable of performing the tasks adequately (McCue et al., 1978). Opponents of appropriateness review (the hospital association and medical society) were not able to have the provisions removed in 1974 or in the renewal legislation (*United States Code,* 1979), although opponents did have the decertification sanctions for enforcement of appropriateness review eliminated in 1974 (McCue et al., 1978). Agencies have only one sanction: making their appropriateness review findings public. It is doubtful that such action will have any measurable effect, especially when Health Systems Agencies do not have the authority to require reporting of data by the hospitals and no sanctions are available for those who refuse to cooperate.

To be effective, appropriateness reviews must be tied to decertification authority and to state reimbursement sanctions under Section 1122. Agencies need the authority to make changes in existing facilities such as closing or merging facilities and services that are found unnecessary or inappropriate. Agencies need regulatory authority not only to collect data but also to enforce findings from the reviews and to utilize incentives for encouraging facilities to comply with recommendations.

FINANCING CONTROLS. Cost containment, a major goal of health planning, is designed to provide more effective use of existing resources to assure equal access to good medical care. The purpose is to eliminate waste while ensuring that everyone can benefit from health care services. Since hospital cost inflation is the principal cause of rapidly growing health expenditures, this is the area where health planning must focus to reduce costs (Gibson, 1980; Califano, 1978; U.S. General Accounting Office, 1980). However, the planning act has been divorced from financial controls over expenditures for health care. Without direct controls over health care costs, the indirect impact through the CON process can be expected to be minimal.

The planning act can have some deterrent effects upon the building of new facilities and new services, but is powerless to reduce overall spending. Health planning agencies must have a direct impact on health expenditures within their area to control costs. Without such controls, CON activities occur in isolation from overall regulation of health expenditures.

One method of controlling costs is the hospital expenditure limit—imposing a mandatory ceiling on the total or the percentage of annual increases in hospital operating and capital expenditures. The objective of such a program is to control the proportion of expenditures devoted to hospital care by forcing hospitals to make allocation decisions within the context of some fixed dollar limit. There are a number of different methods for developing such "cap" goals (Raphaelson and Hall, 1978). Nationwide caps may be difficult because of differences in costs, but regional caps are attractive for developing flexibility for regional circumstances such as rates of inflation, proportions of elderly in the population, and other special circumstances. With a cap on regional expenditures, individual hospitals might get more or less than the average percentage increase, depending upon their particular circumstances related to such factors as operating efficiency, shifts in case mix, and volume of community services. The Rhode Island rate-setting program has been conducted under a statewide cap since 1974. This program has been evaluated as successful in holding costs below the national trend (U.S. General Accounting Office, 1980). If institutions within designated areas were required to spend within a budget for the year, resource allocation decisions could be made based upon priority needs and cost-effectiveness.

Another form of regulation is rate-setting authority and budgetary approval over hospitals. Rate setting is one form of regulatory control that has shown some results in controlling costs, although it is still controversial. This authority needs to be combined with planning and regulatory authority under P.L. 93-641. The federal government could require states to establish a budget and a rate-setting authority for setting expenditure limits based upon analysis of cost data. Only ten states have enacted mandatory rate-setting legislation and obtained demonstration approval from the Department of Health and Human Services to set Medicare reimbursement rates (U.S. General Accounting Office, 1980). Because of the success of the state rate-setting programs, the Carter Administration introduced legislation in 1979 to establish a national budget and rate-setting system for hospitals, but this legislation was strongly opposed by provider associations, and it was defeated. Rate review systems are designed to reduce unit operating expenditures and prices of health facilities for consumers on a prospective basis. Rate review could also serve as a monitoring device for CON decisions, ensuring that approved projects stay within their scope and cost (Urban Systems, 1978). If these two approaches were combined, states could monitor hospitals' prices, new revenues, and supply resources with significantly greater impact.

Organizational and Operational Issues

Two major organizational and operational problems that have developed with the implementation of P.L. 93-641 are addressed in this paper. Financing of the program is considered one critical barrier to effective implementation. The other barrier is the community board structure required by the legislation. Other issues, such as interagency coordination, data systems, planning technology, resource allocation, economic impact analysis, review criteria, and legal resources, although important, are beyond the scope of this paper and will not be discussed.

FINANCIAL CONSTRAINTS. Inadequate federal appropriations levels have caused financing problems for the health planning system in relation to the system's responsibility and authority. In 1975, Congress appropriated $128.6 million for P.L. 93-641 activities, at a rate higher than under the old Comprehensive Health Planning Program. In fiscal 1977, despite increased work loads and inflation, the appropriations were only $125 million. This produced a loss in actual revenues for agencies, especially with dramatic increases in inflation during that period. The total federal funds allocated for planning amounted to less than one-tenth of one percent of the nation's total investment in health care for the same period (Cain and Thornberry, 1977; Connor, 1976). As many states have experienced fiscal crises, state funds for health planning have recently been limited.

The ups and downs of congressional and state appropriations for planning since P.L. 93-641 was enacted have created an atmosphere of unstability (Klarman, 1976; McGraw-Hill, 1978b, h). Congress's failure to renew P.L. 93-641 in 1978 was another major disappointment to health planning agencies, until the legislation was reintroduced and passed in 1979. The low level of agency funding and the instability of program funding contribute to serious staffing problems for many HSAs, such as high staff turnover due to heavy work loads and low salaries and the use of consultants and temporary employees (Bauer, 1979). The high turnover has negative implications for quality and continuity of work and certainly disrupts interagency and intra-agency relationships. Increased federal funding of the program on a long-term basis would be required to develop an effective health planning system.

COMMUNITY BOARD STRUCTURE. The health planning system established by P.L. 93-641 is an attempt to delegate public decision making to consumer and provider board representatives in Health Systems Agencies and the state health coordinating councils rather than to have decisions made by public officials (Vladeck, 1977). The effective operation of the system then depends on informed consumer and provider board members who can make responsible decisions regarding local planning and CON applications (McCue, 1978). Unless the board members understand how the health care system functions, what it costs, what it can and cannot do, and who really pays the bills, complex planning and regulatory decisions cannot be made effectively. Because consumer members often find planning and review issues complex, confusing, and boring, their decisions are not always made from a rational planning perspective.

The problem of provider control of the Health Systems Agency boards has been reported in agencies across the country (Vladeck, 1977; Checkoway, 1979; Clark, 1977). Health providers have greater expertise than consumers and are likely to be heeded by consumers and regulators. Providers are one of the main sources of data, and incentives for participation by providers are much greater than for consumers. There is little pressure on political leaders to take action opposed by politically active providers. Providers are generally more organized, and they have the resources to employ attorneys in legal actions, legislative actions, and appeals in the courts. Health consumers are generally poorly organized and politically ineffective lobbyists (Checkoway, 1979; Urban Systems, 1978; Clark, 1977; Marmor and Morone, n.d.; Marmor and Morone, 1979). Evidence of provider interests dominating the planning agencies is shown in a review by Lewin and Associates (1975) of CON and Section 1122 decisions in 20 states. Lewin et al. found that the states approved more than 93 percent of all projects submitted, with particularly high approval rates for hospital expansions and purchase of equipment and new services. The study showed that consumers on review bodies tended to value ready availability of services over cost-containment concerns and hence tended to support expansion proposals. Other reports have shown that CON regulation is extremely difficult because there is no constituency for the closing of hospitals or controlling hospital costs. Little evidence has been found that CON has been more than minimally effective in cost-containment efforts (Chassin, 1978; Cohodes et al., 1979).

The challenge of educating consumer board members in Health Systems Agencies is great. Checkoway (1979) proposes new initiatives to increase the knowledge and capacity of consumer board members including special board training programs, new curricula, community forums, and full-time staff provided to the consumer members. New educational initiatives no doubt could increase public involvement and effectiveness in health issues and health planning. The question is whether any amount of consumer education or experience can compensate for the greater power held by providers on the boards. And why should providers who have a self-interest in decisions made by the planning system have any role in decision making for the public sector? As board members, in the present system, providers are in a position to dominate and influence decisions that enhance their own interests (Vladeck, 1977).

Health providers have mobilized a great deal of financial resources for political activities to promote their position in all aspects of the health planning system (Feldstein, 1980). For example, the California health industry was successful in obtaining billions of dollars of exemptions from the state's CON legislation. Providers have lobbied at the local, state, and federal levels for legislative loopholes and statutory limitations to CON provisions. Locally, facility representatives have attempted to obtain expansion-oriented standards and criteria for the CON process and the health systems plans (Price, 1978). Facility representatives are active in the planning, CON review, and appropriateness reviews and have blocked monitoring and regulatory activities. Local agency activities are frequently challenged by providers, and conficts between consumers and providers are difficult to avoid. The American Medical Association is one of the most influential, best-known, and wealthiest of all special interest groups. It represents about half of the country's physicians with a yearly budget of about $50 million (Feldstein, 1980; Sinclair, 1978). The AMA spent abut $1.5 million on lobbying in 1978, including a large Washington office, and made major contributions to political campaigns. In 1974 and 1976, the AMA spent more than $3.2 million on congressional candidates (Sinclair, 1978;

McGraw-Hill, 1978a). The American Hospital Association, representing 6,400 hospitals and nursing homes, also has a large legislative office in Washington and makes considerable contributions. The Federation of American Hospitals represents 780 of the 986 investor-owned hospitals and also does a sizable amount of activity in monitoring federal and state health legislation (Sinclair, 1978). Sinclair reported, "These three organizations' ability to activate their networks, their knowledge of which magic button produces a congressional response, and the campaign contributions they can make, give them power." This power has had a substantive impact on federal legislation, including weakening the scope and authority of P.L. 93-641 and killing President Carter's cost-containment legislation proposal in 1978 (Sinclair, 1978; McGraw-Hill, 1979g; McGraw-Hill, 1979i).

If one goal is to give the public real decision-making authority in the health planning system, the legislation will have to be amended so that providers are removed entirely as board members of the agencies, so that all the members are consumers. Even with complete consumer control of boards, health providers would probably continue to dominate board decision making because of the imbalance in power, expertise, and influence of providers over consumers. Perhaps the notion of community control of board decisions in health planning under the present governmental structure is not a viable approach. Public participation in health planning probably is not as effective as the public administrative process used by other health regulatory programs. If the planning legislation were rewritten, the administrative and organizational authority could be given entirely directly to state officials. Not only would the cost of the current "participatory community" program be removed, but the regulatory decisions might better follow the state and federal planning guidelines if the responsibility and authority were vested with public officials at the state or federal levels.

Evaluation

The public in general and consumer health planning board members are not united in their support for changing the health care system and for health planning and regulation as a means of making reforms (Krause, 1975). Health consumers have failed to organize around health issues and, for the most part, do not have enough organized political power to have any impact on health policy or legislation. While some consumers involved in health planning activities have advocated health planning and regulatory legislation, the number of consumers involved has remained small. The failure of the Health Systems Agencies to develop an active consumer constituency has, in the end, resulted in lack of congressional support and negative evaluation of the agencies' impact.

Because hopes and expectations for P.L. 93-641 far exceeded what can realistically be accomplished with the limited resources and authority given to the health planning system, the program's evaluation has been extremely critical. If, instead, health planning were viewed as one effort among many approaches to accomplish changes in health care status and delivery, the program's evaluation would be less negative. Considering that the major planning activities were focused on the delivery system, the notion that health planning would have an impact upon the health of the population was unrealistic. While some agencies directed attention to improving health status by supporting health education, housing, nutrition, birth control, and environmental factors, agencies are limited to community education activities. Changes in health status will have to wait for overall economic, political, and social changes in the society.

The Reagan Administration has proposed to eliminate the health planning program. The administration budget proposed a decrease in the health planning budget from $167 million to $122 million in 1981 and only $58 million for 1982 (Morris Report, 1981b). The 1982 allocations would be primarily earmarked for the states, eliminating the Health Systems Agencies. No federal funds for the planning program are proposed for FY 1983 under the Reagan plan. In explaining this proposal, the Reagan budget document (1981) stated, "We believe that health planning efforts will be continued with non-federal funds." The good programs, as judged by the states, would be continued using state funds and the poor ones would be phased out, according to the budget document (Morris Report, 1981b). The elimination of the planning program is in part proposed as a way to save federal money.

David Stockman, Director of the Office of Management and Budget (1981), described three basic deficiencies in the planning system in what is known as "Stockman's black book": inappropriate regulation, lack of effectiveness, and federal usurpation of state and local responsibilities (Morris Report, 1981a). Stockman's report states:

The health planning program is intended to restrain costs by limiting the supply of facilities and services. However, this approach also inhibits market forces which are needed to strengthen competition and provide less costly services. Moreover, the current structure is seriously defective as a regulatory mechanism in that it relies on non publicly accountable HSA's with strong provider representation. Since the planning process is largely specified and funded and operating with national planning guidelines, it is also viewed as a basic framework for federal regulation of the health care system.

Stockman argues that the program has been ineffective and should be returned to the responsibility of state the local government. In place of the health planning system, Stockman proposes legislative initiatives that would enhance competition between provider organizations. At the same time, Stockman proposes that the Medicaid program be in the form of a block grant to states with a ceiling to control total spending, and he advocates removing some of the federal regulations, which would allow states to institute hospital cost containment and other cost-saving devices.

While it is difficult to marshal evidence to refute Stockman's negative assessment of the health planning agencies, the most appropriate policy proposals to control the high costs of health care and restructure the health care delivery system are certainly open for debate. Unfortunately, this debate may not occur as the administration and Congress move with great speed to institute new policies. The lack of constituencies to support the current planning system and the swing of public opinion away from regulatory approaches have probably sealed the fate of the federal planning system.

SUMMARY AND CONCLUSIONS

The health planning and regulation system is one approach to improving health status and improving the health delivery system with a rational allocation of health service resources. If the goals and premises of health planning and regulation as defined in P.L. 93-641 are accepted, then the problems with the health planning legislation need to be corrected to strengthen the effectiveness of the system. Health planners can begin making a difference by advocating public policy changes that will shift resources away from expensive medical services and toward the prevention of illness and promotion of health. A shift in resources and direction could bring about an actual change in the health status of the population, which is the ultimate goal of planning. By encouraging the development of Health Maintenance Organizations and limiting the expansion of unnecessary services and facilities, the health planning system can begin to make an impact on the delivery of health care. But health planning as presently structured is severely limited in its authority over the health care system. Legislative changes are needed to bring physicians under health planning and regulation. Health Systems Agencies also must have the authority to decertify and close unnecessary services and facilities. At the same time, unless budget and rate-setting control over health facilities is developed in conjunction with health planning and certificate of need, significant cost containment cannot be expected to be achieved. The hope of planning is to develop a more effective health care delivery system with financial incentives for health promotion and prevention of illness, as in HMOs, while the present system is held in check through regulation.

Unfortunately, the Reagan Administration apparently does not agree with the premises of a strong federally operated planning and regulatory system. This philosophical orientation combined with heavy pressure by provider organizations and the absence of consumer support for the current program are reasons for the phaseout of the program. The apparent demise of federal planning under P.L. 93-641 is certainly not the end of health planning. While the present structure may be dismantled in many states, the health planning and regulatory approach is still ideologically strong (Kaiser, 1978; Krause, 1975; Alford, 1975). As states have greater fiscal pressures with federal spending caps on health programs, particularly Medicaid, the states will seek ways to reduce costs. Health planning, rate setting, certificate of need, and other mechanisms will no doubt continue to be used in one form or another.

Providers themselves (hospitals and physicians) will also, no doubt, continue to use health planning as a way to rationalize their expansion and development (Alford, 1975). The competitive models proposed by Enthoven (1979), and the Reagan Administration, while theoretically offering some cost-saving advantages, are not popular with providers (because of the potential instability they could bring to the present delivery system) or consumers (because of the cost-sharing features). For providers the original option of rational planning and regulation may grow in attractiveness as other options are found unacceptable and the costs of health care remain unchecked.

Many changes in the health planning and regulation system can be anticipated in the future. Some new form of accomplishing planning and regulation will no doubt emerge in place of the existing system, but the direction of such a program remains to be developed and shaped, and the weaknesses in the existing system need to be corrected.

REFERENCES

Alford, R. R. 1975. *Health care politics: ideology and interest group barriers to reform.* Chicago: University of Chicago.

Atkisson, A., and Grimes, R. M. 1976. Health planning in the United States: an old idea with a new significance. *Journal of Health Politics, Policy & Law* 1:295–318.

Bauer, K. G. December 1977. *The arranged marriage of health planning and regulation for cost containment under P.L. 93-641 — some issues to be faced.* Report series R58-1, Harvard University Center for Community Health and Medical Care.

Blum, H. L. 1976. From a concept of health to a national policy. *American Journal of Health Planning* 1:3–22.

Bogue, T., and Wolfe, S. M. 1976. *Trimming the fat off health care costs: a consumer's guide to taking over health planning.* Washington, D.C.: Health Research Group.

Cain, H. P. 1978. Issues in the implementation of P.L. 93-641. *American Journal of Health Planning* 3:47–59.

Cain, H. P., and Thornberry, H. N. 1977. Health planning in the United States: where we stand today. In J. Elinson, A. Mooney, and A. E. Siegmann, *Health goals and health indicators: policy, planning, and evaluation.* Boulder, Colorado: Westview.

Chassin, M. R. 1978. The containment of hospital costs: a strategic assessment. *Medical Care* 16:1–55.

Checkoway, B. 1979. Citizens on local health planning boards: what are the obstacles? *Journal of the Community Development Society* 10:101–16.

Clark, W. 1977. Placebo or cure? state and local health planning agencies in the south. Atlanta: Southern Regional Council.

Cochrane, A. L. 1972. *Efficiency and effectiveness: random reflections on health services.* London: Nuffield.

Cohodes, D. R.; Pardini, A.; and Cohen, A. 1979. *Analysis of interstate certificate of need program variation.* Cambridge, Mass.: Urban Systems Research and Engineering.

Common Cause suggests AMA's heavy contributions to Commerce Committee members helped defeat cost cap. 1978. *National Health Insurance Report* 8:6.

Connor, G. R. 1976. State government financing of health planning. *American Journal of Health Planning,* 1:48–51.

Enthoven, A. C. May 26, 1979. Health care costs: why regulation fails, why competition works, how to get there from here. *National Journal,* pp. 885–89.

Ermann, D. January 1978. Cost containment under P.L. 93-641: strengthening the partnership between health planning and regulation. *Harvard University Center for Community Health and Medical Care Report Series,* R58-8.

Feldstein, P. J. 1980. The political environment of regulation. *Academy of Political Science* 33:6–20.

Fineberg, H. V.; Parker, G. S.; and Pearlman, L. A. 1977. CAT scanners distribution and planning status in the United States. *New England Journal of Medicine* 297:216–18.

Gibson, R. M. 1980. National health expenditures, 1979. *Health Care Financing Review* 2:1–36.

Health, United States, 1978. 1978. Rockville, Maryland: Department of Health, Education and Welfare, Health Resources Administration.

Kaiser, L. R. 1978. The future of health planning. *American Journal of Health Planning* 3:1–9.

Kennedy, E. M. 1978. Health planning amendments of 1978. *Congressional Record* 124:3.

Kingsdale, J. M. 1978. Marrying regulatory and competitive approaches to health care cost containment. *Journal of Health Politics, Policy & Law* 3:20–42.

Klarman, H. E. 1976. National policies and local planning for health services. *Milbank Memorial Fund Quarterly* 54:1–28.

Krause, E. 1975. The political context of health service regulation. *International Journal of Health Services* 5:593–607.

Lewin, A. September 1975. *Evaluation of the efficiency and effectiveness of the section 1122 review process.* DHEW contract #HRA 106-74-183. Washington, D.C.

Luft, H. S. 1978. How do Health Maintenance Organizations achieve their savings? rhetoric or evidence. *New England Journal of Medicine* 298:1336–43.

Marmor, T. R., and Morone, J. A. 1979. HSAs and the representation of consumer interests: conceptual issues and litigation problems. *Health Law Project Library Bulletin* 4:117–28.

––––––. N.d. *Representing consumer interests: imbalanced markets, health planning, and the HSAs.* Center for Health Studies, Institute for Social and Policy Studies, Yale University.

McCue, W.; Pierce, C. F., Jr.; and Mott, A. T. 1978. Appropriateness review: which road to take? *American Journal of Health Planning* 3:10–16.

McGraw-Hill Publication. January 23, 1978. *Washington report on medicine and health* 32:47.

––––––. February 6, 1978b. *Washington report on medicine and health* 32:6.

––––––. March 13, 1978c. *Washington report on medicine and health* 32:11.

––––––. May 8, 1978d. *Washington report on medicine and health* 32:19.

––––––. June 12, 1978e. *Washington report on medicine and health* 32:24.

––––––. August 1, 1978f. *Washington report on medicine and health* 32:32.

––––––. October 23, 1978g. *Washington report on medicine and health* 32:43.

––––––. November 20, 1978h. *Washington report on medicine and health* 32:47.

––––––. November 19, 1979i. *Washington report on medicine and health* 33:45.

Milio, N. 1977. An ecological approach to health planning for illness prevention. *American Journal of Health Planning* 2:7–11.

Morris Report. February 13, 1981a. *Health system report* 10:1–8.

––––––. March 13, 1981b. *Health system report* 10:1–8

––––––. May 1, 1981c. *Health system report* 10:1–4.

Price, S. September 1978. *Health law center proposal.* Proposal submitted to the U.S. Department of Health, Education, and Welfare, Los Angeles.

Raphaelson, A. H., and Hall, C. P., Jr. 1978. Politics and economics of hospital cost containment. *Journal of Health Politics, Policy & Law* 3:87–111.

Reeves, P. N. 1977. Issues in health plan development: a critique of the guidelines for plan development under P.L. 93-641. *American Journal of Health Planning* 1:27–35.

Roemer, M. I., and Schwartz, J. L. October 1978. *Doctor slowdown: effects on the* population of Los Angeles County. Paper presented to the meeting of the American Public Health Association, Los Angeles.

Sinclair, W. 1978. How the industry waged war on hospital cost bill. *Washington Post,* November 12–15, 1978, A1.

Sweetland, M., and Bauer, K. G. December 1977. *Linking health planning and regulation to increase cost effectiveness.* Proceedings of a conference, October 1977, Arlington, Virginia and Harvard University Center for Community Health and Medical Care, Report Series R58-3.

U.S. General Accounting Office. 1980. *Rising hospital costs can be restrained by regulating payments and improving management.* Washington, D.C.: Comptroller General of the United States.

United States Code 42, 201. October 4, 1979. Health Planning and Resources Development Amendments of 1979. Public Law 96-79, 96th Congress, Titles 15 and 16 of the Public Health Service Act.

United States Code 42, 300. 1980. Health Planning Technical Amendments of 1980 to Title 15 of the Public Health Services Act.

United States Code. 1974. The National Health Planning and Resources Development Act of 1974. 88 statutes, 2225–76.

United States Code. 1972. Social Security Amendments. 86 statutes, 1386–87.

U.S. Institute of Medicine, National Academy of Sciences. 1980. *Health planning in the United States: issues in guidelines development.* Washington, D.C.: U.S. Government Printing Office.

Urban Systems Research and Engineering and Policy Analysis. November 1978. *Certificate of need programs: a review, analysis, and annotated bibliography of the research literature.* HRP-0301201, Department of Health, Education and Welfare.

Vladeck, B. C. 1977. Interest-group representation and the HSAs: health planning and political theory. *American Journal of Public Health* 667:23–28.

8

PRIMARY HEALTH CARE

Peter Hookey

In recent years the governmental emphasis on primary care incentive programs and the increasing public distaste for the impersonality of superspecialized medicine have combined to create a situation in which primary (health) care identity is valued and claimed by many more physicians than simply those in family practice. Medical care policy makers now commonly use the term "primary (health) care specialties" as a generic term embracing internal medicine, pediatrics, and obstetrics/gynecology as well as family practice. Sometimes general surgery is included.

Only very recently have social workers begun to participate in primary health care on any appreciable scale. A program in a Boston hospital outpatient department is often cited as the first example of such practice (David and Warner, 1918). However, it is probably more meaningful to view the Family Health Maintenance Demonstration associated with Montefiore Hospital in New York as the first project of contemporary policy significance (Silver, 1963; Silver and Stiber, 1957; Friedson, 1961). A key aspect of this inner-city federally funded project was utilization and attitudinal evaluation of the work of the social worker member of the family health care team. The data showed that both physicians and patients were less than enthusiastic in their endorsement of the social worker as a provider of counseling services.

Traditionally, social workers in health care settings have found it much harder to "market" their counseling role than their resource broker role, and this has been very much the case in primary health care settings. The Family Health Maintenance Demonstration findings are probably representative of a variety of subsequent primary health care projects in which the social workers have fought an uphill battle for acceptance in other than narrowly defined roles. However, over more recent years many studies have attested both to the large volume of psychosocial problems presented in primary health care settings (Bishop et al., 1967; Kleinman et al. 1978; Shepherd, 1966, 1974) and to patients' readiness for social work intervention in many situations (Brooks, 1973). While the problem of social workers acceptance in primary care has by no means been resolved, recent professional gains in the legislative area — such as the recognition of state-level vendor status and qualified mental health examiner — are contributing to and symptomatic of its lessening intensity.

During the last quarter century the expansion of the field of social work in primary health care in the United States has been slow but significant. Listed below are references to publications describing some historically significant projects in some key subfields (ordered alphabetically):

> fee-for-service family practice settings:
> Tanner and Carmichael, 1970; Goldberg, 1973; Lincoln, Twersky, and O'Neil-Sale, 1974; O'Connor, 1977.
> fee-for-service internal medicine clinics:
> Margolis and Mendelsohn, 1956; Wegner, Ruiz, and Caccamo, 1966.
> fee-for-service multi-specialty group medicine practices:
> Hobson and Grayburn, 1969; Barkan, 1973.
> fee-for-service pediatric medicine clinics:
> Wishingrad, Schulruff, and Sklansky, 1963; Townsend, 1964; Korpela, 1973; Comfort and Kappy, 1974.
> prepaid group practice and Health Maintenance Organizations:
> Alt, 1959; Golden, Carlson, and Harris, 1973; Bell and Gorman, 1976; Lum, 1976.

Additionally, social workers have participated fairly extensively in inner-city neighborhood health centers (Anderson et al., 1976), and they have begun to join the staffs of some free street clinics and public health clinics. Other types of settings that have sometimes provided a springboard for participation in primary heatlh care have included community mental health clinics (Guillozet, 1975; Maypole and Wright, 1979), family service agencies (Davis and Nevin, 1976), community action organizations (Hookey, 1975, 1977), and industry (Pitz, 1975).

In recent years, one of the strategically important developments has been the growth of social workers' participation on the faculties of residency training programs for the primary care specialties, especially family practice (Tanner and Carmichael, 1970; Lincoln, Twersky, and O'Neil-Sale, 1974). As teachers, mentors, models, and clinician — and client advocate — demonstrators, such social workers are in a position to influence many cohorts of primary care physicians in the direction of closer collaboration with social workers and other health professionals. Of 39 University of Utah family practice residents who were exposed to such influence, 72 percent said they intended to arrange for part- or full-time attachment of a social worker to their future practice clinics (Frangos and Chase, 1976).

CONTEMPORARY AND PROSPECTIVE DEVELOPMENTS AND OPPORTUNITIES

Primary health care is now coming of age in America. Once the lowly step-child of the health care system, it is now the rising star. It is a turbulent and stress-filled subsystem, a stage on which one can observe the actions of a variety of interest groups. In describing and analyzing this stage and its actors from a social work viewpoint one might choose to focus initially on any one of many different aspects. I have chosen to focus first on the issue of intervention emphasis, thence moving on to consider intervention roles, and then delivery systems. Thus, the discussion will focus, in turn, on the philosophies, the methods, and the structures of family health care, with special attention to the actual and potential participation of social workers therein.

Intervention Emphases

The *medical* model has been and still remains the predominant model of primary health care. However, there are pervasive indications that alternatives to the medical model are gaining widespread support (as they have done for some time in the overlapping field of mental health care). These alternative approaches or emphases may be grouped into three categories on the basis of the sources of responsibility for care—namely *professional, personal,* and *shared professional/personal.*

The approaches to be discussed overlap to a considerable extent and vary greatly in the extent of their applicability across various types of situations. Thus the more approximate term "emphasis" will be used rather than the term "model," which tends to suggest a misleading degree of uniqueness and comprehensiveness. The discussion that follows and the labels that are utilized reflect my own assessment of current developments. They are not necessarily representative of other writers in this area, nor would the authors that I cite necessarily agree with my assessments of the nature and type of their contributions.

The *professional* category includes, along with the *medical* model, the *physiological, behavioral,* and *psychological* emphases.

The *physiological* emphasis entails a focus on enabling the client to better comprehend and control his or her own physiological mechanisms, often with the assistance of machines. Perhaps the best-known innovation of this type is the biofeedback technique, in which an electrical sensory/reporting system facilitates the clients' comprehension and control of bodily stress. Social workers have been significantly involved in the application of this technique in primary health care clinics within Kaiser-Permanente prepaid health care plans in California.

The *behavioral* emphasis entails a focus on examination of the relationship between behavior and physical health, helping clients to better understand these relationships, and assisting them in making life-style changes based on such understanding. While the behavioral emphasis and behavioral modification are not synonymous, the latter may often be involved as the methodology whereby the third aspect of the behavioral emphasis is achieved.

The behavioral modification methodology has for some time been commonly utilized by social workers in primary health care settings (see, for example, Brockway et al., 1976). However, the more general participation by social workers in the various aspects of the behavioral emphasis has been less widely reported. The NIMH-funded primary health care demonstration project that is in progress in Washington University, St. Louis, seems likely to focus on the behavioral emphasis in this broader sense (Walter,

1978). To a considerable extent, those social workers whose work focuses on psychosomatic disorders (see, for example, O'Connor, 1977) may be viewed as operating within the behavioral emphasis.

The behavioral emphasis is clearly in a period of expansion. Various sociocultural developments are fueling this growth. Social workers may find much of interest in the activities of the NIMH Task Force on Behavioral Medicine, which may be expected to issue a report shortly (Gallagher, 1979).

The *psychological* emphasis entails a primary focus on intra- and interpersonal psychological data, with the relevance of concurrent or preceding physical disorders being seen as of relatively secondary importance. Few workers in this field would be comfortable with the explicit relegation of physical data to a secondary level of importance. However, there are many who operate on a day-to-day basis as if this were the case, and it is the philosophies that seem to underly everyday practice that are currently being examined.

In this latter context, a distinction between the physiological and behavioral emphases seems meaningful. However, in regard to this latter comparison, it should be noted that many primary health care social workers may be characterized as straddling both emphases. An illustrative case might involve a social worker who historically has operated within the psychological emphasis, who has been persuaded of the salience of the behavioral emphasis in relation to certain conditions (e.g., stress-induced headaches), but who is not ready to adopt the behavioral emphasis as his or her general modus operandi.

As described above, the physiological, behavioral, and psychological emphases have in common the stance of professional authority—the notion that the professionals on the primary health care team—physician, nurse, social worker, etc.—have acquired a level of pertinent wisdom and knowledge that equips them to be especially effective at the task of primary health care, and that the preferred mode of care is dispensational.

The above characterization serves to highlight the comparison with the second category of caring emphases—namely, those emphasizing *personal* responsibility for care. In these emphases the professionals' preferred caring mode is *inspirational*. The professionals' function is seen as helping the client to manage his or her own health with varying degrees of assistance from his or her peers. In recent years, the growth of this emphasis may reasonably be described as phenomenal (Katz, 1978). Included with this emphasis are the contemporary and interrelated movements of self-care (Levin, Katz, and Holst, 1977; see also Hookey, 1979a), personal stress management (Vattano, 1978), lay care (see, for example, Payne, 1976; Collins and Pancoast, 1976), psychodietetic awareness (Cheraskian, Ringsdorf, and Brecher, 1974), jogging (Fixx, 1977), and wellness (Ardell, 1977).

All of these share a belief that good health is the result of a healthy lifestyle; that the choice of life-style is ultimately the responsibility of each individual. While most primary health care social workers would agree that it is appropriate for them to play informational and inspirational roles in relation to life-style changes, there are wide variations in opinion regarding the carrying out of such roles—regarding how often and how vehemently such changes should be advocated and regarding how much and in what ways professionals should be involved in the pragmatics of implementation (e.g., as resource persons in peer support groups; see Jertson, 1975). A particularly controversial issue on which there is sparse social work literature is that of social workers' response to situations where clients' proposed self-care modalities are in direct conflict with the opinions of the professional medical establishment. The continuing controversies over laetrile and home deliveries (McClure, 1978) are cases in point. Illich's writings on the expropriation of care (see, for example, Illich, 1976) provide useful background material on this issue.

Continuing this particular conceptualization of caring emphases, the third category is comprised of emphases in which responsibility for care is shared between clients and professionals, in which the professionals' preferred caring mode is *colleagual* vis-à-vis the client. In these emphases, the professionals seek to utilize their special training and experience in formulating and sharing diagnostically—and therapeutically—oriented observations with clients. The clients, however, are vested with the responsibility for choosing whether to act upon, react to, or reject these inputs. At a theoretical level, such a philosophy may be considered as within the range of both good professional/dispensational care and good self- or lay care. However, as a style of day-to-day practice, this third, midway construct of colleagual care does seem to have a degree of pragmatic utility and distinctiveness. A brief discussion of the *holistic care* emphasis will serve to illustrate the colleagual care mode.

At the outset of this discussion, it should be recognized that the adjective "holistic" has come to be associated with such a spectrum of philosophies of care that it now has limited utility as a unembellished descriptor. At one end of the spectrum there is "wholistic care," which is understood to be a deliberate integration of the physical, psychological, and spiritual aspects of health care, with "spiritual" being unequivocally understood in the sense of Christianity and biblical teaching. "The Bible way of health . . . provides a model of whole person medicine. It stresses nutrition, environment, responsible behavior, stable families, restrained pace of life, and a quality of life centered on revealed meaning" (James Jekel, as reported by Board, 1979).

At the other end of the spectrum there is "holistic care," which also strives for synthesis of the physical, psychological, and spiritual, but whose philosophy includes a generous admixture of establishment knocking and championing of Eastern/mystical/folk forms of care that often run counter to the classical medical world (Carlson, 1977; Miles, 1977; Pelletier, 1977).

The two camps or positions identified above should not be seen as necessarily in opposition—although they may well be, on occasion, in regard to specific ethical issues. Their relationship to each other, and of each to the classical medical model, are perhaps best conceived of in terms of a tripolar juxtaposition, with areas of synthesis, areas of tension, and areas of antithesis. (For an informative and insightful, though clearly partisan, assessment of these relationships, see Alexander, 1978, and Fish, 1978.)

In the field of holistic care, the most clearly articulated model — from both philosophical and organizational standpoints — is that being promoted by Wholistic Health Centers, Inc., a Chicago-based, foundation-supported demonstration/consultancy agency under the direction of Granger Westberg (Westberg, 1970, 1979; Peterson, Tubesing, and Tubesing, 1976; Tubesing, D. A., 1976; Tubesing and Strosahl, 1976; Tubesing, N. L., 1976; and Tubesing, 1977).

Its biblical philosophical base is expounded in detail in the monograph *The Theological Roots of Wholistic Health Care* (Westberg, 1979). The basic organizational structure consists of care delivered by a tightly knit team consisting of a primary care physician, a nurse, and a pastoral counselor (who typically has an extrapastoral degree in a counseling-related discipline such as social work). The team places much emphasis on coordinated planning for each client, a high degree of client participation in selection of treatment regimen, and formal client education on both individual and seminar-group bases.

The first center opened in 1970, and since then several more have been brought into operation, mainly in the Midwest. The setting has usually been a remodeled church facility, but recently plans have been made to experiment with centers in a number of other types of settings (both medical and nonmedical).

As greater financial support for this wholistic care model becomes available, the next type of professional to be brought into the care team would be the social worker (Westberg, 1977). This development will provide opportunities for realizing the considerable community organization potentialities that I feel are latent within the wholistic care model (see Hookey, 1979b).

Intervention Roles

Legitimately, albeit unoriginally, I shall start this section by acknowledging the special contribution of Caplan (1964) in his conceptualization of three levels of preventive activity — primary, secondary, and tertiary. While his original treatise focused on preventive psychiatry, his ideas have been widely generalized to primary health care. While acknowledging Bloom's (1979) recent timely reminder of the very variable contemporary usages of the concept of prevention, the generally recognized distinctions between primary, secondary, and tertiary prevention still provide a useful means of introducing a discussion of the intervention role of social workers in primary health care.

Primary prevention typically involves intervention in the societal environment (economic, social, psychological, cultural, and spiritual) in such a manner as to forestall the development of individual ill health (in the broadest sense of that term) and/or to ameliorate existing disorders. Such activity is most directly suggestive of social workers' community organization role. The involvement of primary health care social workers in community organization activities is not very common in the United States. It is more common in countries such as the Netherlands where social workers are well-established members of primary care teams and where physicians are more supportive of such activity (see, for example, deGroot and Maertens, 1975; see also Hookey, 1978a).

A key form of *secondary prevention* is the identification of individual dysfunctions in latent or pre-acute phases and subsequent provision of educative and/or ameliorative help. An example of primary health care social wprkers' direct involvement in such activities is Henk's use of epidemiological methods to design a screening program for lead-paint poisoning and other hazards in Rochester, New York (Henk and Froom, 1975). Health Maintenance Organizations typically offer free annual physical examinations to their members, and in several instances social workers are becoming involved in psychosocial extensions of these examinations.

Secondary prevention is an arena in which social workers may have a policy-level impact even if they are not involved in the resulting direct service because of lack of resources or other reasons. For instance, social workers may be involved in advocating the incorporation of a psychosocial component in a computerized health hazard screening program, and in designing its programming, even though the organization concerned may decide to use other personnel to respond to client needs revealed by the screening program.

In primary care contexts, *tertiary prevention* entails responding to the acute or chronic problems of clients with the general intent of minimizing the need for subsequent recourse to secondary or tertiary (usually institutional) levels or care. Typically, such responses are provided in the form of individual or group counseling sessions. Such activities constitute the majority of most contemporary primary health care social work practice.

In the terms of the previous discussion of care emphases, one may note that, in general, a shift from tertiary to primary prevention involves a concomitant decrease in the ratio of the professional category of care, and a corresponding increase in the ratio of the more cost-effective personal category of care. From a policy standpoint, the desirability of increased emphasis on primary prevention activities is generally accepted. However, secondary and tertiary prevention activities generally seem more urgent and thus attract all or almost all of the available resources of personnel and money. A possible policy response to this situation—one that would, however, be hard to administer politically—would be for grant-making and revenue-sharing agencies to withhold a portion of their grants until a set minimum portion of the original grant had already been spent on primary prevention activities.

In primary health care settings, social workers' performance in the role of *team member* is of great importance. Being a good team member is most commonly conceived of in terms of collaborating well with other types of professionals in order to provide good care to the client. However, it needs to be recognized that this role is but one of a quartet of functions that emerge when one considers that care is not exclusively dispensational, and that professionals have needs as well as clients. Put more directly, being a good team member also involves the readiness to hear and pass on the client's views and suggestions regarding his or her care, the readiness to act as counselor to other team members, and the readiness to be counseled by other team members.

Currently the three latter functions are far from being routine in primary health care settings. Where they are carried out with determination, the quality of care is enhanced, both directly via better involvement of the clients and indirectly via the nurturance of the team members.

Social workers in primary health care teams do not always have the working job title of "social workers." Some prefer — or are assigned — other titles — for example, "counselor" (Barkan, 1973), medical social worker (Wolfe and Teed, 1967), social service counselor (Hookey, 1977b), psychotherapist (Ghan and Road, 1970), etc. Some within and without the profession argue that such titles enhance appropriate utilization of the social worker by both clients and other team members; others vehemently refute this position, claiming that the social work profession's long-standing public relations difficulties will only be aggravated by inconsistent nomenclature.

Individual workers' opinions on the above issue tend to be related to their feelings on related issues such as intervention emphasis (medical, psychological, behavioral, etc.) and stance toward other professionals. In many teams the social worker's contributions overlap to a considerable extent with those of the psychologist, nurse practitioner, community health nurse, health educator, etc. Some maintain that it is simpler for all such team members to operate with the common designation of "counselor"; others feel that it is more helpful if each operates with a job title reflecting his or her particular profession. Still a further issue is often involved regarding experience and perhaps formal training for work with particular client categories — marital couples, families, the elderly, children, alcoholics, etc. Thus, occasionally primary health care social workers may have a working designation such as marriage counselor, family counselor, pediatric social worker, etc. (Korpela, 1973).

Hokenstad (1977) has discussed five types of specialization identity available to helping persons. Specialization identities may stem from a profession (e.g., "social worker"), from an intervention method (e.g., "advocate"), from a client group focus (e.g., "marriage counselor"), from a service sector focus (e.g., "welfare worker"), or from a problem area focus (e.g., "grief worker"). Currently, increasing numbers of educational institutions are offering degrees Niih designations reflecting these latter types of specializations. According to how one feels about specialization and its various facets, and according to whether one's primary identity is as a professional or as a helping person, these trends may be viewed as regrettable or desirable or with disinterest. (For further discussion of these issues see Hookey, 1979f.)

Assuming the leadership of a group of persons who may represent a variety of types of specializations and blending them into an effective team calls for a special degree of maturity, sensitivity, and insight into the nature of teamwork and the complexities of vocational identity and experience (see New, 1968). While physicians have traditionally been the leaders in primary health care teams, some are now recognizing their lack of preparation for this role, and are willing to defer to other workers who may have had more apropriate training. The case can be made that social workers may often be well suited for *team leadership roles*. For several years they have played this role effectively at the Halsocentralen i Tierp, a prototype integrated primary health and social services system in rural Sweden (Berfenstam and Smedby, 1976). Such developments may be considered analogous to the trend in this country for social workers to assume the directorships of multidisciplinary community mental health centers.

Several contemporary health care trends — notably the urgent need for cost containment — are combining to bring primary health care settings more and more within the legitimate domain of publicly mandated health care planners. This trend comes at a time when many schools of social work are focusing on refining their students' planning skills. Social workers are likely to become increasingly involved in *health planning* (Uhlman and Wesselkampe, 1978). This will provide a new avenue for the promotion of social worker participation in primary health care.

The above discussion has reviewed only some of the roles played by social workers in primary health care settings. Others are touched upon in other sections of this chapter.

Delivery Systems

In this discussion of primary health care delivery systems, I shall first describe what I perceive to be the preferred type of delivery system. Subsequently I shall present a development sequence by which such a system might be achieved, starting from the current situation. With this approach, my own biases will be apparent at the outset, and the reader may make his or her assessment of the ensuing material.

The World Health Organization has defined primary health care as "essential health care made universally accessible to individuals and families in the community by means acceptable to them, through their full participation and at a cost that the community and country can afford. It forms an integral part both of the country's health system, of which it is the nucleus, and of the overall social and economic development of the community" (World Health Organization, 1978, p. 2).

This definition is laudable for its emphasis on universality, accessibility, community focus, lay participation, and cost containment. The latter sentence, dealing with the relationships of primary health care to other human services, is suggestive rather than definitive. I feel that primary health care should not only be "an integral part" of the total "health system," but should further be seen as the "overriding health priority" (see Gottschalk and Selmanoff, 1978, for an excellent explanation of some of the implications of this position).

Second, I feel that primary health care should not only be "an integral part" of "overall social and economic development," but should further be seen as both the entry point and the normal locus and organizational center of the entire human services system. There are two key implications of this preferred state of affairs. They pertain to the nature of the basic primary care delivery units and to the manner in which these units interact with other components of the human services system.

Regarding the former, I concur with a recent World Health Organization working group whose position was that "the basic elements in the nuclear (primary care) team . . . are the general medical practitioner or primary physician, the nurse and the social worker" (World Health Organization, 1973, p. 14). The soundness of this basic democratically oriented, tridisciplinary care unit has been accepted for some years in several European countries, notably in the Netherlands and in Sweden. Such units will preferably be organized on a geographic catchment area basis, especially in rural areas. The social workers on such teams will preferably interact with other human services systems in a similar manner to that currently typical of the primary care physician in the United States. Such physicians typically visit hospitals to participate in the care of clients whom they usually first encounter in the community. For complex disorders they may consult with more narrowly specialized colleagues whose practices tend to center more around the hospital. They may have contracts to act as visiting consultants to public schools, nursing homes, etc.

In a similar manner the social worker would visit hospitals, public schools, nursing homes, correctional facilities, etc., to participate in the helping process in regard to clients whom they had first encountered in traditional primary health care settings — and whose care they would subsequently expect to continue in the community. This would not mean that hospitals, public schools, nursing homes, and correctional facilities would no longer have social workers on staff, but rather that they would tend to have fewer and more specialized social workers, who would engage in direct practice in emergency situations, but whose prime functions would be consultancy and referral to appropriate primary care–based social workers. In such manner, continuity of care would be greatly enhanced, and social workers' relationships to physicians would be enhanced on account of the more similar nature of their practice styles.

In contrast to the stages of human services integration now being practiced in Europe, the American human services scene is organized in a more categorical fashion.

Currently the vast majority of American primary health care is effectively unidisciplinary in effect, though only rarely in a formal sense. Physicians often work with nurses, but their relationships typically are far from democratic.

A very small proportion of primary care physicians have chosen to work closely with social workers, usually by directly hiring them on either a full- or a part-time basis. Several examples of such arrangements have already been cited in the first section of this chapter.

A second (somewhat overlapping) group of primary care physicians have either taken the initiative in establishing collaborative relationships with social workers in social service agency employ and/or in private practice, or have been responsive to social workers' collaborative initiatives. Such relationships may involve telephone referrals and consultations, occasional social contacts, etc. Because such relationships are rarely described in print, it is very hard to know how extensive they are. On the rare occasions when a particular primary health care agency has formalized its relationships with one or more particular local social service agencies, then one may occasionally encounter reports of such alliances (see, for example, Maypole and Wright, 1979).

The above type of collaboration may be facilitated by the colocation of offices. For instance, a public human service agency may choose to base one or more of its staff in a primary health care facility. One of the few examples of this occurred several years ago in King City in rural California, and involved the outposting of a social worker from the regional community mental health center into a small group practice (Guillozet, 1975).

This outposting phenomenon has been much more common in Europe, particularly in the United Kingdom and in Sweden, and also in Japan (Anesaki and Sakagami, 1976).

In the United Kingdom, such outposting is referred to as attachment (or sometimes secondment). Most attachment schemes have involved just one social worker, although Derby once had a city-wide scheme involving a large number of workers (Cooper, 1971). In Scotland, attachment of social workers to new primary health care centers is quite common. Hicks's review of ten published reports of attachments schemes indicated that the median physician/social worker staffing ratio was 5:1 (Hicks, 1976, p. 560).

In what is probably the only controlled client-outcome study of social worker participation in primary health care thus far published, Cooper et al. (1975) found that intervention by a social worker attached to a group of general practitioners resulted in a better mean outcome change with neurotic patients over a one-year period than that obtained for the control group, who were treated by the physicians in informal collaboration with noncolocated local human services agency personnel.

In Sweden, outposting is now probably less common than other forms of primary health care/social services integration (as described below). However, an outposting project in Tynnered, a working-class suburb of Gothenburg, is of particular interest on account of the devolution of statutory powers that has occurred. A social worker was outposted from the local generic social services agency into a three-physician group general practice, and retained her regular statutory authorities under Sweden's Temperance and Children's Welfare Acts (Falklind et al., 1974). This facilitated her direct preventive work in the area of alcoholism and child abuse, and obviated the need for inefficient and time-consuming referrals to other staff at the social services agency headquarters. Such devolution of powers is unfortunately lacking in many other attachment/outposting schemes.

Successful outposting schemes tend to increase trust and interprofessional appreciation among physicians, nurses, and social workers, in both the practice and policymaking spheres. They pave the way for more comprehensive types of services integration, whose initiation tends to depend on the preexistence of high levels of trust.

More comprehensive services integration may involve, as a first stage, the functional merger of field-level primary health care and community social services in a particular locality. Administratively, this is more easily achieved in a country such as the Netherlands where the community social services are usually already generic and public. For instance, the establishment of an integrated colocated primary human services center in Hoensbroek essentially involved negotiations among three cadres of professionals — those providing medical, nursing, and public, generic social services — who had previously operated relatively autonomously (Dubois, 1971, 1976). In comparison, in the United States such negotiations will tend to be considerably more complex, since analogously comprehensive mergers will often need to involve private primary health care clinics, public health clinics, community mental health centers, family services agencies, and protective services agencies.

In many cases, colocations of these agencies will require the construction of a new multi-service facility whose architecture is designed to facilitate the primary care team process. Occasionally, one existing agency will have the capacity to extend its facilities in order to play physical host to the others, and in appropriate circumstances one can envisage any of the above types of agencies acting as host.

In the larger towns and cities of the United States, all of the above agencies are prime candidates for mergers. The resulting integdaied primary human services center will tend to have so many professional staff members that the formation of subgroups or "primary care unit teams" will be necessary to facilitate the development of meaningful teamwork relationships. In this regard, the tactics adopted at the Vardcentralen i Tierp merit careful study (Berfenstam and Smedby, 1976). This integrated human services center was built several yars ago to serve approximately 20,000 people in Tierp County in central Sweden. The center's staff divided themselves into several primary care unit teams, each comprising a physician, a social worker, and a nurse and each service a different geographic sector of the county. Each team met weekly, and the meetings were chaired by the social workers.

In the vast rural areas of the United States there are more compelling grounds for anticipating that primary health care clinics will become the locus of development for integrated primary human services centers. For instance, currently a small town of 3,000 or so persons might be served by a group family practice clinic having three physicians and three nurses. The nearest offices of the region's public health clinic, community mental health center, family service agency, and protective service agency may all be many miles distant in a larger city.

As interprofessional trust levels arise, the family practice clinic may first add a social worker to its professional staff. The specialized agencies mentioned above may subsequently integrate themselves and reorganize into several primary care unit teams. Those team members who were particularly experienced in the specialized functions of their previous agencies would make themselves available as consultants to other team units and/or other centers. These consultants could then participate in "circuit-riding" systems whereby they would regularly visit several of the above type of small-town clinics on a one- or two-day-a-week basis, providing emergency on-call service as needed at other times. Thus each small-town clinic would have effectively become a small integrated primary human services center providing to its clients the same range and quality of care available in the larger cities.

Apart from the obvious advantages of such arrangements in regard to continuity and comprehensiveness of client service, they will also contribute to the attractiveness of professional practice in rural areas, many of which are now chronically underserved. The staff members of a well-functioning integrated primary human service center often enjoy a camaraderie and a sense of shared burdens. These subjective feelings are the positive antithesis of the kinds of professional isolation experiences that have driven large numbers of solo physicians reluctantly to leave many American small towns. Thus this projected incremental reorganization of primary human services may well achieve, by virtue of its intrinsic appeal, what the National Health Service Corps and the various federal rural health initiatives are currently struggling to achieve (with very variable success) by extrinsic incentives.

The operating efficiency of the primary human services integration movement will be greatly enhanced if it is accompanied by a growth in individual rather than agency locus of professional statutory responsibility, especially in regard to social workers. This development represents the logical extension of the devolution-of-authority concept discussed above in connection with outposting schemes.

Integrated primary human services centers have the potential of providing a natural focus for the promotion of self-care and the facilitation and coordination of lay support energies.

In Milio's words, self-care "cannot be conceived as an individualistic or even family enterprise isolated from the community infra-structure. . . . [It] must be seen as a community concept" (Milio, 1977). However, it needs to be recognized that currently "one of the major factors motivating the creation of self-help and self-care in the health field is a widespread disenchantment with professional practitioners, agencies, and institutions" (Katz, 1978, p. 2). To some extent this disenchantment stems from the current pervasive fragmentation and insularity of human services systems and professionals. Thus we may anticipate that the primary human services integration movement will provide a climate more amenable to closer collaboration with self-care and lay support movements. With wisdom and sensitivity on the part of all concerned, at both practice and policymaking levels, we can hope for an eventually harmonious synthesis of professional, self-, and lay care.

In this country, lay care has been viewed by professionals largely in terms of a support mechanism that may supplement concurrent professional care, and thereafter supersede it (in the chronological sense). It is in the usage of lay persons as "case finders"—i.e., as facilitators of access to services and preventive intervention — that there is perhaps the greatest potential for innovation, especially in conjunction with the development of integrated primary human services centers.

In this regard the Polish lay "social volunteer" system merits special study (Wojciechowski, 1975). For purposes of this system, the population of Poland is divided into geographical units each containing approximately 600 persons — in a city perhaps the size of a city block, or a few square miles in the countryside. Within each unit, a lay volunteer is assigned responsibility for keeping in close touch with the residents, providing concrete and/or emotional support services in straightforward cases, and for referring to the local primary care center those persons in specific need of professional social and/or medical services. Their work involves both case finding and being available for self-sought help. The volunteers are typically mature, well-educated persons — for example, retired schoolteachers — who by virtue of their prior status and experience are already known and respected in their community. They are reimbursed for any out-of-pocket expenses in connection with their activities. Their work is often supervised and coordinated by the social workers based in the local primary care center. Over a period of time, these social volunteers develop an awareness of those "trouble spots" within their area to which they should give special attention. At least in the Warsaw area, the volunteers, with student help, make "once a year . . . case-finding visits to all households in their area, giving special attention to the elderly and invalids. The result is an annual list of people with social or health problems which are then followed up" (Kohn, 1977, p. 36).

The preventive potential of case finding may also be realized via fostering collaborative relationships between primary human service staff and members of those occupational groups whose work provides particular opportunities for case finding and referral. The Swedes have focused on rural mailmen in this regard. Other strategically placed groups include bartenders and the police.

The staff of integrated primary human services centers will of course need to have referral relationships with staff in other parts of the total human services system — with the staff of public schools, hospitals, correctional facilities, etc. Over a period of time, one may envisage that the practice of referral will tend to be progressively displaced by the practice of "mutual permeability" — a modus operandi that is much more conducive to continuity of service. Thus a social worker on the staff of a primary human services center would normally plan to continue to meet directly with his or her client wherever his or her service needs are most appropriately met, whether it be in the center, at the client's home, in his or her public school, in the local hospital, in a correctional facility, etc. The implications of this operating style are that some institutional social services personnel will tend to move out into primary human services settings (in order to provide the staffing levels that enable the above kind of continuity of services). Concurrently, those who remain based in institutional settings will tend to become more specialized, serving as consultants to community level workers. However, fairly often there will be occasion for them to provide services — usually of a crisis intervention nature — to institutionalized clients who are not already on the case load of a primary human services center worker. In such circumstances, the practice of mutual permeability would suggest that it would be at the discretion of the institutional staff whether to refer clients once they return to the community or whether to continue to work with them by visiting them in community settings. The latter choice might be more appropriate in those instances where need for future episodic institutional services is anticipated.

In the kinds of human services systems envisaged above the role of the clergy requires special clarification. In formulating their role, it is necessary to recognize the current trend in this country toward the development of increasingly differentiable secular and religious life-styles. Those with secular life-styles may eschew all contact with the clergy or may value such contact only in conjunction with infrequent milestone-type events — birth, marriage, divorce, death, etc. In regard to such life-styles, it will be quite adequate for primary human service staff to develop informal, low-intensity collaborative relationships with area clergy.

In contrast, those with religious life-styles are increasingly articulating their yearning for primary human services that are organizationally closely integrated with the counseling services of area clergy and are philosophically compatible with them. These yearnings suggest the need for the nationwide accessibility of the kind of wholistic religion-based care described earlier in this chapter in the context of intervention emphases (see Cunningham, 1977).

Thus, in regard to the evolving role of the clergy, the composite demand patterns of American society will probably be met by a nationwide network of wholistic care centers (in the specific sense indicated above) that are located in the larger towns and in the cities, and that are enmeshed in, operated in collaboration with, and complemented by a larger-scale integrated primary human services network of the type previously described.

The delivery system scenario that has been developed during the course of this chapter section constitutes the kind of system that I hope and anticipate will evolve in this country. It is a delivery system and practice style that provides for comprehensiveness and continuity of services and for mutually stimulating interchange between workers in community and institutional environments.

The above outline encompasses more than the *primary health care* system — it depicts a total *primary care* delivery system. Primary care, if interpreted literally, is much more inclusive than primary health care; in fact, it is essentially interchangeable with the term "primary human services." For the sake of clarity I have used the latter, less semantically ambiguous term in the foregoing discussion (and later in this chapter). This is because many writers tend to use the term "primary care" as synonymous with primary health care. However, I tender the suggestion that it may be helpful for social workers to begin to use the term "primary care" in its more literal case (usually after appropriate definition). This will help promote a very desirable day-to-day consciousness, on the part of physicians, nurses, etc., that primary health care is but one part in the much larger field of primary care — and of the corollary that the better all parts of the field are integrated and coordinated, the higher will be the quality of care in each of the parts.

ADVOCACY AND POLICY DEVELOPMENT

In discussing various aspects and trends of primary health care services, I have made a few passing comments regarding the behaviors of social workers that may facilitate the enhancement of social worker participation in primary care settings. In this section I shall focus more explicitly and systematically on these issues, beginning with the topic of local-practice-level advocacy, and subsequently shifting the focus toward the influencing of health care policy formulation.

Local-Practice-Level Advocacy

The following discussion of local-practice-level advocacy is organized under the headings of advocacy target, advocacy content, and advocacy methodologies.

ADVOCACY TARGET. In the field of primary health care, physicians are the most powerful, most influential, and most prestigious professional group. Innovative projects in which they are co-opted as partners will generally proceed much more readily than those in which they are treated as adversaries. Admittedly, when physicians are partners with socail workers and others in systems change efforts, the potential always exits for physicians to exploit the unequal balance of the partnership and to steer the direction of change toward an end point that the social workers may view as undesirable. However, it is my opinion that the likely frequency of such usurpation is too readily overestimated by some social workers. Looking ahead, such partnerships will take place in an era in which we may expect a progressive rapprochement between the ideological and the practical philosophies of primary care physicians and social workers. This latter expectation is based in part on the recent developments in primary care physician education that were summarized earlier in this chapter.

As well as being at the pinnacle of authority in primary health care, physicians usually have a very marked "gatekeeper" role with regard to the entry of social workers into primary health care systems (Hookey, 1977a, 1979c). In view of the above, it seems reasonable to view physicians as the key targets of advocacy regarding the enhancement of social worker participation in primary care settings.

ADVOCACY CONTENT: SERVICE QUALITY ISSUES. As social workers endeavor to justify their participation in primary health care, the issue of enhanced effectiveness of client service is a very natural, legitimate, and strategic starting point. At present, there is no shortage of descriptive, uncontrolled studies with which to supplement an advocacy presentation. However, there is a very definite shortage of controlled research focusing on client outcomes — and this is the only kind of research that is of any consequence to the significant proportion of physicians who are very experimental-research-oriented. There is an urgent need for the results of this kind of research in the United States. The previously described study in Britain by Cooper et al. (1975) is certainly pertinent here, but its salience to many American physicians is diminished by its being carried out in the cultural context of socialized medicine.

As social workers discuss with primary care physicians their current or prospective contributions relating to specific client dysfunctions and particular role functions, the issue of uniqueness of contributions will often surface. To attempt to detract attention from this issue or to overrate or become defensive about the uniqueness of social workers' contributions will detract from the effectiveness of advocacy. Each advocate needs to be able to honestly formulate and articulate the nuances of the special contributions of social workers vis-à-vis those of psychologists, health educators, nurse practitioners, clergy, etc. Each advocate will develop a subtly different formulation, but this is not to be regretted — rather, it reflects our uniqueness as individual helpers.

This is no academic issue. Very commonly, the above types of professionals are in effective competition with social workers for the role of primary counselor on a primary health care team. In other instances they already have or will have membership on the team along with the social worker.

In general, social workers are ill advised to claim that a particular primary health care team needs a social worker per se. Rather, a less direct approach is often more effective — namely, to suggest that the team needs to offer a certain comprehensive range of services; that the existing members may not have the training and/or inclination and/or time to provide some of these services adequately; and that a social worker has the capacity to take care of this deficit. Granted, this approach leaves open the possibility that another type of professional may be chosen as better able to fill the void. However, such competition is enduring — it will not evaporate in the face of the former, less client-centered, more profession-centered approach.

ADVOCACY CONTENT: ECONOMIC ISSUES. Traditionally, social workers have found it difficult to quantify the dollar costs and benefits of their services. This difficulty is understandable in view of the kinds of services we provide. However, the need to struggle with cost-benefit issues is nowhere more pressing than in regard to participation in primary health care. Very often, social workers aspiring to enter this field will find themselves — whether willingly or reluctantly — discussing cost-benefit issues with business managers hired to promote the physicians' business interests, or directly with physician-entrepreneurs. In such situations advocates need to be able to address the cost-benefit issues as seen from three perspectives: of the physicians-as-businesspersons, of the clients-as-consumers, and of the public-as-taxpayers. Each of these perspectives will be discussed briefly below.

Physicians-as-businesspersons perspective. Although most physicians could afford to pay a social worker a good salary, realize no financial return from the latter's activities, and still have a net income much greater than that of the social worker, this scenario is enacted only very rarely. However, few physicians expect the alliance with a social worker to generate a dollar profit for them, although this could happen, indeed has happened on very rare occasions. More typically, the kinds of physicians who are interested in teaming up with social workers are ready to accept that the alliance may increase their net costs, but are also very interested in discussing how this cost could be minimized. The pertinent cost-benefit equation sets the costs of the alliance (usually salary and overhead expenses) against the sum of the direct fiscal benefits (usually fees-for-service and any consultation fees) and any indirect fiscal benefits that may result from changes in the physician's productivity (patient visits per week) and/or drug prescription rates. (For a detailed discussion of this perspective, see Hookey, 1979c.)

Clients-as-consumers perspective. Physicians and their business managers are interested in the clients-as-consumers perspective on account of both direct (altruistic) and indirect (consumer-relations) motivations. The effective advocate of social worker participation in primary health care will need to be familiar with pros and cons of various service reimbursement alternatives (fixed fee, waivable fixed fee, sliding scale fees, free service); with state- and country-wide norms for fee rates, collection/write-off percentages, and annual fee incomes; and with opportunities for client reimbursement from locally prominent insurance carriers (and with the related vendor-status limitations and physician-supervision stipulations). For further details and illustrative data regarding this perspective, see Nason and Delbanco, 1976; Twersky and Cole, 1976; and Hookey, 1978b, p. 215.

Public-as-taxpayers perspective. Physicians and their business managers are concerned about the public-as-taxpayers perspective on account of their community-service motivation — and also because, as members of the public, they share in any community-wide costs or benefits. From this perspective, the major cost-benefit issue is the extent to which the expenses of the deployment of social workers in a community's primary health care settings are offset by or exceeded by the savings stemming from prevention-related reductions in the extent and thus the costs of secondary-level services necessitated by acute but often preventable dysfunctions. For an example of this type of analysis, see Collins, 1975. Research and evaluation from this community-wide perspective will tend to be particularly complex, speculative, and inexact. However, much more of it is urgently needed, from both process (consciousness-raising) and outcome (advocacy underpinning) standpoints.

ADVOCACY METHODOLOGIES. Given the above-discussed tactics regarding advocacy target and content, what pragmatic methods will most effectively accomplish the advocacy task?

In addressing this question, it may be advisable to start by recognizing the severe limitations of some of the traditional media-based approaches commonly used for social work advocacy. Primary care physicians virtually never read social work journals. They rarely read medical journal articles that are not primarily concerned with their particular specialized clinical interests. They have a reputation for being somewhat impervious to well-meaning advice directed to them via consumers' and/or planners' community forums, or via newspaper coverage thereof.

Regarding alternative methodologies, social workers may be able to learn much by studying the tactics of the pharmaceutical drug companies, for whom the physician is a vital sales enabler. Drug companies do not rely on their prodigious journal advertising. They also field large numbers of traveling sales representatives ("detail men") whose job it is to make face-to-face contact with physicians in their offices. A classic innovation diffusion study by Coleman et al. (1966) documented the particularly important role of detail men in the spread of the adoption of a prescription drug by physicians in three areas of the Midwest.

Elsewhere (Hookey, 1977a) I have drawn out the several specific implications of this study regarding the strategies of social work advocates. The major implication is that direct face-to-face contact with physicians and their business managers is a particularly effective way to promote social worker participation in primary health care. Such contacts can be arranged, given sufficient ingenuity and perseverance, but available contact time will normally be short, and careful preparation and rehearsal are necessary if it is to be used most effectively. Such contacts may be made by individuals seeking a job for themselves, by job brokers who act as facilitators and intermediaries between interested physicians and potential social worker employees or associates (Liberson, 1978), by advocates operating under the aegis of local NASW chapters, etc.

The importance of direct advocacy in physicians' offices cannot be overestimated. However, it may be helpfully complemented by public-speaking activities at county medical society meetings, regional medical association conferences, etc.

Influencing National Health Care Policy Formulation

In shifting to a focus on national policy, it is well to recognize the potentially significant "filter-up" effects of the local-practice-level advocacy described above. However, our focus now is on more direct methods of influencing national policy — in particular on demonstration projects and on legislative activity.

DEMONSTRATION PROJECTS. Several current demonstration projects incorporate some of the issues addressed above and promise to have significance with regard to the future development of national policy regarding social work in primary care settings.

In the United States, the first two federally funded demonstration projects in this field have been financed by the National Institute of Mental Health. They are based in New York (Miller, 1978) and St. Louis (Walter, 1978). Both are designed as five-year social work training projects. At this writing, both projects still are in the tool-up (first year) phase, and it is too early to report even preliminary results. However, it is already clear that financial accountability aspects of evaluation — including experimental/control group cost-benefit comparisons — will be given special attention.

The issue of the economic aspects of interdisciplinary primary health care is a key focus of the monitoring system for the Health Care Institute in Detroit (Wainstock and Gardner, 1978). Social workers are among the seven types of professionals participating in this ongoing demonstration project — the others being clinical pharmacists, clinical psychologists, health educators, nurse clinicians, nutritionists, and primary care physicians. An especially significant feature of this project is that the plans call for a novel system of third-party-payer reimbursement, whereby the reimbursable unit of service is the institute visit — irrespective of the number of different provider encounters occurring during the visit (Wainstock and Gardner, 1978, p. 11). If this system proves viable, it will indicate that it is possible to avoid the complexities of the traditional provider contact-based reimbursement system and the related intricacies of physician approval and cosignature in the cases of non-physician provider contacts.

A fourth project that merits special attention is the Canadian government-funded Primary Care Counseling Project, which is currently in operation in and near Kingston, Ontario (Burbridge, 1978). This three-year project has funded the placement of social workers in primary health care physicians' offices in several different locations, both rural and urban. The final report will provide a very comprehensive set of evaluative data, including experimental/control group comparisons regarding clinical intervention outcomes, client satisfactions, service utilization patterns over time, and relative costs of services. The result will be of particular interest to American observers insofar as they are originating within the context of a virtually universal provincial health insurance system, one that may prove to have several similarities to whatever national health care organization/financing system is eventually implemented in the United States.

Demonstration projects are a well-established mechanism by which national policy may be influenced. Of late, however, two factors are combining to jeopardize the contributions of some demonstration projects: the accelerating rate of change in human service systems and the increasing time lag between the design and the reporting of projects (on account of bottlenecks at the funding allocation and publishing stages). In such circumstances, it behooves project designers to experiment with a formulation which may still be timely by the time it is tested and disseminated. It behooves proposal assessors to give full consideration to what may at the time seem farfetched formulas. In particular, I believe it is none too soon to begin the design of demonstration projects pertaining to the kind of integrated primary human service system outlined earlier in this chapter.

It is hoped that the above concerns will be addressed in due course by the recently mooted President's Council for the Health Services, the blueprint for which calls for a 40 percent representation of social/behavioral scientists (Barclay, 1979, pp. 3–4).

LEGISLATIVE ACTIVITY. In this context, I shall focus on issues pertaining to just one prospective and very significant legislative development — namely, the impending enactment of some form of national health care organization/financing system in the United States. Clearly, it would be myopic to ignore the potential impact of this impending legislation on the primary health care systems and trends discussed in this chapter.

Lack of space precludes an attempt to analyze and compare the various proposed versions of this legislation from the standpoint of social worker participation in primary health care. In any case, such analysis might well be obsolete before this chapter is published. In these circumstances it seems more appropriate to posit just a few of the many policy analysis questions that stem from the various discussions and positions presented thus far. These questions would seem to be of relatively more enduring salience. It is to be hoped that their answers, as of particular future dates, will provide a means for social workers to compare competing legislation and to participate in the legislative process — whether as public speakers, testifiers, lobbyists, supporters of lobbyists, voters, etc.

These questions are: To what extent does this legislation encourage and/or reimburse the provision of psychotherapy/counseling services by nonphysicians? . . . by social workers? How restrictive is any mandatory physician supervision of such activity? In what ways does this legislation recognize and cater for the substantial overlap of "health" and "mental health" care at the primary care level? To what extent is this legislation compatible with the longer-term trend toward integrated primary human services systems? Does the legislation facilitate full and appropriate harnessing of the vast potentials for self- and lay care that exist in this country? Does this legislation provide incentive mechanisms to promote greater emphasis on primary and secondary prevention activities in primary care settings? Does this legislation encourage interdisciplinary initiatives in education for primary care workers?

ON RESPONSIBILITY

The field of social work in primary health care may well become one of the largest fields of social work practice, particularly if the anticipated trend toward integrated primary human services systems is realized.

One implication of this is that social work will tend to become to the common man what psychology has already become to the intelligentsia — namely, a form of religion. In making this latter assessment, I am identifying with Paul Vitz, whose position is documented in detail in his book *Psychology as Religion* (1977). The claim that psychology has become a religion is basically a neutral sociological statement. It acknowledges the power and popularity of pyschology, but it leaves unsaid how these potentials are being used. However, Vitz's position with regard to the latter is indicated by subtitle: "The Cult of Self-Worship." His position, with which I concur, is one of general — though not unmitigated — criticism, of serious concern regarding the way that much contemporary psychology is feeding a pervasive and ultimately destructive narcissism.

How psychologists utilize their ascribed — or sometimes self-styled — status as secular priests is not necessarily predictive of how social workers will utilize their increasing authority in the realms of ethics.

However, I think that there are, in fact, strong indications that in general social workers' performances are paralleling those of psychologists. (To some extent, this is to be expected, insofar as many psychologists and social workers share common philosophical underpinnings).

Let us listen to one observer and critic from within the social work profession:

Individualism has run amok. . . . The labored quest for fulfillment and self-actualization is encouraging narcissism in individual development and further weakening the institution of the family. . . . [But] is there a need to sermonize about civic duties and family cohesiveness to those dedicating their lives to the betterment of their fellow man?

I believe it is necessary because social workers are part of the problem. They [are] fostering . . . an individualistic ethic which is regulating societal and family concerns to secondary status. Social workers are encouraging the very narcissism they are increasingly being called upon to treat. (Glick, 1977, pp. 579, 583)

Glick's criticism is well put, clear, and unequivocal. I concur with it. I have presented it because, frankly, I am concerned that the anticipated widespread permeation of primary health care by social workers will lead to a new wave of dysfunctional self-centeredness. Having this concern, I feel it would be irresponsible of me not to express it in this context.

On a more positive note, I wish to express my endorsement of the stirrings within the profession toward a return to emphasis on interpersonal responsibility in the senses of altruism and other-centeredness, and toward a revaluing of traditional moral standards (see, for example, Hardman, 1975). I want to express my hope that these will be the values that social workers will champion as they practice more and more frequently, and more and more authoritatively, in primary health care settings.

REFERENCES

Alexander, B. 1978. Holistic health from the inside. *Spiritual Counterfeits Project Journal* 2:5–17.

Alt, E. S. 1959. Social work consultation in a prepayment medical care plan. *American Journal of Public Health* 49:350–54.

Anesaki, M., and Sakagami, H. 1976. Development and future demand/supply of medical social workers. *Iryo to Fukushi* (Journal of Japanese Association of Medical Social Workers) 29:19–32.

Anderson, E. J.; Judd, L. R.; May, J. T.; and New, P. K. 1976. *The neighborhood health center program.* Washington, D.C.: National Association of Neighborhood Health Centers.

Ardell, D. B., ed. *High-level wellness.* 1977. Ammaus, Pa.: Rodale Press.

Barclay, R. W. May 4, 1979. Health research. *Washington Newsletter* (of the American Public Health Association). pp. 3–5.

Barkan, T. 1973. Private casework practice in a medical clinic. *Social Work* 18:5–9.

Bassoff, B. Z. 1976. Interdisciplinary education for health professionals: issues and directions. *Social Work in Health Care* 2:219–28.

Bell, C., and Gorman , L. M. 1976. The HMOs: new models for practice. *Social Work in Health Care* 1:325–35.

Berfenstam, R., and Smedby, S. 1976. Collaboration between medical and social care. *Socialmedicinsk Tidskrift* 53:365–72.

Bishop, M.; Parrish, H.; and Baker, A. S. 1967. Function role activities of the private practice. *Clinical Pediatrics* 6:36–38.

Bloom, M. March 1979. *A working definition of primary prevention related to social concerns.* Paper presented at the meeting of the Council on Social Work Education, Boston.

Board, C. S. March 9, 1979. Healing body, soul and spirit. *Evangelical Newsletter.*

Brooks, M. B. 1973. Management of the team in general practice. *Journal of the Royal College of General Practitioners* 23:239–52.

Brockway, B. S.; Werking, J.; Fitzgibbons, K.; and Butterfield, W. 1976. Social work at the grass roots: practicing in the doctor's office. In B. Ross and S. K. Khinduka, eds., *Social work in practice.* Washington, D.C.: National Association of Social Workers.

Burbridge, P. 1978. Personal communication.

Caplan, G. 1964. *Principles of preventive psychiatry.* New York: Basic Books.

Carlson, R. Fall 1977. Holistic health: concept, movement, modality. *Holistic Health Review.* P. 5.

Cheraskian, E.; Ringsdorf, W. M., Jr.; and Brecher, A. 1974. *Psychodietetics: food as the key to emotional health.* Briarcliff Manor, N.Y.: Stein and Day.

Coleman, J. S.; Katz, E.; and Menzel, H. 1966. *Medical innovation: a diffusion study.* New York: Bobbs-Merrill.

Collins, A. H., and Pancoast, D. L. 1976. *Natural helping networks.* Washington, D.C.: National Association of Social Workers.

Collins, J. 1975. A cost effectiveness model. In W. T. Hall and G. C. St. Deris, eds., *Quality assurance in social services in health programs for mothers and children: proceedings of an institute.* Pittsburgh: University of Pittsburgh School of Public Health.

Comfort, R. L., and Kappy, M. S. 1974. Pediatrician and social worker as a counseling team. *Social Work* 19:486–89.

Cooper, B. 1971. Social work in general practice: the Derby scheme. *Lancet* 1:539–42.

Cooper, B.; Harwin, B. G.; Depla, C.; and Shepherd, M. 1975. Mental health care in the community: an evaluative study. *Psychological Medicine* 5:372–80.

Countryside Council Human Services Task Force. 1975. *Report on human services integration.* Marshall, Minn.: Countryside Council.

Davis, H., and Nevin, N. 1976. *The introduction of a social worker into a private medical clinic.* Ottawa, Ontario, Canada: National Health and Welfare, Welfare Grants Division.

Davis, M. M., and Warner, A. R. 1918. *Dispensaries: their management and development.* New York: Macmillan.

deGroot, M., and Maertens, N. November–December 1975. The hard practice at the Hoensbroek health center. *De Eerste Lijn.* pp. 8–13.

DuBois, V. 1971. The Hoensbroek — north health care center illuminated from another side. *Huisarts en Wetenschap* 14:137–38.

—————. 1976. The shaky equilibrium of the team of a health care center. *Huisarts en Wetenschap* 19:178–80.

Falklind, H.; Larsson, S. O.; Lewerentz, B.; Lindholm, G.; Nystrom, S.; and Wohrm, A. 1974. The Tynnered project: integration of primary health care and social welfare activities. *Lakartidningen* 74:596–98.

Fish, S. 1978. Transcendental meditation: holistic health and the nursing profession. *Spiritual Counterfeits Project Journal* 2:39–41.

Fixx, J. F. 1977. *The complete book of running.* New York: Random House.

Flexner, A. 1910. *Medical education in the United States and Canada.* New York: Arno Press (1972 reprint).

Frangos, A. S., and Chase, D. 1976. Potential partners: attitudes of family practice residents toward collaboration with social workers in their future practices. *Social Work in Health Care* 2:65–76.

Friedson, E. 1961. *Patients' views of medical practice.* New York: Russell Sage Foundation.

Gallagher, J. 1979. Personal communication.

Ghan, L., and Road, D. 1970. Social work in a mixed group medical practice. *Canadian Journal of Public Health* 61:488–96.

Glick, P. M. 1977. Individualism, society and social work. *Social Casework* 58:579–84.

Goldberg, R. L. 1973. The social worker and the family physician. *Social Casework* 54:489–95.

Golden, A. S.; Carlson, D. G.; and Harris, B. 1973. Nonphysician family health teams for Health Maintenance Organizations. *American Journal of Public Health* 63:732–36.

Gottschalk, J., and Selmanoff, E. D. October 1978. *Creating the desired future.* Paper presented at the meeting of the American Public Health Association, Los Angeles.

Guillozet, N. 1975. Community mental health: new approaches for rural areas using psychiatric social workers. *Medical Care* 13:59–67.

Hardman, D. G. 1975. Not with my daughter, you don't! *Social Work* 22:278–85.

Henk, M., and Froom, J. 1975. Outreach by primary care physicians. *Journal of the American Medical Association* 233:256–59.

Hicks, D. 1976. *Primary health care: a review.* London: Her Majesty's Stationery Office.

Hobson, C. J., and Grayburn, D.W. 1969. Social work in group medical practice. *Group Practice* 18:25–30.

Hokenstad, M. C., Jr. 1977. Higher education and the human service professions: what roles for social work? *Journal of Education for Social Work* 13:52–59.

Hookey, P. November 1975. *Social work in a rural foundation Health Maintenance Organization: the bootheel project.* Paper presented at the meeting of the American Public Health Association, Social Work Section, Chicago.

――――― . 1976. Education for social work in Health Care Organizations. *Social Work in Health Care* 1:337–45.

――――― . 1977. The establishment of social worker participation in rural primary health care. *Social Work in Health Care* 3:87–89.

――――― . 1977b. Do social workers belong in group practice? *Group Practice* 26: 12–14.

――――― . 1978a. Social worker participation in primary health care: an overview of current developments in industrialized nations. *Annals of the New York Academy of Sciences* 310:212–20.

――――― . 1978b. Social work in primary care settings. In N. Bracht, ed., *Social work in health care.* New York: Haworth.

――――― . 1979a. Review of L. S. Levin, A. H. Katz, and R. Holst, *Self care: lay initiatives in health.* New York: Neale Watson Academic Publications, 1977. In *Social Work in Health Care* 4:349–51.

――――― . 1979b. *Wholistic primary care: opportunities for ministry and potentials for abuse.* Workshop presented at the meeting of the National Association of Christians in Social Work, Columbus.

――――― . 1979c. Preparing social workers for effective practice in integrated human service agencies. In F. W. Clark and M. L. Arkava, *The pursuit of competence in social work.* San Francisco: Jossey-Bass.

_____ . 1979d. De Eerste Lijn: a dutch pressure group of international signif-icance. In M. van Beugen, ed., *Caring in the first line*. Assen, Netherlands: van Gorcum.

_____ . 1979e. Cost-benefit evaluations in primary health care. *Health and Social Work* 4:151–67.

_____ . 1979f. Primary care and community services. In J. Fry, ed., *Primary care: world patterns*. London: Heinemann Medical.

Illich, I. 1976. *Medical nemesis: the expropriation of health*. New York: Pantheon.

Jertson, J. M. 1975. Self-help groups. *Social Work* 20:144–45.

Katz, A. H. October 1978. *Is there a future for self-care, self-help in community health?* Paper presented at the meeting of the American Public Health Association, Los Angeles.

Kleinmann, A.; Eisenberg, L.; and Good, B. 1978. Culture, illness and care: clini-cal lessons from anthropologic and cross-cultural research. *Annals of Internal Medicine* 88:251.

Kohn, R. 1977. *Coordination of health and welfare services in four countries: Austria, Italy, Poland and Sweden*. Copenhagen, Denmark: Wprld Health Organization.

Korpela, J. W. 1973. Social work assistance in a private pediatric practice. *Social Casework* 54:537–44.

Levin, L. S.; Katz, A. H.; and Holst, E. 1977. *Self-care: lay initiatives in health*. New York: Neale Watson Academic Publications.

Liberson, M. 1978. Personal communication.

Lincoln, J. A.; Twersky, R. K.; and O'Neil-Sale, D. 1974. Social work in the family medical center. *Journal of Family Practice* 1:34–37.

Lum, D. 1976. The social service health specialist in an HMO. *Health and Social Work* 1:29–50.

Margolis, H. M.; and Mendelsohn, H. 1956. The medical social caseworker in a private medical practice. *Journal of the American Medical Association* 161:309–13.

Maypole, D. E., and Wright, W. E. 1979. The integration of services of a medical clinic and a community mental health center in a rural area. *Social Work in Health Care* 4:299–308.

McClure, M. October 1978. *Medicine in community: primary health care on the farm*. Paper presented at the meeting of the American Public Health Association, Los Angeles.

Miles, R. B. Fall 1977. What is holistic health? *Holistic Health Review*. P. 4.

Milio, N. 1977. Self-care in urban settings. *Health Education Monographs* 5:136–45.

Miller, R. S. 1978. Personal communication.

Nason, F., and Delbanco, T. L. 1976. Soft services: a major cost-effective com-ponent of primary medical care. *Social Work in Health Care* 1:297–308.

New, P.K.M. 1968. An analysis of the concept of teamwork. *Community Mental Health Journal* 4:326–33.

O'Connor, K. K. 1977. Treatment for adults with psychosomatic symptoms. *Health and Social Work* 2:90–110.

Payne, L. 1976 The story of IG and the department of social apology. *Social Work Today* 7:354–56.

Pelletier, K. 1977. *Mind as healer, mind as slayer: a holistic approach to preventing stress disorders*. New York: Dell.

Peterson, W. M.; Tuesing, D. A.; and Tubesing, N. L. 1976. *Wholistic health care: the process of engagement*. Hinsdale, Ill.: Wholistic Health Centers.

Pitz, J. 1975. Personal communication.

Rogers, D. E. 1977. The challenge of primary care. In J. H. Knowles, ed., *Doing better and feeling worse: health in the United States*. New York: Norton.

Shepherd, M. 1966. *Psychiatric illness in general practice.* London: Oxford University.
———— . 1974. General practice, mental illness, and the British national health service. *American Journal of Public Health* 64:3.

Silver, G. A. 1963. *Family medical care: a report on the Family Health Maintenance Demonstration.* Cambridge, Mass.: Harvard University.

Silver, G. A., and Stiber, C. 1957. The social worker and the physician. *Journal of Medical Education* 32:324–30.

Tanner, L. A., and Carmichael, L. P. 1970. The role of the social worker in family medicine training. *Journal of Medical Education* 45:859–65.

Townsend, E. H. 1964. The social worker in pediatric practice. *American Journal of Diseases of Children* 107:115–21.

Tubesing, D. A. 1976. *Whole person health care: an idea in evolution.* Hinsdale, Ill.: Wholistic Health Centers.

———— . 1977. *Wholistic health: a whole person approach to primary health care.* New York: Human Sciences.

Tubesing, D. A., and Strosahl, S. G. 1976. *Wholistic health centers: survey research report.* Hinsdale, Ill.: Wholistic Health Centers.

Tubesing, N. L. 1976. *Whole person health care: philosophical assumptions.* Hinsdale, Ill.: Wholistic Health Centers.

Twersky, R. K., and Cole, W. M. 1976. Social work fees in medical care. *Social Work in Health Care* 2:77–84.

Uhlman, G., and Wesselkampe, S. 1978. The role of the social worker in health planning. *Human Services in the Rural Environment* 3:1–5.

Vattano, A. J. 1972. Power to the people: self-help groups. *Social Work* 17:7–15.

———— . 1978. Self-management procedures for coping with stress. *Social Work* 25:113–19.

Vitz, P. C. 1977. *Psychology as religion: the cult of self-worship.* Grand Rapids, Mich.: Eerdmans.

Wainstock, E. J., and Gardner, H. H. May 1978. *A model for primary health care service financing and reimbursement.* Paper presented at the meeting of the Second International Congress of the World Federation of Public Health Associations, Halifax, Nova Scotia, Canada.

Walter, C. 1978. Personal communication.

Wegner, M.; Ruiz, J. A.; and Caccamo, L. P. 1966. The social worker in the private practice of internal medicine. *Archives of Internal Medicine* 118:347–50.

Westberg, G. 1970. The parish pastor's finest hour. *Journal of Religion and Health* 9:170–77.

———— . 1977. Personal communication.

———— . 1979. *The theological roots of wholistic health care.* Hinsdale, Ill.: Wholistic Health Centers.

Wishingrad, L.; Schulruff, J. T.; and Sklansky, A. 1963. Role of a social worker in private practice of pediatrics. *Pediatrics* 32:125–30.

Wojciechowski, S. 1975. Poland's new priority: human welfare. In D. Thursz and J. L. Viglante, eds., *Meeting human needs: an overview of nine countries.* Beverly Hills, Calif.: Sage.

Wolfe, S., and Teed, G. 1967. A study of the work of a medical social worker in a group practice. *Canadian Medical Association Journal* 96:1407–16.

World Health Organization. 1973. *Trends in the development of primary care.* Copenhagen, Denmark: World Health Organization.

———— . 1978. *Primary health care: a joint report by the director-general of the World Health Organization and the executive director of the United Nations Children's Fund.* Geneva, Switzerland: World Health Organization.

9

LONG-TERM HEALTH CARE

Neil F. Bracht

The prevention and treatment of social conditions associated with chronic illness and disability pose complex problems for health care professionals and social policy leaders. The increase in chronic illness and accompanying medical, social, and economic costs have highlighted serious gaps in both the delivery and the financing of social and health services. In their study of chronic illness and the effects of continued care, Katz and his associates state that "few if any communities in the United States are prepared to meet the simplest needs of the existing population of chronically ill persons who live at home. In spite of vigorous efforts at demonstration and innovation, the development of ambulatory clinics, day care centers, home care, and homemaking services have been slow. For the disabled patient confined to his home, modern medicine tends to become more remote and his contact with it more episodic and haphazard." (Katz, 1972). As the number of chronically ill, disabled, and aged persons increases, alternative public policy options will be reviewed and new program directions will be seen as urgent priorities for implementation. Social workers are already in key community and professional postions associated with care of the chronically ill, and they can influence new social health policies and services.

While models (Morris and Harris, 1972; Nielsen, 1972) exist for the successful linkage of health and social support systems necessary for care of the chronically ill, several factors inhibit needed actions to improve long-term care. First, the lack of strong federal initiatives (e.g., increased home health benefits under Medicare) provides little incentive for local area reform efforts. Second, there is a deeply ingrained penchant for the practice arenas of acute care and treatment among professionals. Third, obvious differentials in status, rewards, and financial reimbursement exist between professionals who work in the more visibly exciting and technologically advanced world of acute care and life-saving treatment and those who labor among the chronically sick and infirm. Fourth, part of the problem in directing adequate resources to chronic patients occurs because the health system has no effective way of controlling the introduction of costly new technologies or evaluating their total cost-benefit to society. A recent advocate of coronary artery bypass graft operations (38,000 in 1973 costing $400 million) said the United States should prepare to do 80,000 coronary arteriograms a day. Dr. Hiatt of the Harvard School of Public Health comments on this forecast: "Rough calculations indicate that radiologic assessment alone would cost $10 billion a year. If today's ratio of arteriograms to bypass surgery were to prevail, the cost of the resultant surgery would exceed $100 billion a year" [a figure almost equivalent to today's total health dollar resources] (Hiatt, 1975). By contrast, an equal number of miners, some 77,000, currently receive disability benefits for chronic black lung disease, yet follow-up and continuity of health care for their condition are largely neglected. For each new CAT scanner purchased, yearly estimated operating costs range from one-quarter to one-half million dollars. In analyzing some of these paradoxes of modern health care, one physician recently remarked, "Medicine's highpowered technology and quick-cure image differs considerably from the reality of what most needs to be done, that is, care of chronic illness, personal counseling services, and social support networks" (Airie, 1975).

Disease patterns of contemporary industrial societies have changed considerably. Unlike the diseases that devastated and decimated large numbers of our population in the early nineteenth century, today's new "social diseases" are largely chronic in nature. They are insidious, developing over time, and disabling significantly large but seldom-seen populations in this country. The new "social diseases" of hypertension, lung cancer, heart disease, obesity, and drug abuse are closely linked to the stresses and lifestyle of our affluent nation. The cost of mental illness in the United States, measured conservatively, was nearly $40 billion in 1974. Despite the advances of medical science, no modern industrialized country has, through its health system, been able to cope effectively with the complex chronic and social illnesses that predominate. There is much evidence to indicate that positive physical and mental health status is determined more by social-environmental factors than by medical care services (Syme, 1974).

This examination of the problems and the opportunities for policy and program change in the care of those with chronic illness will include the following areas:

1. the social epidemiology of chronic illness and disability — its scope and distribution;
2. the personal and family adjustments associated with chronic illness;
3. the social costs of chronic illness and disability; and finally
4. social policy changes indicated in order to meet the needs of the chronically ill.

SOCIAL EPIDEMIOLOGY OF CHRONIC ILLNESS

How serious is the problem of chronic disease and disability? The following statistical overview gives us some idea of the breadth and depth of the problem we confront. In this discussion, *disease* refers to the presence of some morbid physical or mental state that is either latent or manifest; *illness* means a disease with manifest clinical symptoms; and *disability* refers to a demonstrable loss or limitation of normal function from whatever cause lasting three or more months. In this latter category we usually refer to limitations of activity. These can be either major activities, such as going to school or housekeeping, or restricted activities in such areas of mobility as walking, wheeling, eating, bathing, etc. A disability is said to be either total or partial depending upon how much work a person reports being able to do. To illustrate the use of these terms: in one community, 20 percent of the population showed some evidence of heart disease, 7 percent reported they were ill because of their disease, and only 1 percent was judged as having a moderate or severe disability due to the disease.

While definitions of illness and disability are often imprecise and open to differing interpretations, use of the phrase "long-term care" poses equally difficult definitional problems. Who is a long-term patient? Does every disabled person represent a long-term care service need? Is the functionally independent self-treating diabetic a long-term care person? As Sherwood (1975) notes:

There are, of course, many persons for whom there would be little question about their long-term care status or their need for long-term care. For example, it is probably reasonable to assume agreement that someone is a long-term care person who has reached, either suddenly or gradually, a state of collapse or deterioration in human behavioral functioning which requires—for survival, slowing down the rate of deterioration, maintenance, or rehabilitation—the services of at least one other human being. At the same time the boundaries defining who should or should not be considered a long-term care person remain fuzzy and there is need for research that might help clarify this issue.

Estimating the proportion of persons who require long-term services or institutional care varies widely and is influenced by rapidly developing alternatives to institutional care. Morris and Anderson (1975) describe the need for personal care services in the United States. They call for a more distinct management role for social work in coordinating and operating that part of the health subsystem which deals with long-term care and handicapping conditions. This notion is supported by Brody (1975), who says:

It is a simplistic fiction that the need for medical and nursing care is the "reason" for institutional care. Available evidence points to the complex interweaving of individual and family, health, social, economic and environmental factors with decisions being constrained by current social policy. Whatever form long-term care takes, in the community or in congregate facilities, it is a *social/health solution* to *social/health problems.*

SCOPE OF CHRONIC ILLNESS

Overall, it is estimated that 50 percent of the American population has one or more chronic conditions. Some 23 million persons, or 14 percent of the population, have chronic conditions that cause activity limitation. Three-fourths of these, or 19 million, are limited in major activities—that is, working or going to school—and 6 million are simply unable to carry out their major activities. Another 1.8 million people need help in moving about; many of these are the elderly. Interestingly, 1.6 million of those who cannot carry out major activities are children, and over half of those are mentally retarded. In 1972, 23 percent of the children under 17 years of age

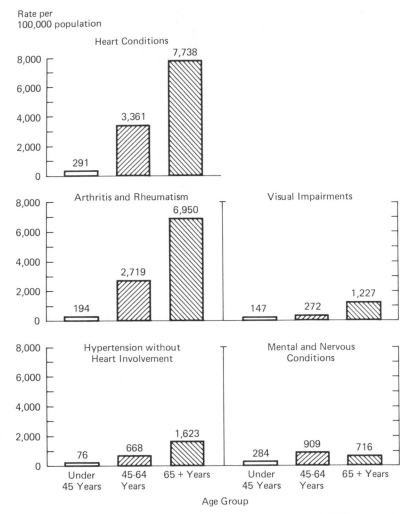

Source: U.S. Department of Commerce, Bureau of the Census, *Statistical Abstract of the United States: 1974* (Washington, D.C.: U.S. Government Printing Office, 1974). Tables 135, 3.

Figure 9.1. Incidence of Selected Chronic Conditions Causing Activity Limitation by Age, 1972 (Rate per 100,000 population)

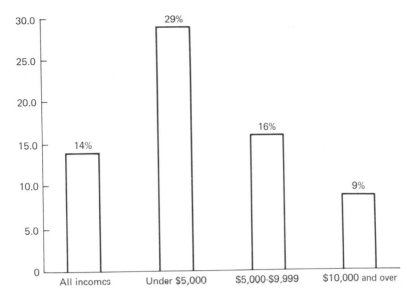

Source: *Health Interview Survey, 1974,* National Center for Health Statistics, U.S. Department of Health, Education, and Welfare.

Figure 9.2. Proportion of Population with Activity-Limiting Chronic Conditions, Calendar Year 1974

had chronic conditions. The EPSDP screening program for low-income children showed between 20 percent and 40 percent of the children screened with chronic conditions. Fewer than half of these were under any kind of health care. Major chronic conditions causing activity limitation are shown in Figure 9.1.

The chronic diseases that affect Americans can cause serious disability and impairment. The proportion of the population with activity-limiting chronic conditions is shown in Figure 9.2 with striking differential rates by income levels. It should be noted that the percent of population with activity limitation is 14.1 percent. Figure 9.3 shows the average number of disability days per person and days of restricted activity and work loss days. Table 9.1 illustrates that nearly 3.2 million people have limitation in mobility, either confined to their house, need help in getting around, or have trouule getting around alone.

In 1974 there were 2.5 million persons receiving disability insurance benefits under Social Securtiy. By 1978 this number had reached 3.1 million. The 1985 level is projected at 4 million. About half of these are disabled workers. The total number of disabled persons is estimated at between 8 and 14 million. The leading diagnosis for those receiving disability payments under the age of 40 is schizophrenia. After the age of 40 it is heart disease, followed by emphysema and arthritis (after the age of 55). Other data enlarge our view of the impact of disability and chronic conditions:

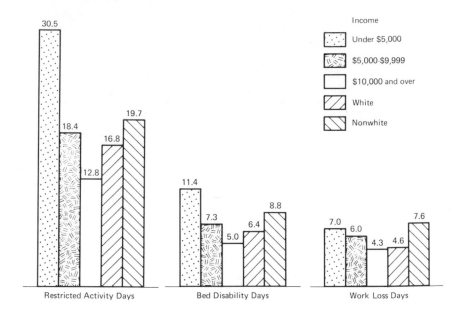

Source: *Health Interview Survey, 1974.* National Center for Health Statistics, U.S. Department of Health, Education, and Welfare.

Figure 9.3. Average Number of Disability Days per Person per Year, Calendar Year 1974

1. Approximately 2 million handicapped children require care in the United States. Another 1.5 million have asthma, and 50,000 children have sickle-cell anemia.

2. Approximately 200,000 mentally retarded individuals reside in our institutions.

3. Some 20,000 residents in homes and training facilities for the blind.

4. State rehabilitation agencies accept annually over 100,000 persons below the age of 21.

5. Five percent of live-born infants have a significant abnormality, of which 50 percent will die by the age of five. For those living beyond that age, the need for long-term care is substantial.

Certain rates of chronic disease are increasing. Leading the group is chronic respiratory disease. Diabetes is believed to be increasing at a level of about 6 percent, and cirrhosis of the liver, which had a death rate of 9.2 per 100,000 in 1950, has now risen to 15.7. This is, in large part, due to increased rates of alcoholism. Emphysema and chronic bronchitis combined had a 12.6 per 100,000 death rate in 1960. By 1970 the death rate for em-

Table 9.1   Percent of Persons of All Ages with Limitation of Mobility by Selected Demographic Characteristics: United States, 1972

Demographic characteristic	Population all ages (thousands)	Percent of population of all ages with limitation of mobility			
		Total	Confined to the house	Needs help in getting around	Has trouble getting around alone
Total[a]	204,148	3.2	0.9	1.0	1.3
Sex					
Male	98,445	2.9	.8	.9	1.2
Female	105,704	3.4	1.0	1.1	1.3
Color					
White	178,727	3.1	.8	1.0	1.2
All other	25,421	3.7	1.2	1.0	1.6
Region					
Northeast	48,011	3.1	1.0	1.0	1.1
North Central	55,974	2.7	.6	1.0	1.1
South	64,128	3.9	1.1	1.1	1.6
West	36,036	2.7	.7	.9	1.1
Residence					
Metropolitan	131,100	2.9	.8	.9	1.1
Nonmetropolitan	73,049	3.7	.9	1.2	1.6
Family income					
Less than $5,000	40,835	8.6	2.6	2.7	3.2
$5,000 to $9,999	59,134	2.5	.6	.8	1.1
$10,000 to $14,999	51,074	1.3	.3	.4	.6
$15,000 and over	40,983	1.1	.2	.4	.5

[a] Includes unknown income.

Note: Among reported chronic conditions, arthritis and hearing impairments rank 1st and 2d, respectively. Heart conditions cause more limitation of activity than any other condition, however.

Source: Health—United States, 1975, Public Health Service, U.S. Department of Health, Education, and Welfare.

physema alone was 19 per 100,000. Approximately 70,000 males die each year of lung cancer, a largely preventable chronic disease. Recent hospital discharge reports from V.A. hospitals found that hypertension among hospitalized veterans had increased from 25,229 in 1971 to 52,206 in 1976. Chronic ischemic heart disease accounts for more than half of the diagnoses of heart disease during this five-year period.

Today there are as many persons being treated in nursing homes and related institutions as in general hospital beds. But this is not the whole picture. As Strauss says so poignantly: "Even cursory scrutiny shows that most patients visiting the hospital for specialized treatments are not there because of acute diseases but because they currently suffer from an acute phase of one or another chronic disease: cancer, cardiac, kidney, respiratory, and the like" (Strauss, 1975). Traeger prefers the term "intercurrent illness." She says: "Chronic disease states, in general, are not characterized by an unbroken state of extreme ill health and incapacity which begins at the moment of diagnosis and ends in a custodial bed" (Traeger, 1975). And what about the chronically ill in boarding homes? Pearl Roberts (1974) found in a study of 334 homes in Pennsylvania that almost all 589 residents in these homes required medical care and that 50 percent should have been in an intermediate nursing care facility or hospital.

There are distinct differences in the way chronic disease and disability affect the population—differences according to age, sex, marital status, ethnicity, and education. For example, black persons are twice as likely to be disabled as whites. Also, lower levels of educational attainment are correlated with higher degrees of disability and impairment. Looking at other variables we find:

Age

As we know, old age is not synonymous with chronic disease. Shanas, in her studies of the elderly, both in this country and abroad, notes that in all countries nearly three-quarters of the elderly population are ambulatory and healthy. On the other hand, the elderly do have more chronic illnesses than other age groups. For those over 65, 39.6 percent will have chronic conditions, as contrasted with 14.2 percent of those between 45 and 65. The number of people over the age of 75 is growing at a faster rate than those between the ages of 65 and 75. It is now projected that nearly 11 million individuals who are 75 years of age or over will require long-term services by 1990. Two to 4 percent of the aged are bedfast, 12 percent to 14 percent are homebound, and 48 percent need help with simple tasks. Shanas's study (Shanas, 1974) also shows that of those over 65, nearly one-fourth who live in the community require home care services. Pfeiffer's (1973) community study provides evidence of significant impairment (either moderate to complete) among the elderly at 41 percent. Older people in institutions differ from their noninstitutional peers. They are advanced in years (average age 82) and have a higher incidence of chronic physical and mental impairment

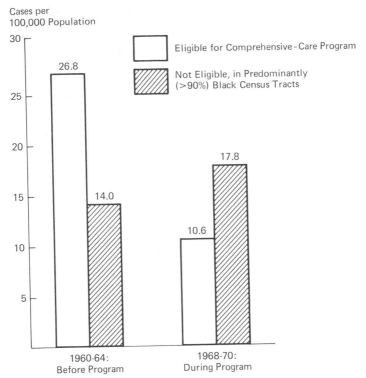

Cases per
100,000 Population

Eligible for Comprehensive-Care Program

Not Eligible, in Predominantly
(>90%) Black Census Tracts

26.8

14.0

17.8

10.6

1960-64:
Before Program

1968-70:
During Program

Source: L. Gordis, "Effectiveness of Comprehensive-Care Programs in Preventing Rheumatic Fevers," *New England Journal of Medicine,* vol. 289, no. 7, table 3, p. 333.

Figure 9.4. Incidence of Rheumatic Fever and the Effect of Eligibility for Comprehensive-Care
Programs: Baltimore, 1970.

resulting in functional disability (perhaps as many as four disabilities per
person). Some studies indicate that 10 percent to 20 percent of the elderly
living in urban areas are mentally impaired.

Moving to a different aspect of the age differential, it is important to
point out that from one-sixth to one-third of all chronic illnesses are
estimated to originate in childhood. Some chronic conditions are preventable. In Figure 9.4 the findings from a study conducted by Gordis (1973) in
this city (Baltimore) demonstrated that (over a three-year period) in an urban area offered comprehensive medical care services, rheumatic fever
rates were about one-third lower than comparable parts of the city without
comprehensive health care services. These census tracts were predominantly black. The implications for reductions in valvular heart disease and
nephritis are apparent, and long-term economic savings could probably be
demonstrated if such prevention programs were expanded.

Ethnicity

Space is not adequate to summarize the voluminous data on ethnic differences in chronic disease categories. We need not dwell on the striking difference in disease rates between blacks and whites, which has long been available for study and action in this country. Richardson (1969) has documented these statistics, concluding that the poor in the United States are sicker than the nonpoor and use fewer ambulatory health services. "If anything, however, these crude value measures of utilization applied to a national sample tend to understate both the severity and complexity of the problem." The relationship betwen social and economic conditions in health status is clear. Thirty-eight percent of American Indians have incomes below the poverty level. Thirty-five percent of blacks and 23 percent of Hispanics live below the poverty level. Data from the national health survey consistently shows race-related differences in the utilization and receipt of health care services for these groups. Life expectancy for Indians is approximately seven years less than that of the nonwhite population. Interestingly, the rate of cardiovascular disease among Indians is lower than the rest of the population. There is among Asian-Americans an upward trend in certain kinds of cancers and heart diseases, much of which is associated with "Anglo" diets. Among the Japanese, it is interesting to note that, for every heart attack sustained by a Japanese male in Japan, there are four among Japanese-Americans in Hawaii and ten for Japanese-Americans on the United States mainland (Matsumoto, 1971).

Occupational Status

Variations by occupational status are also interesting. Overall, chronic conditions affect 3.7 percent of professional and technical workers versus 9 percent of farmers, farm managers, and other blue-collar workers. It is important to note that significantly large proportions of the disabled are unemployed or out of the labor force.

PERSONAL AND FAMILY ADJUSTMENTS ASSOCIATED WITH CHRONIC ILLNESS

What do all of these statistics add up to and what are the implications? Simply stated, many individuals suffer from chronic illness. Some will experience serious psychological assault to their body image. They may lose a sense of mastery and autonomy over their life. In some instances there will be substantial loss of self-sufficiency. The needs of the chronically ill and their families are frequently quite complicated. Their total adjustment to life may be altered. Suchman (1958) found that one out of five patients reported that their current diagnosis called for changes in eating, drinking, or smoking. In addition, 50 percent were concerned about carrying on normal activities, 22 percent about loss of independence, 37 percent about the cost of treatment, 30 percent about the loss of work, and 15 percent about the interruption of personal plans.

Half a million AFDC families have one incapacitated parent, and there are 37,000 families with both parents disabled. Engel (1962) notes: "Studies of morbidity in families reveal a tendency to chain-reaction-like responses; other members may become sick or disturbed. The ultimate catastrophe under these circumstances may be that the whole family breaks up." In a recent study of the impact of disability on family structure, Franklin (1977) found that more marriages among the disabled end in divorce than among the nondisabled. She also states:

The educational, geographic and economic resources available to these families, especially those of the severely disabled, were less abundant than for the general population. The extended family generally provided no greater support to the disabled than to the healthy population. So the nuclear family was forced to cope with its problems as well as it could. Men and women withdrew at a slower rate from their sex-assigned roles. Decreased participation in most aspects of living highlighted the patterns of the disabled in their family settings. Chronic poor health impoverished not only those it afflicted but also those living with them.

In a recent report by Kaplan (1976) it was found that 89 percent of the families studied could not cope adequately with the consequences of childhood leukemia. Strauss, in his excellent book *Chronic Illness and the Quality of Life,* gives some insight into what parents face with a chronically ill child. He says:

When life may hang on proper carrying out of a regimen through machinery, that anxiety may be almost unbearable during the early phases of learning to use and live with a machine. One family, whose child had cystic fibrosis, remarked that they no longer went out at night. (I don't even trust my sister to do the right things.) Both parents were so acutely anxious about the mist-tent pump and the possibility of its going bad, that they constantly listened for any change in noise or rhythm and also constantly checked the water bottle to make certain it was not empty. (Strauss, 1975)

Sexual dysfunctioning following chronic illness conditions is often neglected in both the assessment and the treatment of the condition. Both diabetic and myocardial infarct patients show increased rates of sexual dysfunction. One hospital study found that:

Although patients and physicians focused upon physical disease, personal and social attributes produced disability as great as that caused by physical disease. Of the 155 patients discharged alive, 14 percent were not disabled, 24 percent were disabled from physical disease, 44 percent were disabled from psychosocial disturbances, and 18 percent were disabled from a combination of these causes. (Duff and Hollingshead, 1968)

Clearly, the social-psychological aspects of care for the chronically ill are growing in importance, yet the provision of such services strain existing budget resources.

SOCIAL COSTS

In a study of the Workman's Compensation program, Brinker and Murdock (1973) found that severely injured workers suffered a substantial drop in income, forcing them to move to poorer housing. Their children were also adversely affected; they had a lower rate of college attendance and held poorer jobs than children in the control group. The economic costs from premature disability or death have been studied, but it is, of course, difficult to estimate the entire cost of work days lost, school days lost, and other activities that are curtailed because of illness. The average income of the totally disabled is half that of nondisabled persons.

Several recent studies have directed attention to the potential of increased mortality rates in the relocation of elderly from one level of care to another. In speaking of the elderly we cannot escape the implications of the increased population projections for those over 75. Already two and a half times more of our medical care dollar is spent on the elderly than on the 19–64 age group. Between 1960 and 1970, long-term beds increased by 30 percent. Nursing home care costs are now estimated at $9.5 billion, up $1.5 billion from the previous year.

Many families with moderate incomes cannot cope with the catastrophic nature of certain chronic illnesses. A recent study of 115 families by the National Cancer Foundation revealed that the average cost for a cancer patient who died in these families during the past year and a half was approximately $19,000. Health insurance only covered, on the average, $8,000. Similar problems exist among the severely or totally disabled adult. In general their medical bills are twice those of the nondisabled, and they possess less health insurance coverage. This is especially serious since the disabled are two to four times as likely to be hospitalized. In these families the need for home health and other social support and family counseling services grows, yet the need for these services emerges at a time when concern over the already burgeoning costs of health care are causing many medical leaders to call for a retrenchment in the scope of medical care services. Simply put, many are calling for tighter boundaries around medicine and a retreat from a broader concept of health benefits in which professional results are harder to measure. This move toward narrow medical intervention, especially as it concerns chronic and long-term illness, is doomed to failure. As Bess Dana has said: "The prevention of disease and disability, whether physical or mental, is intimately connected with the conditions of human life."

PUBLIC SOCIAL POLICY IMPLICATIONS AND RECOMMENDATIONS

The needs of the chronically ill and those requiring long-term care must receive renewed attention by the American public and health care policymakers. Our goal in this country must be to develop an *explicit* policy on long-term care for the chronically ill, infirm, and disabled. Strong advocacy on the part of social workers is required to prevent the unnecessary physical and mental deterioration of large numbers of people that will result if a "second-class" level of care continues for the chronically ill. Obvious differentials in status, rewards, and incentives exist between health and social work personnel who work in the exciting and technologically advanced world of acute care and life-saving programs and those who labor among the chronically sick and infirm. Part of the crisis in obtaining adequate resources for chronic care relates to the overwhelming preference for *cure* as opposed to *care* modes of intervention among existing health professional providers.

What can be done? First, committed professional educators in all of the disciplines must develop academic content and patient experiences that place equal attention on care as well as cure; on prevention as well as treatment. In individual clinical work, assessment of the impairment to individual functioning must supersede the heavy focus on the diagnosis of pathology. Case management and program coordination skills must be highlighted in curriculums. Knowledge of natural support networks and self-help groups must be enhanced. Social work students, in particular, must understand the interrelationships among life-style, diet, and environment and how they contribute to changing illness patterns in American society, and the resulting impacts on families and personal productivity. The old social diseases of VD and TB are clearly being replaced by the "new" social diseases of modern society, such as hypertension, lung cancer, drug abuse, heart disease, obesity, and industrial accidents. These new social diseases have, in large part, social causes that are amenable to social intervention. A clearer role for social work and other social behavioral disciplines is now developing. Much can be done to implement strategies aimed at assisting individuals in their motivation to alter deleterious health habits. The same applies to assisting community groups to organize around environmental concerns linked to health hazards. Social workers in industrial employee assistance programs have many new opportunities for directly attacking occupational health problems.

Second, social work research most likely to influence policy and program directors will come from studies directed at two target areas. First, measures of both the capacity for or impediments to social functioning performance are germane to program needs for the chronically ill. In a recent hospital study of the effectiveness of postdischarge follow-up (Mannino and Shore, 1974), showed how marital status, family stage, family type, and family position have an interactive effect that produces less favorable outcomes for patients discharged from a state hospital. Nielsen (1972) was able to measure differences in the change in contentment among older persons following hospitalization. Self-health appraisals by elderly persons is another promising development. Jorgensen and Kane (1976) have developed a scale related to the performance of nursing home residents. The second target area for research must be directed at the service systems for long-term care. The fragmentation, and in some cases the complete absence, of services can pose serious problems for the chronically ill. These gaps in services and deleterious conditions must be documented and their impact on clients assessed. Solid research findings are a great ally in advocating badly needed reforms.

Other areas of policy related research include:

1. The effect of personal income deficiencies and unnecessary institutionalizations.

2. Impact of multidisciplinary assessment for the chronically infirm client. Does a comprehensive assessment program work?

3. Adequacy of subsidized housing for the chronically impaired person.

4. Community progress in eliminating environmental barriers for the handicapped.

5. Impact on "near poor" of publicly supported programs for "poor" only.

6. Studies that document the need for and value of social services in nursing homes.

7. Needs of the chronically ill and their families in different racial and ethnic groups.

8. Daily maintenance needs of the home-bound client, including basic money management assistance.

Third, it is incumbent upon providers and consumers to be actively involved in the new Health Systems Agencies. Not only do HSAs set health planning priorities at local and regional levels, but they must review and approve a wide range of federal grants that come into a particular region. The lack of effective and coordinated services for the long-term patients and the chronically ill must be assertively brought to the attention of those professional and public citizens who help determine health care policy. For example, only one of every four disabled persons actually receives rehabilitation services. The chronically ill themselves must be involved in decision-making processes. The development of long-term care demonstration centers funded by the National Agency on Aging Office is a welcome addition of federal resources to the local area. Demonstration programs, if successful, must receive permanent funding. In some ways we have had sufficient demonstration activities to point to successful models for long-term care. What we now need is collaborative and concerted local, state, and federal action to implement programs that truly link health and social service systems.

Fourth, the entrepreneurial traditions of American medicine are reflected in an overemphasis in hospital reimbursement for acute care problems along with reimbursement of highly specialized surgical and medical techniques. Home care, self–care, and alternative health care services are not emphasized because medicine as it is being practiced still focuses on repairs of the human machinery at a time when theoretical and empirical evidence indicates that health is determined more by socioenvironmental factors and concrete social services than by health services. Cost containment for the health care field reached new heights of consciousness, but, in the end, those most likely to feel the brunt of cost-saving procedures are the chronically impaired, the poor, and others who have little voice in determining medical care priorities. If cost containment produced a shift in resources for the growing needs of the chronically ill, some benefit could be derived from this trend. The zealots of technologically advanced equipment and programs, however, will still have the loudest and strongest voice. Who will argue for the pressing need to shift from our dominant acute care focus? Social workers and other concerned colleagues can unify to meet this challenge. The NASW's recent policy statement on long-term care (NASW

News, 1979) can serve as one unifying theme for collective action. One target of action is the public Medicare-Medicaid programs. Medicare and Medicaid were never, unfortunately, designed to deal w..h long-term care. Services have been inpatient-, acute-care-oriented. Less than one percent of Medicare funds is spent on home health care services. It is deplorable to note that some elderly couples have had to obtain a divorce in order to qualify for Medicaid eligibility (so as not to go into major debt because of long-term nursing care). The new Federal Bureau of Health Care Financing must vigorously address new policy options and abandon those regulations that are deleterious to the *"health"* of recipients.

Mechanic (1973), who has studied health systems in several countries, comments:

The system of medical care in any country reflects the traditions of the past and the social priorities for the future. Health care is a vast industry and subsumes many groups with conflicting perspectives and interests. How these interests are weighed, negotiated, and resolved determines, in part, the organization of health services and the various priorities given to different aspects of health care.

Because of these conflicting perceptions and multiple interests, the American health care system is full of paradoxes. For example, medicine's high-powered technology and quick-cure image differ considerably from the reality of what most needs to be done, that is, care of chronic illness, personal counseling services, and social support networks (Airie, 1975). Chronic illness and accompanying restorative and rehabilitative demands increase exponentially as new biomedical engineering feats of medical science prolong life. The benefits from such feats as the control of genetic disorders, DNA discoveries, breakthroughs in reducing antigen rejection to allow for organ transplants, prevention of viral diseases and certain kinds of cancer, and the application of advances in space medicine to health maintenance (such as biofeedback machines) seem self-evident. However, the most dramatic effect of these events is that they put further strains and stresses on an already fragmented system that is overloaded with technology directed to acute care conditions when chronic care and rehabilitation are the major overriding problems. The challenge of leadership for the social work profession has never been more pressing.

REFERENCES

Airie, T. June 1975. *New society*. No. 5.

Brody, E. May 1975. *Long-term care: the decision-making process and individual assessment*. Paper presented at the meeting of the National Conference on Social Welfare, San Francisco.

Brinker, P., and Murdock, W. 1973. Children of the severely injured. *Journal of Human Resources* 8:242–44.

Dana, B. 1973. Health, social work, and social justice. In B. Ross and C. Shireman, eds., *Social work practice and social justice*. Washington, D.C.: National Association of Social Workers.

Duff, R., and Hollingshead, A. 1968. *Sickness and society*. New York: Harper and Row.

Engel, G. 1962. *Psychological developments in health and disease.* Philadelphia: Saunders.

Franklin, P. 1977. Impact of disability on the family structure. *Social Security Bulletin* 40:3-18.

Gordis, L. 1973. Effectiveness of comprehensive-care programs in preventing rheumatic fever. *New England Journal of Medicine* 289:332-35.

Hiatt, H. 1975. Protecting the medical commons: who is responsible? *New England Journal of Medicine* 293:235-40.

Jorgensen, L. A., and Kane, R. 1976. Social work in a nursing home: a need and an opportunity. *Social Work in Health Care* 1:480-81.

Kaplan, D. 1976. Predicting the impact of severe illness in families. *Health and Social Work* 1:71-82.

Katz, S. 1972. *Effects of long-term care.* Washington, D.C.: Center for Health Service Research.

Mannino, F., and Shore, M. 1974. Demonstrating effectiveness in an aftercare program. *Social Work* 19:351-54.

Matsumoto, Y. S. 1971. Social stress in coronary heart disease in Japan. In H. P. Dreitzel, ed., *The social organization of health.* New York: McMahon.

Mechanic, D. 1973. Health and illness in technological societies. *Hastings Center Studies* 1:7-18.

Morris, R., and Anderson, D. 1975. Personal care services: an identity for social work. *Social Service Review* 49:157-74.

Morris, R., and Harris, E. 1972. Home health services in Massachusetts, 1971: their role in care of the long-term sick. *American Journal of Public Health* 62:1088-93.

NASW News. 1979. Policy statement on long-term care. *NASW News* 24:22.

Nielsen, M. 1972. Older persons after hospitalization: a controlled study of home aid service. *American Journal of Public Health* 62:1088-93.

Pfeiffer, E. November 1973. *Multidimensional quantitative assessment of three populations of elderly.* Paper presented at the meeting of the Gerontological Society, Miami Beach.

Richardson, W. 1969. Poverty, illness and the use of health services in the United States. *Hospitals* 43:249.

Roberts, P. 1974. Human warehouses: a boarding home study. *American Journal of Public Health* 64:277-79.

Shanas, E. 1974. Health status of older people: cross-national implications. *American Journal of Public Health* 64:261-64.

Sherwood, S., ed. 1975. *Long-term care: a handbook for researchers, planners, and providers.* New York: Spectrum.

Strauss, A. 1975. *Chronic illness and the quality of life.* St. Louis: Mosby.

Syme, S. L. 1974. Behavioral factors associated with the etiology of physical disease. *American Journal of Public Health* 64:1043-45.

Traeger, B. May 1975. *The community in long-term health care.* Paper presented at the meeting of the National Conference on Social Welfare, San Francisco.

10

COST CONTAINMENT

John H. Noble, Jr., and Ronald W. Conley

Three interrelated trends, perceived by some as alarming, have emerged in the United States during the past 25 years. First, the share of the gross national product (GNP) that is being spent on hospital care is increasing rapidly. Between 1950 and 1977, the share of the GNP that goes to hospital services rose from 1.3 percent to 3.5 percent. As a proportion of all personal health expenditures, hospital servies have expanded in the same 27-year period from 35.6 percent to 46.0 percent of all personal health care spending (U.S. Department of Commerce, 1978). Second, the share of the GNP that is expended by the public sector (federal, state, and local) has also been rising steadily and was almost 33 percent of GNP in 1977 (President of the United States, 1978). Third, health costs, as a percentage of federal outlays, have grown to 9.6 percent of federal spending in 1979 as compared to 8.5 percent in 1975, and are projected to rise to almost 10 percent of federal outlays during 1979 (President of the United States, 1978).

Widespread dissatisfaction with these trends is causing policymakers to search, almost frantically, for ways to reduce or even to reverse them. There is fear that if health care expenditures continue their rapid rise, then given the reality of limited resources, either an undue proportion of the nation's resources will be diverted to health care or the achievement of other public objectives will be impeded. As observed by Rosenthal (1978, p. 34), "we are moving from pursuing health goals 'at any price' to a realization that limited resources require deliberate choices." Rosenthal was urging the adoption of cost containment as an antidote to undue past reliance on the simple expansion of health resources as the way to achieve the positive goals of public health care policy.

The growth of social services is being restrained as one consequence of the effort to hold down public spending, and the prospect is for even more restraint in the future. It is our contention that constricting the growth of the social services is self-defeating because it will lead ultimately to an increase in medical costs greater than the expected savings in social services costs. Moreover, such a policy may even cause the quality of health care to atrophy, since the social services play an important role in maintaining the good health and social adjustment of persons with acute and chronic conditions.

Table 10.1   Health Care Spending in the United States and the Federal Republic of Germany (FRG) Compared, 1960–75

Year	Personal health care, U.S.[a]			Statutory health insurance, FRG[b]		
	$ billion	Average growth (percentage)	GNP average growth (percentage)	DM billions	Average growth (percentage)	GNP average growth (percentage)
1960	10.153	—	—	9.513	—	—
1965	15.921	11.4	7.2	15.785	13.2	8.8
1970	35.841	25.0	8.6	25.179	11.9	8.4
1975	73.918	21.2	11.1	60.974	28.4	8.8

[a]Third-party payments for personal health care, including expenditures by private insurance carriers, government, and philanthropic and other sources. In 1977, these payments represented 69.7 percent of total health care spending in the U.S.
[b]Statutory health expenditures in the FRG covered 90 percent of the population in 1979; private insurance covered an additional 7 percent.

Source: Pflanz, M. and Geissler, U. (1977), Table 1, p. 293; Statistical Abstract of the U.S. (1978), tables 146 and 708, pp. 102 and 440.

THE U.S. AND WEST GERMAN EXPERIENCES

The pattern of growth in overall health care spending and in outlays for hospital services in the United States parallels in many ways the experience of the West Germans.[1] From 1960 to 1976, the share of the West German GNP that is spent on hospital care grew from 0.51 percent to 1.72 percent. As a proportion of all expenditures under the statutory health insurance scheme, spending for hospital services rose from 16.5 percent in 1960 to 28.7 percent in 1975 (Pflanz and Geissler, 1977; Stone, 1979). About 90 percent of the West German population receives medical care through a statutorily prescribed program, so that the ratio of hospital costs to all health care expenditures in West Germany would be only a little less than these percentages. As Tables 10.1 and 10.2 show, the annual rate of growth of spending in the United States and in West Germany for hospital services and for health care in general has consistently exceeded the nominal growth rate of the GNP of both countries.

Alarmed by their experience, the West Germans passed legislation (effective as of July 1, 1977) authorizing aggressive measures to curtail the growth of health care expenditures (Stone, 1979). That mandatory controls were placed on all medical costs *other than* those incurred in hospitals is an

Table 10.2 Hospital Services Spending in the United States and the Federal Republic of Germany (FRG) Compared, 1960–75

Year	United States			Federal Republic of Germany		
	$ billions	Average growth (percentage)	GNP average growth (percentage)	DM billions	Average growth (percentage)	GNP average growth (percentage)
1960	8.5	—	—	1,568	—	—
1965	13.2	11.1	7.2	2,947	13.5	8.8
1970	25.9	19.2	8.6	6,009	15.3	8.4
1975	48.4	17.4	11.1	17,500	23.8	8.8

important peculiarity of the West German cost-containment legislation. The measures mandated to control nonhospital medical costs included:

An annual mandatory ceiling on expenditures for physicians' and dentists' services and for prescription drugs must be negotiated among health insurance plan participants—the National Health Commission, the Federal Association of Insurance Doctors, the Federal Association of Insurance Dentists, and the Federal Association of Sickness Funds. Arbitration is compulsory if agreement cannot be reached. Moreover, there is a maximum permissible rate of health expenditure growth that is explicitly linked to certain economic indicators (e.g., average wages or salaries of all employed persons, the costs of medical practice, etc.).

Physicians must provide ambulatory care on the basis of a fee schedule, but their total billings cannot exceed the total amount of funds available for providing services to the members of each insurance fund. If some physicians exceed their allotted share of services, then the rate of reimbursement for all the services provided by all participating physicians is to be cut back uniformly (e.g., 80 percent of the rate set by the fee schedule).

Lists of therapeutically equivalent drugs are to be published, and physicians are to prescribe the less expensive brands. Fines are to be imposed on physicians whose drug expenditures consistently deviate from the "norm" in the absence of an epidemic or sudden increase in drug prices.

Hospital-based physicians who were previously precluded from performing outpatient diagnostic tests or giving follow-up care will be allowed to do so in order to cut down on needless duplication of services caused by the strict separation of hospital and ambulatory care.

Automatic exemptions from the cost-sharing provisions of the West German health insurance system for all pensioners, handicapped per-

sons, and recipients of income transfer payments have been eliminated.

Home health services are to be provided when provision of these services
will eliminate the need for hospitaliztion.

Other measures authorized by the cost-containment legislation include
spreading the cost burden of caring for the elderly more equally by
broadening the risk pools of the health insurance funds and by
redistributing funds according to a "need quotient" formula. Strictly
speaking, these measures are not oriented to cost containment as much
as to spreading the cost burden of ill health more evenly.

The events preceding the enactment of the cost-containment legislation
provide insights into what might be accomplished through "voluntary" as
compared to "mandatory" cost controls, particularly if the voluntary controls are accompanied by the threat of mandatory controls in the event of
failure. Stone (1979) offers evidence to show that, prior to the passage of the
cost-containment legislation and during the debate leading up to it,
dramatic, across-the-board slowing occurred in the annual growth rates of
spending for physicians' and dentists' services, drugs and appliances, and
hospital care. The rate of growth of expenditures on apothecaries, for example, declined from 12.9 percent in 1975 to 8.0 percent in 1976; and the
growth rate of spending for dental services dropped from 21.5 percent to
3.8 percent during the same period. The rate of growth of expenditures for
hospital services declined from 15 percent in 1975 to 9.5 percent in 1976.
Stone explains these changes as the result of the threat of tough cost-control
legislation which caused spending for physicians services to decline as well
as spending for "all other types of services for which physicians are
gatekeepers" (pp. 26–27). In addition, the slowing trend in hospital costs
continued during the 1976–77 interval even though they were exempt from
mandatory controls. Presumably, this occurred as the result of the continuing threat that hospitals would be encompassed in future cost-containment
legislation should increases in hospital costs exceed other medical costs
under mandatory controls.

The United States seems destined, at least in the immediate future, to
take the voluntary approach to hospital cost containment. The recent attempt to impose mandatory controls was defeated by a wide margin in the
U.S. House of Representatives. The United States, unlike West Germany,
has no mandatory controls on any part of its health care system. Only time
will tell whether the voluntary approach will work in the United States, or
whether mandatory controls – or at least the threat of their imposition – are
needed to restrain the costs of hospital and other health services.

Considerable uncertainty surrounds the issue of what policies will
restrain the escalating costs of health care, because the precise causes of increasing costs and the extent of their singular and interactive causal influences are not well understood anywhere in the world. As characterized
by Pflanz and Geissler (1977, p. 295), rising health expenditures are a
worldwide trend, whose causes are attributable to greater consumer demand for services induced by "growing awareness of the value of health, in-

creased acceptance of the 'right to health,' extended definitions of illness,
. . . changing demographic, socio-economic, and morbidity structures of
the population, . . . the progress of medical science," and an increased supply of health care resources, particularly "the tremendous, virtually unchecked increase of manpower and other resources in health care." This
uncertainty about causality makes identification of the theoretically proper
mix of corrective policies very difficult, and heightens the risk of error for
the choice of policy arrived at by the political process.

COMPETING U.S. APPROACHES

On November 15, 1979, the U.S. House of Representatives voted its approval of H.R. 5635, a hospital-cost-containment bill introduced only a
month previously by Congressman Richard A. Gephardt (D-Mo.). This
bill, among other things, set voluntary goals for hospital cost containment,
established a National Commission on Hospital Costs to monitor price increases and to study their underlying causes, and authorized a new grant-
in-aid program of $10 million for the first year and such sums as necessary
for the two succeeding years to help states set up their own voluntary or
mandatory hospital-cost-containment programs. The hospital industry and
the American Medical Association gave strong support to this bill, partly
because it embodied their beliefs in the superiority of voluntary as opposed
to mandatory cost controls, and partly because by shifting the locus of these
efforts to the states where their influence is greater than at the national
level, they hoped to insulate themselves — at least temporarily — from the
threat of mandatory controls.

The Gephardt bill effectively quashed two major hospital-cost-
containment bills that had been under consideration: a bill supported by
the Carter Administration and one sponsored by Senators Herman E.
Talmadge (D-Ga.) and Robert Dole (R-Kan.). The bill supported by the
Carter Administration (H.R. 2626; S. 570) and that of Senators Talmadge
and Dole (S. 505) had certain features in common. They would have
developed a uniform cost accounting system to keep track of individual
hospital performance; changed the "reasonable costs" reimbursement
machinery of Medicare and Medicaid in ways that would provide explicit
rewards and penalties for efficiencies and inefficiencies, as the case might
be;[2] granted numerous exemptions to hospitals meeting specified criteria;[3]
delegated broad authority to the Secretary of Health, Education, and
Welfare (HEW) to define and operationalize many of the principal concepts and procedures of the proposed new systems; and established a national commission to study the phenomenon of spiraling hospital costs and
to report to Congrss its recommendations for bringing them under control.
Both bills were envisioned by their sponsors as transitional: experience
under the initial system that was adopted would lead to some future permanent system of hospital cost containment.

The bills also differed on many important features. The Carter administration's bill accepted the voluntary goal, set by the hospital industry, of
limiting hospital cost increases in 1979 to 11.6 percent, but made provision

for mandatory controls if the voluntary effort failed. These mandatory controls would have applied to hospital costs paid by all parties — Medicare, Medicaid, private insurance carriers, and individuals. The Talmadge-Dole bill, on the other hand, would have established mandatory controls for the Medicare and Medicaid programs only, and not by reference to any a priori goal, such as the hospital industry's voluntry goal of limiting hospital cost increases in 1979 to 11.6 percent, but instead on the basis of actual costs incurred by homogeneous classes of hospitals.

The Carter administration's bill would have calculated the voluntary national limit on hospital cost increases for 1980 and succeeding years on the basis of a national index consisting of four components: (1) the actual percentage increase in average hourly wage rates and wage-related expenses for nonsupervisory staff; (2) the average percentage increase in the national market basket of other goods and services that hospitals purchase; (3) an allowance for population growth; and (4) a 1 percent increase for "net intensity," nowhere explicitly defined but referred to as an allowance made to reflect the fact that hospitals often provide new services as the result of technological innovation whose additional costs cannot be offset through improved productivity and economies of scale. Hospitals failing to meet the national voluntary limit would be given an opportunity to justify the higher expenditures using local versions of the four components of the national index: (1) the individual hospital's own data on nonsupervisory wage and wage-related increases and the proportion of its total costs accruing from these sources; (2) area, regional, or state market basket price indices rather than national indices if available; (3) a state, SMSA, or county rather than national allowance for total population growth; and its own weighting of expenses arising from the different cost categories of the hospital's nonwage market basket. In addition, individual hospitals could have justified an above-average increase in costs if the percentage of its aged patients increased. If requested, all of the individual hospital's expenses for charity patients and uncollectible bills would have been omitted from the calculation of cost increases.

The Carter administration's bill would have imposed mandatory controls on all hospitals that failed to comply with the voluntary limits (a strange definition of voluntarism!) — even on hospitals located in a state which as a whole met the voluntary limit if they exceeded the voluntary limit for two successive years. The mandatory controls would have placed a limit on growth of each hospital's average inpatient revenues per admission. These limits would have become known to the hospital at the close of its accounting period after it had filed its Medicare cost report. Before this time, each hospital would have had to depend on estimates of nonwage market basket cost increases for the nation, calculated periodically by HEW, as well as on its own experience of wage-related expenses and other factor costs, to estimate what its charges should be and whether it was staying within or exceeding the anticipated limit. At the end of the accounting year, government programs and private insurance carriers would have then adjusted their reimbursements to each hospital according to the current methods of settling over- and underpayments in connection with final Medicare cost reports. Payments received from all other patients in excess of the limit set for the average inpatient charge per admission would have been placed in escrow and drawn on when the hospital's inpatient charges in succeeding years fell below future mandatory limits.

To reward or penalize hospitals for staying below or exceeding the mandatory limit, as the case might be, the Secretary of HEW was to develop a system for classifying hospitals on the basis of patient case mix, metropolitan versus nonmetropolitan setting, and the like, and a method to measure the relative efficiency of hospitals within homogeneous classes. Graduated bonuses and penalties were to have been assessed on the basis of each hospital's group norm, with a bonus of up to 1 percent of allowable reimbursement to be paid for restraining costs to a growth rate of less than 90 percent of the group norm, or a penalty of up to 2 percent of allowable reimbursement for exceeding the growth rate of the group norm by more than 130 percent.

In contrast, the Talmadge-Dole bill would have set per diem target rates for each hospital on the basis of the average per diem operating costs for a group of similar hospitals classified by bed size, type of hospital, urban versus rural location, or other criteria established by the Secretary of HEW. "Routine costs" were to be defined as they now are by Medicare but to have excluded the routine variable costs of capital and related costs; education and training programs; interns, residents, and nonadministrative physicians; energy costs; and malpractice insurance costs.

Numerous adjustments to these routine operating costs would have been allowed in order to accommodate the special circumstances of individual hospitals. For example, newly opened hospitals and any hospital trying to make up for past failure to meet fully the standards and conditions of participation as a provider in the Medicare program were to have that portion of their routine operating costs attributable to these conditions exempted from calculation of the hospital's adjusted target rate. The Secretary of HEW was to have been responsible for projecting anticipated annual increases in the costs of the mix of goods and services that comprise the hospital's routine operating expenses according to an appropriately weighted index, and for adding this as an adjustment to the target rate of reimbursement for the accounting period. Somewhat as in the administration's proposal, an end-of-the-year adjustment was to have been made to correct for actual as compared to the projected cost increases, or for changes that might have occurred due to a shift in the hospital's classification during the accounting interval.

Hospitals able to keep actual routine costs below the target rate for their hospital class would have received one-half the difference between their actual routine costs and the target rate, with a maximum allowable bonus of 5 percent of the target rate. In the system's first year, hospitals exceeding their target rate would have received payment of actual costs up to a limit of 115 percent of the target rate. In the system's second and succeeding years, the target rate for each hospital would have been somehow based on the actual increase in the average per diem operating costs of the hospital class to which it belonged, but the calculation of the class average was to exclude "one-half of costs found excessive" (U.S. Senate, 1979).[4]

The Carter administration's bill, like the Gephardt bill, contained a provision for establishing a grant-in-aid program to help the states set up and operate their own cost-containment programs. But whereas the Gephardt bill would provide funding for voluntary or mandatory programs, the Carter administration's bill would have funded only mandatory programs. The Talmadge-Dole bill took a quite different approach to the support of state efforts. It would have had the federal government pay a percentage of the costs of state hospital-cost-containment programs commensurate with the proportion of hospital costs paid by Medicare and Medicaid, either as part of allowable administrative expenses under Medicaid or through a waiver of existing Medicare regulations, but on condition that the state program be mandatory and demonstrate to the satisfaction of the Secretary of HEW its capacity for controlling hospital costs at least as well as the otherwise applicable federal program. If, for any reason, a state program failed over a two-year period in this regard, the Talmadge-Dole bill would have provided for recoup of excessive reimbursements by reducing the otherwise permissible hospital cost limits in succeeding accounting years.

Congressman Gephardt and those joining with him in dissent against the Carter Administration's proposal expressed their aversion to mandatory controls in general and to federal intervention in particular. While directed against the Carter administration's bill, their objections could almost equally be leveled against the Talmadge-Dole scheme. In their view, implementing the proposed federal system "establishes a cumbersome, inappropriate method for reducing the cost of hospital care" that would "result in unworkable controls, distortions in the allocation of health resources, rationing, and reduced quality of patient care" (U.S. House of Representatives, 1979, pp. 66 and 70).

More specifically, Congressman Gephardt and his fellow dissenters pointed out that growth in the "intensity" of both routine and specialized services often associated with higher-quality care, not hospital inefficiency, account for the rising hospital costs.[5] They regarded the Carter administration's bill as insensitive to the real need in many cases for intensive service delivery and as possibly dangerous because it could cause some people to go without the benefits to be derived from advances in medical knowledge and technology. They argued that lowering the rate of inflation, as measured by the consumer price index, by less than one-tenth of 1 percent by 1981 was not worth the risks. Moreover, they saw the Carter administration's bill as failing to address numerous factors, not within the control of the hospitals, that contribute to rising hospital costs: economy-wide inflation in the costs of hospital purchases; higher costs of malpractice insurance; the increasing costs of the regulatory burden imposed by federal, state, and local governments; greater hospital utilization by the poor and elderly under the Medicare and Medicaid programs; and overutilization of inpatient services due to the greater convenience, safety, and profits it affords physicians.

Last, Congressman Gephardt's dissenting group argued that hospitals could circumvent the mandatory controls of the Carter administration's bill in a number of ways, some of which could prove detrimental to the quality of health care. Since controls, for example, would be on inpatient revenues per admission, hospitals could still maximize revenues by increasing admissions, or by switching patients to outpatient care even though continued inpatient care was more appropriate, or by contracting with autonomous entities not subject to the controls to provide services that are now directly provided and billed for by hospitals. They regarded as particularly perverse the incentives provided by the Carter administration's bill to discharge patients prematurely or to switch inappropriately to outpatient care in the absence of an adequate supply of home health care and social services in many communities throughout the country. Neither the poor nor many of the privately insured population are very adequately covered for outpatient treatment, some of whom may require rehospitalization as the result of either the inadequate outpatient care they receive or the ill effects of being prematurely discharged in order to circumvent the system of controls by artificially inflating the hospital's total admissions. To the extent that this happened, the end result would be higher expenditures for hospital care and increased spending for outpatient services, borne both by third-party payers and by patients out of pocket.

The Gephardt bill died in the 96th Congress. Hospital costs increased 12.5 percent in 1979, 0.9 percent more than the hospital industry's voluntary goal of an increase no greater than 11.6 percent. Since 1979, costs of hospital care have been rising at an annual rate exceeding 17 percent (American Hospital Association, 1981).

The election of President Reagan in November 1980 has reinforced the voluntary approach to hospital cost containment. Citing the need to stimulate greater competition within the health care industry in order to restrain costs, the Reagan Administration has proposed phasing out the federally funded health planning program, consisting of 213 local Health Systems Agencies and 57 state planning organizations. It has argued that the health planning program "imposed additional regulatory burdens on the industry with little appreciable impact on controlling health cost increases nationally" (U.S. Department of Health and Human Services, 1981, p. 9).

HOSPITAL SPENDING AND THE SOCIAL SERVICES

Given the constraint of limited resources, any increased spending for hospital care will necessarily diminish resources available for the production and provision of other goods and services. It is basically for this reason that there is so much concern about the rapid growth of personal health care expenditures (which encompass spending for hospital services) in both the public and private sectors of the economy.

The government share of personal health care expenditures has been steadily rising since 1965, growing from 43.7 percent to 57.5 percent in 1977 (U.S. Department of Commerce, 1978). During that period, substan-

tial shifting among the different categories of government spending has occurred. More recently, federal spending for hospital services in the
Medicare and Medicaid programs has accelerated and begun to squeeze
not only Medicare- and Medicaid-funded community health care but also
the social services programs, the latter broadly defined to include expenditures under Title 20 of the Social Security Act, the Developmental
Disabilities Bill of Rights and Assistance Act, the Rehabilitation Act, the
Community Mental Health Centers Act, the Administration of Aging programs, and the Alcohol and Drug Abuse Community Services programs.

The "squeeze" is occurring because Medicare and Medicaid, unlike the
social services programs, are considered "entitlement" programs, whose
covered services must be reimbursed by the federal government for all eligible persons. In a sense, Medicare and Medicaid have "open-ended" federal
budgets, the sizes of which are more or less determined by the quantity of
covered services consumed by eligible persons (subject, in Medicare, to a
degree of consumer cost sharing and, in Medicaid, to appropriation by the
state of the requisite matching funds). Whenever it is necessary to hold the
line or cut back on the overall federal budget, the budget cutters cannot
touch the "entitlement" programs without resorting to new legislation
changing eligibility, coverage, or both eligibility and coverage. This, of
course, Congress is understandably loath to permit, and so the budget cutters in the administration and Congress turn to the annual level of appropriations of the "nonentitlement" programs, such as the social services,
as the place to find "savings." As is apparent from Table 10.3, over time the
relative share of the federal human services budget expended in "nonentitlement" programs has diminished.

Table 10.3 shows how much the federal government spent for health care
and social services in 1970 and 1976 and is estimated to spend in 1979 and
1985. The declining importance of the social services and community
health care is apparent. Particularly noteworthy is the estimated decline to
5 percent in 1985 of the share of total federal spending for health care and
social services that will go to the social services programs. In contrast, the
share of the acute inpatient hospital sector will steadily rise from 52 percent
in 1970 to an estimated 56 percent in 1979 and 65 percent in 1985. Table
10.4 and Figures 10.1 and 10.2 compare current and constant (1970)
growth rates for federal expenditures on community health services, acute
inpatient care, long-term care and mental hospitals, and the combined
social services programs. In current dollars, each of these sectors is
estimated to continue to increase through 1985. In constant 1970 dollars,
however, which show changes in real purchasing power, all but one of the
budgets will increase. It is estimated that the constant dollar budget for the
social services will begin to decline in 1982.

The significance of these trends is obvious. Without major changes in
public policy, spending for acute inpatient hospital services and long-term
care in nursing homes and chronic disease institutions will continue to
squeeze the social services programs, some portion of which can be considered substitutes for care in the more restrictive settings. The lack of
funds for community-based services will present serious barriers to achieve-

Table 10.3 Shifting among Federal Budgets of Community Health Services, Acute Inpatient Care, Long-Term Care and Mental Hospitals, and Combined Social Services Programs, 1970–85 (estimated in billions of dollars)

Program	FY 70 Budget	FY 70 Percentage of total	FY 76 Budget	FY 76 Percentage of total	FY 79 Budget	FY 79 Percentage of total	FY 85 Budget	FY 85 Percentage of total
Community health services (CH)[a]	$ 2.70	26	$ 6.57	23	$ 9.81	20	$ 22.27	16
Acute inpatient care (AIC)[b]	5.44	52	14.44	50	26.65	56	91.23	65
Long-term care[c] and mental hospitals (LTC and MH)	1.179	11	3.636	13	6.333	13	19.726	14
Combined social[d] services programs (CSS)	1.179	11	4.161	14	5.147	11	6.878	5[f]
Total[e]	$10.50	100%	$28.81	100%	$47.94	100%	$140.10	100%

[a] Community health services: the sum of 56.8 percent of Medicaid and total Medicare amounts reimbursed for physician services, prescribed drugs, dental services, outpatient, clinic, home health, and other. This represents the federal expenditure.

[b] Acute inpatient care: the sum of Medicare and 56.8 percent of Medicaid total amounts reimbursed for "general hospital" expenses. This represents the federal expenditure.

[c] Long-term care and mental hospitals: the sum of Medicare and 56.8 percent of Medicaid total amounts reimbursed for mental hospitals, T.B. hospitals, SNFs, and ICFs. This represents the federal expenditure.

[d] Combined social services programs: the sum of the appropriations for Title 20 of the Social Security Act, Developmental Disabilities, Rehabilitation Act, community mental health centers, Administration on Aging, Alcohol and Drug Abuse Community Services programs, assuming Title 20 is not allowed to expand after it reaches its authorized ceiling in 1979.

[e] Estimates for FY79 are based on projections of the compound growth rate for the period 1974–76 for Medicaid; namely, 18.03 percent for community health services, 18.47 percent for acute inpatient care, and 21.48 percent for long-term care and mental hospitals. For the Medicare components, the projected growth rates are 11.91 percent for community health services, 23.41 percent for acute inpatient care, and 4.79 percent for long-term care.

[f] With Title 20 expanding, 1985 = $13.401 billion; total = $148.5 billion.

Source: HEW, note 4, Annex pp. 10–2 to 10–3.

Table 10.4 Program Budgets in Current and Constant 1970 Dollars (billions), 1970–85 (estimated)

Program	FY 70		FY 76[a]		FY 79		FY 85	
	Current dollars	Constant dollars	Current dollars	Constant dollars	Current dollars[b]	Constant dollars[c]	Current dollars[d]	Constant dollars[e]
Community health services (CH)	$2.7	$2.7	$ 6.57	$4.47	$ 9.81	$ 5.59	$22.27	$ 8.69
Acute inpatient care (AIC)	5.44	5.44	14.44	9.82	26.65	15.19	91.23	35.58
Long-term care and mental hospitals (LTC and MH)	1.179	1.179	3.636	2.48	6.333	3.64	19.726	7.73
Combined social services programs (CSS)	1.179	1.179	4.161	2.83	5.147	2.93	6.878[f]	2.68

a FY 76 includes the transitional quarter appropriations.

b Current dollars for FY 79: the 1979 amounts are based on projections of the compound growth rates for Medicaid, 1974–76, of 18.03 percent for community health services, 18.47 percent for acute inpatient care, and 21.48 percent for long-term care and mental hospitals. For the Medicare components, the projected growth rates are 11.91 percent for community health services, 23.41 percent for acute inpatient care, and 4.79 percent for long-term care.

c The GNP implicit price deflator used for FY 79 was 159.13 (FY 1972 = 100), estimated by the Office of Management and Budget on the basis of projecting the recent average yearly increase of 6.17 percent.

d Current dollars for FY 85 were estimated using the compound growth rates for 1974–76. (See footnote b and, for community social services programs, see footnote f.)

e The constant dollar amounts for FY 85 are derived by using the projected GNP implicit price deflator for FY 85 of 233.01 (1972 = 100). The FY 85 projection of 233.01 is based on the assumed growth rate of 6.17 percent per year which was used by the Office of Management and Budget to project the GNP implicit price deflator during 1977–79.

f Estimated spending for combined social services programs is based on the compound growth rate for FY 74–76 of 8.75 percent for the combined programs, excluding Title 20. Title 20 is estimated to reach its ceiling of $2.5 million in FY 79. The ceiling amount is contained in the FY 79 estimate and the FY 85 estimate. If Title 20 were allowed to grow, CSS in 1985 would be $13.401 billion in current dollars and $5.25 in constant dollars.

Source: HEW, note 4, Annex pp. 10–5 to 10–6.

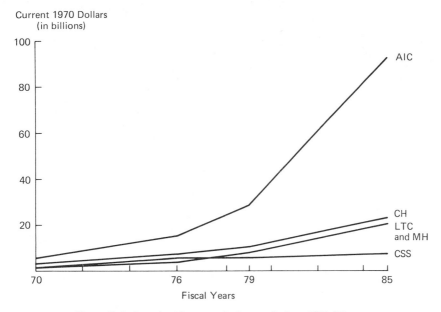

Figure 10.1. Growth of Programs in Current Dollars, 1970–85

ment of legislatively mandated and judicially decreed deinstitutionaliza-tion, which is prescribed under the philosophy that all citizens have a right, should they become eligible for Medicaid, Title 20 social services, or any other government intervention, to care that is appropriate to their needs and least restrictive of their personal liberties.

To maintain the 1976 proportion of the total amount spent for commu-nity health at 23 percent and the combined social services programs at 14 percent throughout 1979–85, and at the same time not to exceed the estimated total 1985 budget for the four program sectors,[6] would require accelerating the growth rate of spending for community health and the combined social services from their current annual rate of 15.8 to 24.0 per-cent during 1979–85, while simultaneously slowing the growth rate of spen-ding for long-term care and mental hospitals and acute inpatient hospital care from their current annual rate of 22.4 to 20.8 percent.

A MODEL OF MEDICAL COST CONTAINMENT

The term "medical care" encompasses a wide variety of distinct services that are provided to persons with acute or chronic illnesses in order to produce a product that may be generally described as improved health and/or reduced suffering. More specifically, medical care is provided to avert death, pro-mote healing, alleviate pain, prevent or retard deterioration of physical and mental health, improve the level of physical and mental functioning, etc.

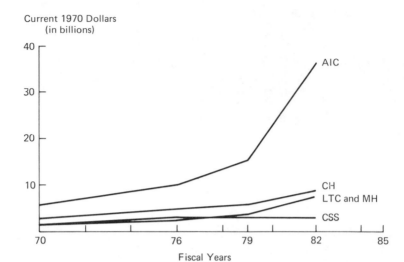

Figure 10.2. Growth of Programs in Constant 1970 Dollars, 1970-85

The specific medical services needed by individuals at given points in time vary widely because of differences among the illnesses and injuries that people suffer and their individual capacities to recover from, or cope with, their conditions.

The total cost of medical care is a function of the types of services delivered and the price that must be paid for these services. In symbols:

$$C = p_1q_1 + p_2q_2 + p_3q_3 + \ldots + p_nq_n$$

where:

q_i refers to the amount of a specific type of medical service delivered, and p_i refers to the price per unit of this service. C can be interpreted in several ways. It can refer to (a) the total cost of medical care in the United States; (b) the total cost of medical care annually for a particular person; or (c) the cost of a particular episode of illness or injury.

"Cost containment" clearly implies that policies are adopted that result in lower outlays for medical care than would have occurred in the absence of these policies. But the different definitions that may be given to C illustrate how the term "cost containment" may refer to quite different concepts. The term can alternately mean:

1. restraining total national outlays for medical care;
2. restraining outlays per person (which is very different from restraining total outlays if the population size is changing); and
3. restraining outlays per episode of illness (in which it is quite possible for total outlays and average outlays per person for medical care to be increasing at a much faster rate than expenditures per episode of illness if the number of episodes per person treated is increasing).

Narrower definitions of "cost containment" are also possible. The term, for example, can refer to (a) containing only some portion of medical costs, such as hospital care; (b) limiting costs in the public programs, primarily Medicare and Medicaid; or (c) restraining only the cost per unit of medical services but without limiting the number of units delivered.

We believe that the primary focus of cost-containment policies should be on the cost per person in the United States, taking into account changes over time in the age composition of the population and changes in the prescribed methods of providing care. In light of this, some cost-containment policies would seem more appropriate than others, as will become apparent.

There are three basic ways of controlling the cost of medical care, whether we are referring to total national costs, outlays per person, or costs per episode of illness: (1) the quantity of services can be curtailed; (2) the prices charged for particular medical services can be reduced; and (3) the composition of the services that are consumed can be altered by substituting less expensive services for more expensive ones (e.g., providing generic instead of brand-name drugs). In the equation, this would be equivalent to reducing the q_is, the p_is, or changing the q_is so that relatively more of the less expensive q_is are purchased. Each of these possibilities is examined in turn.

REDUCING THE QUANTITY OF MEDICAL CARE. The quantity of medical care can be reduced in two ways: (1) the demand for medical care can be curtailed, or (2) the resources available to supply medical care can be limited. The demand for medical care can be limited in a number of ways.

The number of persons becoming ill or suffering injuries can be reduced by adopting relevant preventive techniques. Vaccinations to prevent tetanus, diphtheria, and other diseases have reduced the demand for medical care substantially. Annual physical checkups may prevent or delay the onset of other serious diseases, although it is a matter of uncertainty whether the costs of some of the preventive techniques, such as routine X-rays and other diagnostic tests used to screen populations at risk, are lower than the costs of treating the cases that would develop in the absence of prevention. The demand for medical care, it should be noted, can be curtailed by many nonmedical interventions, such as accident prevention, assurance of proper diet, and the like.

A second way of reducing the demand for medical care is to eliminate unnecessary medical procedures. The development of Professional Standards Review Organizations (PSROs) to evaluate the appropriateness of medical procedures employed by physicians is justified on the grounds that inappropriate procedures will be cut back. Coinsurance and deductibles are features of insurance policies that attempt to discourage unnecessary demand for medical services by requiring the persons covered to pay part and, in some instances, the total costs of medical care.

Curtailing the demand for medical care not only limits the number of episodes for which medical charges are made, but may also bring downward pressure on the prices of medical services if medical providers have to compete with one another in providing services.

Limiting the supply of medical services is sometimes justified on the grounds that medical providers can, and do, create their own demand. If a hospital is built and not immediately filled with patients, admissions may well be made of cases that might formerly have been treated in a physician's office, or the length of stay in the hospital may be extended an extra day or two or even longer in the cases of conditions that require protracted post-hospital convalescence. Similarly, physicians who are not besieged with calls for appointments may be tempted to ask people to come in for a visit whom they might have otherwise advised to go to bed with an aspirin and ample fluid intake, or to request patients to return for a follow-up examination whom they might have otherwise advised to return only if complications had developed, or to increase the number of follow-up examinations beyond the necessary number. It has even been suggested that surgery is sometimes recommended when less radical forms of treatment are more appropriate.

The supply of medical services can be reduced in many ways; e.g., the supply of hospitals and medical personnel can be reduced by denying licenses to build medical facilities and by cutting back on the amount of financial assistance available to medical students, forcing some students to drop out of school because of unmanageable tuition costs.

By our previous logic, such restriction of the supply of medical services will limit the quantity of medical care provided to consumers without reducing the quality of medical services because the extra day or two in the hospital or the extra office visit was not really needed. Whether or not this will restrain the overall costs of medical care, however, depends on how the remaining providers of medical care react to an increasing demand for their services. According to the usual economic assumption, when the availability of a good or service is reduced relative to the demand, the price will rise. But advocates of this form of hospital cost containment somehow assume that if the supply of physicians and hospital beds is curtailed, the remaining physicians and hospitals will respond not by raising prices but by cutting back on the provision of medical care in nonessential areas. This assumption can be put to an empirical test.[7] There is reason to worry, however, about whether instead of cutting back on nonessential medical services, physicians will reduce the services that are provided to persons least able to pay their fees. Even the most optimistic advocates of this approach of limiting the supply of medical care to contain costs acknowledge that the rationing device of higher prices will almost certainly be employed if the supply of medical services is cut drastically.

Another way of curtailing the supply of medical care is to place a limit on overall expenditures for all persons served by a particular program. No private insurance scheme could impose this type of limit on its beneficiaries, since it would run the substantial risk of seeing some persons covered by the insurance policy go without contractually promised medical services. Because the public programs do not so much represent a binding contract to deliver specific services to individuals as a political decision to spend for specific purposes up to some predetermined level, they are likely candidates for "capping," particularly Medicaid. A federal "cap" on Medicaid would force states to: (a) limit medical care to Medicaid recipients; (b) pay from state funds for additional amounts of medical care; (c) reduce the prices that they will pay for medical services; or (d) develop less costly ways of providing medical services.

REDUCING THE PRICE OF MEDICAL CARE. The prices paid for medical care can be reduced in two ways. First, a limit can be placed on the amount that will be paid for a particular operation, condition, injury, or medical procedure (e.g., hysterectomy, hernia, bone fracture, or X-ray or blood test). This is the approach frequently taken by private insurance companies that provide medical coverage. Second, somewhat less precise approaches can be taken that place limits on annual expenditures per person, per episode of illness, or on annual hospital utilization. These "meat-cleaver" approaches are also employed by insurance companies, and frequently cause insufficient allocation of funds to cover the needs of some individuals whose conditions require treatment beyond the limits of the insurance.

CHANGING THE COMPOSITION OF MEDICAL SERVICES. Seeking and adopting less costly ways of producing goods or providing a service are normal behaviors in most industries as competition among firms compels each one to try to obtain price advantage over its rivals, or to look for ways to offset any price advantage that a competitor may have. Unfortunately, the competitive drive to lower costs is weak to nonexistent among providers of medical services.

Competition exists in most private industries because consumers usually: (a) are able to choose among alternative goods and services produced by different companies that serve the same or similar purposes; (b) are cost-conscious as well as product-conscious; (c) can defer their purchases while they compare the different available alternatives; and (d) have the time and resources with which to familiarize themselves with the costs and characteristics of the alternative products.

Persons who seek medical services, however, frequently care little about costs because their primary concern is to obtain the best possible medical care in order to maintain the quality of their life, if not life itself; frequently require immediate medical attention; normally rely on the judgment of a physician concerning what composition of services to receive and pay for — a judgment that may not always be unbiased; and typically lack the time and information with which to compare the costs and effectiveness of the different providers and, in fact, may be loath even to raise the crass issue of cost with the provider for fear of offending and/or inviting the retribution of lower-quality care. In consequence, the pressure to adopt less expensive ways of providing medical care does not emerge from careful consideration of alternatives, but from the drying up of the till, i.e., the exhaustion of the private assets of the patient, or an increasing reluctance by society to continue to be taxed to support medical care programs containing few apparent controls on their growth.

The reluctance of the consumer to compel cost-consciousness by medical providers is partly offset by the cost-consciousness of large private health insurers who apparently are not as ashamed as the consumer to seek ways of reducing costs. The growing number of prepaid group health plans is another sphere where strong motivation exists to restrain medical costs.

Despite the lack of competitive dynamism in the health care industry, ways are being found to tilt the composition of medical services toward those which are less expensive. Examples include use of generic instead of brand-name drugs; less frequent use of X-rays; greater use of nursing homes as a substitute for hospital care; limiting hospital stays; and provision of home health and other in-home services.

MIXED STRATEGIES. As previously observed, any proposal to limit medical costs must either reduce the amount of services provided, curtail the cost per service, or change the composition of the services provided. Particular cost-containment methods may, however, combine more than one of these objectives or approaches. Limiting the availability of funds for medical care, for example, may not only serve to restrain costs but also stimulate the search for more effective ways of providing medical care, either through technological change or by the substitution of less expensive services for those currently provided.

The use of Health Maintenance Organizations (HMOs) has been strongly recommended as a means of controlling medical costs. Prepaid medical plans provide strong incentives to restrain the costs of medical services. Since the overall HMO budget is fixed, the HMO will try to avoid providing unneeded services, and will seek to reduce the demand for medical care through preventive medicine. In addition, HMOs will search for and adopt whatever means seem likely to lower the unit costs of services. For example, use of a central laboratory can reduce, through economies of scale, the cost of laboratory tests. Centralized record keeping and billing can lessen the amount of time spent on these activities by practicing physicians. Finally, HMOs can generally tilt the composition of their services toward those which are equally effective but less expensive.

The capitation method of paying for medical care, used in England, pays the physician a flat fee for each person on his or her registry in exchange for meeting all the general medical practice needs of those persons. It has some of the characteristics of HMOs and is justified by the same arguments.

There are some other interesting approaches to limiting medical costs. In West Germany, as previously mentioned, fee schedules are negotiated between insurance funds and the County Association of Insurance Doctors in an effort to limit the unit costs of medical services (Stone, 1979). The recent strong push to prevent Medicare and Medicaid fraud and abuse in the United States serves the multiple purposes of reducing the demand for unneeded services, limiting the cost per service when deemed excessive, and even eliminating some charges for which no service was provided. Utilization review, as practiced by PSROs, seeks to identify instances where inappropriate medical services were provided and to lay the groundwork for minimizing the future provision of inappropriate services.

EFFECTS OF SOCIAL SERVICES
ON MEDICAL COSTS

Medical care is usually conceived of as consisting only of those services provided by, or supervised by, a licensed medical practitioner, such as a medical doctor or nurse. Thus, the services of a chiropractor may not be considered a form of medical care. Nevertheless, a condition of poor health will often create the need for services other than those generally regarded as purely medical. Examples of these other services include income support, personal and family counseling, information and referral, legal assistance, attendant care, help in obtaining meals, chore services, transportation, recreational opportunities, and so on. These services are often categorized and labeled as "social services" (although income support is usually made a separate category). The important point here is that the "social services" are a critical component in the total package of services often needed by a person who suffers poor health.

There are several ways in which the social services affect the delivery of health care services:

The social services may serve as a *substitute* for medical services, i.e., the provision of the social service will reduce the need for medical services. In some cases, the distinction between a social service and a medical service is only a matter of which provider or facility rendered the service, not the nature of the service itself.[8] If a special diet is prescribed by a physician, then it is usually described as medical care; but if prescribed by a dietitian, it may be listed as a social service. Basic room and board will be described as a medical service if provided in a hospital or nursing home, but as a social service if provided in a board-and-care home exercising a modicum of supervision.

In other cases, the social services may limit the need for medical services even though the type of social service provided bears little resemblance to the types of medical services that are thereby displaced. Several examples come to mind.

People — particularly those who are older and/or disabled — may exhibit signs of emotional illness and develop real or imagined physical complaints when they find themselves unable to cope with such personal problems as the inability to find a suitable job, dissatisfaction at their present job, worries about relationships with spouse or children, grief over the death of a close relative or friend, etc. Provision of social services to assist people to cope with these problems often has the beneficial effect of reducing the accompanying emotional or physical complaints.

Persons recovering from an illness or injury often require social services to come to grips with impaired functioning and performance of the normal activities of daily living. Some may not have a home to which to return from the hospital. Assistance in locating suitable housing will reduce the length of time that may be inappropriately spent in a hospital for the lack of an alternative. And if, as often happens, the person faces a lengthy period of convalescence, then helping to locate a suitable facility offering less intensive care than the hospital, or making arrangements for in-home assistance, becomes necessary. The provision of housekeeping services, daily meals, income support, and other in-home services is increasingly viewed as the way to avoid overly restrictive care in nursing homes, only one step removed from the institutional environment of hospitals.

The social services may also be a *complement* to medical services; i.e., the nature of the medical problem may be such that successful medical attention will lead to an increase in the need for social services.[9] Successful medical treatment may lead to such social service needs as counseling to assist the person to adjust to restored community living; vocational rehabilitation; help in locating suitable housing; and chore services to assist home-bound persons to live as independently as possible.

The need for continuing social services will usually be greater for persons suffering chronic in contrast to acute health problems and for conditions that require a long convalescence as compared to those for which recovery is rapid. In some cases, the need for social services will be far greater than the initial need for medical services, particularly if there remains a permanent physical or medical impairment that necessitates long-term supportive care (e.g., saving the life of an accident victim who has suffered extensive brain damage).

A social service can simultaneously act as both a complement and a substitute for medical services. Thus, assisting a hospital patient to find a suitable residential living arrangement may, at one and the same time, shorten the length of hospital stay (substitute) and be a necessary consequence of successful medical treatment (complement).

Because the social services are an essential component of the care of so many persons with conditions that require medical treatment, it follows that the total cost associated with the proper care of persons in poor physical or mental health is more inclusive than medical costs alone. Suppose that we expand the original formulation of the cost of medical care to encompass all of the medical and social services costs of treating conditions requiring some level of medical care. In symbols:

$$K = p_1 q_1 + p_2 q_2 + \ldots + p_n q_n + r_1 s_1 + r_2 s_2 + \ldots + r_n s_n$$

where:

K refers both to the cost of medical services (C) and the cost of the social services arising from a specific medical condition; s_i refers to the amount of a specific social service provided; r_i refers to the price per unit of the social service, and p_i and q_i are defined as before. K, in effect, is the total treatment cost of a specific health problem.

Because the social services are both substitutes and complements to medical services, it follows that policies which effect medical costs may also have unforeseen and sometimes undesirable effects on the costs of the social services, and vice versa. Consider the implementation of policies designed to restrain medical care costs. In some cases, such policies may reduce both medical and social services costs (e.g., if prevention limits the prevalence of severe physical or mental conditions). In other cases, the medical-cost-containment policy may have no effect on social services costs (e.g., if unnecessary medical procedures are curtailed, or the composition of medical services is altered without affecting their quality).

Suppose medical services are constrained by limiting the price that can be charged for them. If this is accomplished without causing adverse effects to patients, the only result will be less money being paid to medical practitioners — presumably a net social benefit, although the benefit is primarily one of redistributing income from the medical profession to the general public. But suppose that compulsory price constraints induces some medical practitioners to limit the quantity of their services.[10] Or suppose the quantity of medical services provided are limited by a reduction in the supply of these services. What are the likely consequences? Several possibilities can be envisioned.

Some medical services may have been unnecessary to begin with, and possibly these will be the services that are curtailed. We suspect, however, that any large decline in medical services will either increase the demand for substitute social services, or will cause some portion of the legitimate need for medical care to go unmet. Instances come to mind where the social services could replace medical care with either a neutral or a harmful effect. In some cases persons with psychiatric problems may turn to a social worker for counseling and the net effect on mental health will be neutral or even beneficial. A harmful effect may result if aged persons with significant medical needs are forced to subsist in a board-and-care home when they require the more intensive care offered by a nursing home.[11]

The major concern, of course, is that the social services substituted for medical care will prove less effective than the replaced medical services. Public decisions to achieve cost-containment goals are not apt to be very sensitive to the subtleties of appropriate and inappropriate substitution. Generally, legislative decisions take the form simply of reducing the supply of medical personnel below some level, or of "capping" the publicly financed health insurance programs. It is for "others" to figure out how to live within these restraints.

The converse, i.e., the substitution of medical for social services, can also happen, and in fact is more likely to occur given the existing structure of public programs. Public programs represent a large portion of K, and are set up so that those which fund medical services are usually open-ended while those which fund the social services are usually "capped." The simplest way to restrain overall public spending is to limit the growth of the "capped" social services programs. The inevitable effect of doing so, however, will be to increase the demand for medical services in order to replace the unavailable social services, thus driving up the total cost of medical services and replacing social services with medical services which are frequently less suitable. Many examples of this kind of substitution exist.

Sometimes the shortage of nursing home beds, particularly in intermediate care facilities, is cited as a cause for excessive lengths of hospital stays. Termed "administrative days" in the Medicaid vernacular, these excessive days in the hospital are defined as time spent in an acute hospital by patients who no longer need acute care but are awaiting placement into a nursing home. Wiener (1979) reported that the number of "administrative days" in Massachusetts had increased two and one-half times since 1975.[12] Interestingly, his investigation disclosed that the number of administrative days of hospitalization was more closely associated with the number of acute hospital bed vacancies than the unavailability of nursing home beds, supporting those who argue that supply creates its own demand in medical care facilities and, therefore, reducing the supply of such facilities to some level publicly decided as adequate will prove cost-beneficial.

COST CONTAINMENT RECONSIDERED

The ultimate social goal of medical care is the maintenance of as high a level of good health and social adjustment as possible within a given budget constraint. The budget constraint itself can be considered a variable that can be expanded if it is believed that the resultant improvement in people's health warrants the use of additional resources, or contracted if it is believed that the resources saved are more valuable than any diminution in health that may occur.

Within a given budget, services should always be delivered in the most efficient manner. Thus, unnecessary services should be curtailed and less expensive services utilized in preference to more expensive ones when quality remains unaffected, or when the gain in the quality of the services is not worth the additional costs. It should be emphasized that the goal of cost containment does not necessarily mean that costs should be minimized, but rather that costs should be restrained by eliminating unneeded services and by operating at maximum efficiency.

Good health, and what is equally important, good social adjustment, are achieved by provision of a variety of medical and social services—often jointly essential, although within limits they can be substituted for one another. From a social standpoint, cost containment should not be narrowly construed as referring to one narrow segment of these services. Such a policy is self-defeating if the restraint, for example, is placed on social services programs and causes an increase in the demand for even more expensive and less appropriate medical services.

Accordingly, cost-containment policies should be broadly viewed so that the cost variable being measured is the total cost of maintaining good health and good social adjustment in persons suffering acute and chronic conditions. Ironically, considerable savings in medical costs may be gained by pursuing a more generous funding policy with respect to social services programs.

We believe that an imbalance now exists in the relative availability of medical as compared to social services. What is more, the spending trend is toward an even greater imbalance. If current trends persist, as we have pointed out, the social services share of the 1985 federal budget for all health and social services will drop to 5 percent, while the share of acute inpatient hospitals will increase to 65 percent. Just to maintain the relative shares of these competing programs at the 1976 level, it would be necessary to adopt coordinated policies that substantially accelerate spending for appropriate substitutes for inpatient care of the increasing number of chronically ill persons in the population, while limiting the growth of inpatient expenditures.

Since the age composition of the U.S. population is shifting toward the elderly at the same time that the total population is increasing, it is probably unrealistic to aim for the 1976 relative shares among the program sectors as normative. However, the line should be held as much as possible against high growth rates for hospital spending in favor of higher growth rates for the social services. We believe that the current direction of growth in these sectors is wrong, and that the trends must somehow be reversed in order for people to stay out of, or limit their stay in, institutional settings of every variety — acute care hospitals, mental institutions, nursing homes, and the like.

Voluntary cost containment, if taken seriously, should increase the demand by hospitals for reliable information about what kinds of patients are likely, prior to discharge, to need extensive planning for provision of social services if they are to make a successful transition to living at home as independently as possible. This information should include what difficulties the patient and/or family had experienced in coping with living conditions prior to hospitalization, as well as how the patient's current illness and convalescence may affect that adjustment. Hospitals will also want to accumulate information about the efficacy of the surrounding social agencies in helping patients with different conditions and varying levels of functioning to readjust successfully to life upon discharge from the hospital.

Systematic rather than "hit-or-miss" methods of gathering these kinds of information will be necessary, including investment in hospital social service information and accountability systems (Volland and German, 1979). When coupled with efforts throughout the entire hospital to identify and make changes that might reduce costs (and actually documenting and verifying the results of cost-saving projects), there is reason to believe that voluntary hospital-cost-containment efforts will succeed (Solomon, 1979). If the Reagan Administration's proposed deregulation of the health care industry does indeed lead to greater competition among hospitals, they may have incentive to develop *hospital-based* management information systems capable of tracking the effectiveness of cost-savings projects and the impact of social services interventions on behalf of specific classes of patients. But if no greater competition than now exists among hospitals emerges, the outlook is bleak. Hospital prices, like those for oil, seem likely to rise unrestrained by anything other than what the market will bear.

REFERENCES

American Hospital Association. 1981 *National hospital panel survey report.* Chicago.
Deputy Assistant Secretary for Planning and Evaluation. September 1, 1978. *Interim report of the task force on deinstitutionalization of the mentally disabled — decision*

memorandum. Unpublished memorandum to the Secretary of the Department of Health, Education, and Welfare.

Linden versus *King* (D. Mass.; CA No. 79-862-T).

Marshall, J., and Funch, D. 1979. Mental illness and the economy: a critique and partial replication. *Journal of Health and Social Behavior* 20:282–89.

Ninety-sixth Congress, U.S. Senate. March 1, 1979. S. 505, to provide for the reform of the administrative and reimbursement procedures currently employed under the Medicare and Medicaid programs, and for other purposes. Washington, D.C.

Pflanz, M., and Geissler, U. 1977. Rapid cost expansion in health care system of the Federal Republic of Germany. *Preventive Medicine* 6:290–301.

President of the United States. 1978. *Economic report of the President.* Washington, D.C.

Rosenthal, G. 1978. Controlling the cost of health care. In M. Zubkoff, I. Raskin, and R. Hanft, eds., *Hospital cost containment.* New York: Prodist.

Smith, R. 1979. Carter attempt to limit doctor supply faces tough going in Congress. *Science* 203:630–32.

Solomon, S. June 18, 1979. How one hospital broke its inflation fever. *Fortune.* Pp. 148–54.

Stone, D. 1979. Health care cost containment in West Germany. *Journal of Health Politics, Policy and Law* 4:176–99.

U.S. Department of Commerce, Bureau of Census. 1978. *Statistical abstract of the U.S.* Washington, D.C.

U.S. Department of Health and Human Services. 1981. *The fiscal year 1982 revised budget.* Washington, D.C.

U.S. House of Representatives. 1979. *Hospital Cost Containment Act of 1979: Report of the Committee on Ways and Means on H.R. 2626.* Washington, D.C.

U.S. Senate, Committee on Finance. 1979. *Background materials relating to S. 505 and other health care cost containment proposals.* Washington, D.C.

Volland, P., and German, P. 1979. Development of an information system: a means for improving social work practice in health care. *American Journal of Public Health* 69:335–39.

Wiener, J. July 3, 1979. *Draft long term care component, state health plan II.* Unpublished memorandum to Long Term Care Subcommittee, Health Policy Group, Commonwealth of Massachusetts.

NOTES

1. Established in 1883 by Bismarck, the national health insurance system in West Germany is the world's oldest scheme.

2. Under prevailing cost-based reimbursement methods, hospitals are alleged to have little incentive to control their costs, since any increases can be passed along to third-party payers — private insurance carriers, Medicare, and Medicaid. In fact, the opposite incentive may be felt because of the lack of effective limits on what costs can be recognized as "reasonable."

3. The administration's bill would have exempted hospitals if they were within a state with an approved mandatory cost-control program, or if they were presumed to have effective cost-control mechanisms in place (e.g., 75 percent of their patients are members of a federally qualified HMO), or if they were presumed to meet a special need (e.g., small nonmetropolitan hospitals with 4,000 or fewer admissions per year). By these criteria, less than 50 percent of the 5,776 community hospitals in the United States and roughly 50 percent of total hospital expenditures would have

been exempt from mandatory controls (U.S. Senate, 1979). No comparable estimate is available on the possible impact of exemptions allowed by the Talmadge-Dole bill.

4. The language describing how this calculation would be made is ambiguous.

5. The drafters of the administration's proposal were sensitive to the inadequacy of the measure of hospital efficiency that they had adopted. They explicitly recognized that "total costs per admission," if reflective of the types of patients and conditions cared for, would be a better gauge of relative efficiency than "routine costs per day," and hoped to shift to a better measure in future years as improvements were made in the classification methods of accounting scheme on which the cost-containment program was to have been based (U.S. Senate, 1979, p. 33).

6. The 1985 fiscal year total for the four program sectors was estimated by projecting the 1974–76 compound growth rates for each of the sector components during the 1979–85 period, and totaling them.

7. There is considerable controversy about how the laws of economics work in medicine. Existing data on how physicians respond to varying levels of demand are ambiguous. According to some economists, limiting the number of physicians would cause health care costs to decline because physicians are thought to generate patient demand in order to maintain or increase income. Other economists argue that this will not happen because fees — at least for general practitioners and general surgeons — are actually lower or the same where physician density is higher and correction is made for the higher living costs of these areas of the country. Furthermore, physicians in these areas tend to shorten their working hours, despite higher fees, and to show lower overall earnings. Thus, unless physicians increase their working hours as part of the response to a cutback on their numbers, fees are unlikely to change much (Smith, 1979).

Actually, we are probably faced with a multidimensional, nonlinear model of medical supply and demand. One way to reconcile the prevailing theories is to note that if an excess supply of medical facilities and personnel exists, the provider reaction — given the indeterminate nature of the market for medical services — may well be to stimulate demand artificially without raising prices for specific services. If the supply of medical services is reduced, providers may respond by limiting the provision of unnecessary care without raising the costs of services. Eventually, however, the unnecessary services will be eliminated. Providers at that point are certain to ration medical care by raising their prices.

8. When provided by agencies or programs whose mission is the delivery of health care, the costs of providing these ambiguous services appear in the national health budget. When delivered by social service agencies or programs to persons who are also receiving medical care — perhaps even at the expense of the social service agency or program — the costs of providing these same services appear in the national social services budget.

9. In economics, "substitute goods" refers to those goods which provide similar service, causing the consumption of one good to decline when the consumption of the "substitute good" increases (e.g., wood, coal, and oil; fish, chicken, and beef; public versus private transportation, etc.). "Complementary goods" are those which collectively provide a product to the consumer such that an increase in the consumption of one good leads to an increase in the consumption of its complements (e.g., razors and razor blades; popcorn and salt; automobiles and gasoline, etc.).

10. In the long run, fewer persons may seek medical training and thereby reduce the supply and provision of medical services in the more distant future.

11. Here we should note that strong sentiment exists at the present time for moving many aged and physically and mentally disabled persons out of nursing homes

into less restrictive nonmedical settings. In Massachusetts, the aged and physically and mentally disabled residents of Medicaid-certified intermediate care facilities throughout the state are suing state authorities in a class action for placement in less restrictive care settings. See *Linden* versus *King* (D. Mass.; CA No. 79-862-T).

12. For corroborative evidence relating to mental hospitalization, see Marshall and Funch (1979).

11

NATIONAL AND STATE
HEALTH INSURANCE

Milton I. Roemer

Organized programs to finance and provide health services, like the field of social work, originated in efforts to help the poor. From the city-state doctors of ancient Greece to the hospitals of the medieval Christian Church to the Poor Law doctors of early-nineteenth-century Europe to the public assistance medical care programs of current times, social efforts were directed mainly toward treating the sick who were poor and homeless (Goldmann, 1945).

For the self-supporting, organized actions to assure medical care when needed have also been taken for centuries, but the mechanisms have differed. The principal strategy has been for groups of people to make periodic payments into a fund, from which money could be withdrawn to help a member of the group at a future time of sickness. Starting in Europe on a self-help basis in the early years of the Industrial Revolution, this "voluntary health insurance" among working-class families has evolved through many stages toward statutory programs that offer health care protection to whole national populations (Frankel and Dawson, 1911).

EARLY DEVELOPMENTS IN U.S. VOLUNTARY
HEALTH INSURANCE

In America, as in Europe, insurance for medical care started in the nineteenth century as a mechanism for supporting the costs of treatment (as well as the replacement of wage loss during sickness) in working populations. The early need was most prominent in isolated industries—at mines, lumbering camps, railroad construction sites—where local doctors and hospitals did not exist. In order to assure that medical care was available to the workers and their families, local management would deduct small amounts from each month's wages to establish a sickness fund; sometimes employers would also contribute. From this fund, the salary of a doctor and perhaps a nurse and other personnel would be paid. Where large groups of workers were concentrated, a hospital might be built and financed.

These health insurance plans in isolated industries affected only a small fraction of the American population. In certain large cities, somewhat equivalent insurance plans were organized by fraternal lodges composed mainly of European immigrants, but these also involved relatively few people and typically paid only for limited doctor's care. In the early twentieth century, some private insurance companies began to sell individual (not group) policies that insured against income loss, and some medical care costs, due to sickness or accident (Follman, 1963).

Not until the Great Depression starting in 1929, however, did the insurance idea become developed in a major way to meet health care costs in America. The initiative at this time was taken, not by workers, but by hospitals, which found themselves half empty because patients could not afford the charges. A mechanism, initiated quietly by individual hospitals in Dallas, New Orleans, and Philadelphia, suddenly appeared attractive; these hospitals sold low-cost insurance to employee groups to cover future hospitalization costs. In New Jersey, several hospitals joined together to form a nonprofit corporation to market such insurance. By 1934, the idea had become so widely accepted that it was endorsed by the American Hospital Association; a set of standards was issued for these "hospital insurance" plans, and the movement adopted a symbol: the Blue Cross (Goldmann, 1948).

In spite of initial opposition by the medical profession (as "socialized medicine"), by 1939 these views changed, and in California the state medical association organized a similar nonprofit insurance plan to pay doctor bills during hospitalized illness. The California Physicians Service concept soon spread to other states, and in 1946 the American Medical Association endorsed the movement, symbolizing state plans with the Blue Shield emblem (Somers and Somers, 1961). In both Blue Cross and Blue Shield plans, the insurance fund would pay the hospital or doctor directly for the service, so that the patient had no financial obligation at the time of sickness; hence, they were considered "service plans."

Observing the success and the financial feasibility of these nonprofit programs, in the 1940s and especially after World War II, the commercial insurance industry set out to market similar group insurance for hospitalization and hospital-related medical care. Since many insurance companies were already selling policies for pensions or disability cash benefits to groups of industrial workers, they made rapid progress in selling this new form of group insurance for health care. Commercial insurance companies had the further advantage of selling indemnity policies, in contrast to the "service plans" sponsored by providers. Thus, the insurance company would indemnify the patient for fixed amounts for various hospital or medical services; if the actual charges were higher, the patient would have to pay the difference (Dickerson, 1963). This enabled these carriers to keep insurance premiums relatively stable, when hospital and medical charges were rising. Moreover—unlike the "Blue" plans, which charged the same premium to all population groups (so-called community rating)—the insurance companies engaged in "experience rating," which yielded lower premiums for lower-risk groups, thereby attracting their patronage (Health Insurance Institute, 1978). Higher-risk demographic groups were left for the nonprofit plans to enroll.

Thus, although starting much later than the voluntary health insurance plans sponsored by workers or their employers, the "Blue" plans started by health care providers and the plans sponsored by commercial insurance companies soon came to dominate the field. By 1960, a solid majority of the American population was enrolled in insurance programs that protected for all or most of the costs of hospitalization. The largest share of insured people were in commercially sponsored programs, followed by those in the provider-sponsored "Blue" plans, with only a small fraction enrolled in the pioneer consumer-sponsored plans (Health Insurance Institute, 1978).

The consumer-sponsored or "independent" plans typically provided more comprehensive health services, delivering ambulatory care through group practice clinics (such as the Kaiser-Permanente Medical Care Program in California or the Health Insurance Plan of Greater New York); although members of these "prepaid group practice" plans were entitled to more services per insurance dollar, the programs constituted a deviation from traditional medical custom, and their rate of growth was relatively slow (Reed, Henderson, and Hanft, 1966; MacColl, 1966).

About 1950, the commercial carriers launched a new idea that enabled them to offer benefits much more comprehensive than hospitalization, while still not organizing group clinics along the lines of the consumer-sponsored plans. This was the "major medical expense" policy — providing indemnification for a wide range of medical and related services, often including drugs and certain types of dental care as well as overall physician services, once the benefits of "basic hospital and inpatient medical insurance" were exhausted and the individual had incurred personal expenses of a stated amount (such as $100 or $500). At this point the insurance indemnifies for 80 percent of any approved health care expenditure. The major medical expense concept was soon adopted by the "Blue" plans, as well. It has grown rapidly (covering 148 million people in 1976), as a response to the criticism of the strong focus on hospitalized services in the programs of both commercial and provider sponsorship (Health Insurance Institute, 1978). Yet these policies do nothing to change or disturb the prevailing patterns of private medical or hospital care. Another response, also designed to maintain conventional delivery patterns, came from certain county medical societies, which organized "medical care foundations" offering insurance for comprehensive physician's care through individual practitioners.

In spite of the general success of the overall voluntary insurance movement in protecting people against the high costs of hospitalized sickness and catastrophic expenses for other types of medical care, there were certain important gaps in their coverage. Enrollment was substantially weaker among lower-income groups, among rural people, and among the aged. Persons past 65 years of age, in fact, were an important share of the other two population categories as well. On retirement, their insurance protection would ordinarily lapse — just at the period in life when, with more chronic disease, medical needs were usually greatest.

In 1957, therefore, a movement was started to fill this important gap in voluntary health insurance coverage, through mandatory national legislation (Corning, 1969). Representative Forand introduced in the U.S. Congress an amendment to the Social Security Act that would provide for pensioners not only monthly cash benefits, but also payment of the costs of hospitalization.

THE GOVERNMENT HEALTH INSURANCE MOVEMENT

Before discussing the enactment of statutory national health insurance for the aged, occurring in 1965, we should realize that this was not the first entry of American government into the health insurance field.

As far back as 1798, the launching of a network of marine hospitals at the young nation's major ports was financed by mandatory deductions from the wages of merchant seamen, under a law introduced by Alexander Hamilton (Straus, 1950). This limited social insurance program for medical care did not spread to cover other occupational groups, perhaps because, as we have seen, later actions were taken on a voluntary basis (in isolated industries, etc.). Moreover, reflecting changes in the position of workers and the general political scene in America, in the 1880s the seamen's wage deductions were replaced by a tonnage tax on shipowners, and in 1912 the Marine Hospital Service was converted to the U.S. Public Health Service, supported completely by general revenues.

In 1910, following the example of Europe, the first action was taken by a state government, that of New York, to mandate insurance of industrial workers against the costs of work-connected injuries—both in compensation for wage loss and for medical care (Somers, 1954). Although this initial law was declared unconstitutional by the New York courts, the judicial decision was soon reversed, and gradually all states (the last being Mississippi in 1952) enacted such worker's compensation laws. Over the years these laws have gradually been extended in the types and numbers of workers protected and the range of medical services provided (now typically covering occupational diseases as well as injuries) (Skolnik and Price, 1970).

By 1915, parallel efforts were made in about a dozen states to extend the workmen's compensation idea to provide health care insurance for all injuries or sickness in workers, whether job-connected or not. In a few states, such legislation came close to passage, but it was not enacted in any. The principles embodies in these bills were much like the original German legislation—applying only to low-income workers and requiring them to be enrolled in some existing insurance program or, if lacking, in a government-sponsored fund (Millis and Montgomery, 1938).

By 1920 World War I was over, and a conservative period set in. The social insurance idea was dropped, and the only significant health legislation enacted was the Sheppard-Towner Act of 1921, providing federal grants to the states for preventive maternal and child health clinics; even these were terminated in 1929 (Mustard, 1945). With the onset of the Great Depression, problems of unmet need for medical care became prominent again; when the Social Security Act became law in 1935, however, its health provisions were limited to grants-in-aid to the states for public health purposes. Even Title 1 on public assistance for the needy required "cash

grants" to the individual, so that these funds could not be used for organization of medical care programs by state governments even for the poor.
President Roosevelt had considered a health insurance provision in the law,
but decided against it, for fear that opposition to it would jeopardize the
passage of the whole act (with old-age insurance, unemployment compensation, etc.) (Schottland, 1963).

In July 1939, however, Senator Wagner, sponsor of the Social Security
Act, set out to fill the gap by introducing the first National Health Bill with
health insurance objectives. This legislation would have offered grants to
the states to assist them in developing state health insurance programs,
presumably along the lines of the earlier 1915–20 proposals. A few months
later, however, World War II broke out, and all social legislation was put
aside to pursue the war effort (Harris, 1966).

In the midst of World War II, "postwar planning" was launched in
several fields. The Beveridge Report, *Social Insurance and Allied Services,*
came out of Great Britain in 1942, laying the groundwork for the British
National Health Service, which was indeed enacted in 1946 (Beveridge,
1942). Similarly, in 1943 a new National Health Bill was introduced in
Congress by Senator Wagner along with Senator Murray and Representative Dingell. While this bill called for federal subsidy of hospital construction, expanded support for medical research, and other actions, its clearly
most controversial feature was its provision for a nationwide program of
mandatory health insurance covering all wage-earners and dependents (but
not self-employed), through a central social security fund (i.e., not using
grants to the states) (Falk, 1951).

The Wagner-Murray-Dingell Bill generated a storm of opposition from
the medical profession and private insurance industry, and went through
several amended versions over the next 15 years. Although the omnibus bill
did not pass, the sections on hospital construction subsidy (the Hill-Burton
Act of 1946), medical research, and other parts were enacted separately.
Also, and quite important, the national debate over this legislation served
as a strong stimulus to the growth of voluntary health insurance, reviewed
above. With the selection of a Republican administration (under President
Eisenhower) in 1952, the postwar campaign for comprehensive national
health insurance (NHI) came to an end. A few years later, the issue became
narrowed down to health insurance protection of the aged, as noted above
(Harris, 1966).

For eight years after Congressman Forand introduced his 1957 bill,
which would have added hospitalization benefits to Social Security old-age
pensions, there was national debate on this issue. The same bitter opposition as had confronted the Wagner-Murray-Dingell NHI Bill was directed
against social insurance for hospital (and later medical) care of the aged.
Voluntary health insurance plans improved their offerings to permit
coverage of workers (usually at higher rates) after retirement. The
American Medical Association spent millions on a campaign of opposition
to "Medicare" (as the newspapers had come to label the proposed legislation) as "the beginning of socialized medicine." Nevertheless, in July 1965,
the Social Security Act was amended by addition of Title 18, which

established a national system of payment for medical and hospital services for nearly every American 65 years and over (Feingold, 1966).

MEDICARE AND AFTER

As applies to most controversial legislation, the Medicare amendments to the Social Security Act embody many compromises. While the funds are raised through a nationwide Social Security tax on virtually all workers, employers, and self-employed persons, reimbursements for services are made through scores of "fiscal intermediaries"—essentially existing private health insurance plans, both nonprofit and commercial—throughout the country. These agents of the government carry no risks and simply process the payment of medical, hospital, and related bills on behalf of the government; yet they are vested with responsibility to monitor the program and make certain that the services rendered and paid for are "medically necessary" (Myers, 1970).

Although the Medicare law accepts existing patterns of health care delivery with fee-for-service remuneration, it establishes no schedule of fees. It simply authorizes reimbursement of hospitals for all "reasonable costs" and payment to doctors of "customary and prevailing" charges in the community. With such open-ended authorizations, it was inevitable that the costs of medical care would rise sharply soon after 1965. Several investigations of the performance of fiscal intermediaries by the U.S. General Accounting Office (GAO) showed extreme laxness in the way that they carried these responsibilities. Little was done by them to control unnecessary hospitalization or excessive length of stay of Medicare patients. Even less was done to monitor the services of doctors (U.S. General Accounting Office, 1972).

The law itself incorporates various copayments and deductibles, payable by the patient. Approximately the cost of the first day of hospitalization is a deductible (i.e., it must be paid by the patient), and for medical and related services the patient must pay the first $60 of expenses incurred each year. After this, the patient must pay 20 percent of all acceptable charges. Moreover, the doctor may decide whether he will "accept assignment" (which means direct payment to him by the intermediary of 80 percent of customary and prevailing charges) or not. If he does not accept assignment—the policy of the great majority of doctors at present—he may charge the patient whatever he wishes, but the patient may seek reimbursement from the intermediary only for 80 percent of the "prevailing and customary charge" for the specific service (Myers, 1970).

On the brighter side, socially speaking, the Medicare law includes certain measures intended to promote quality and economy in the care of the aged. Each participating hospital must have resources and policies that meet minimum standards. Among these is a "utilization review" mechanism, designed to monitor the propriety of admissions and durations of hospital stay. When this process was found to be of little effectiveness, in 1972 it was tightened up through establishment of a nationwide network of Professional Standards Review Organizations (PSROs) on a regional basis

(Roemer, 1975). In addition to financing hospitalization, Medicare pays for service in skilled nursing homes, and also for care by home health agencies. There are limits to all these services, but the intention is clearly to encourage use of less expensive care for long-term patients, when appropriate.

Also, soon after enactment of Medicare, Congress legislated the Regional Medical Programs (RMP) for control of heart disease, cancer, and stroke — the major causes of death in the nation, especially among the aged. These RMP grants were designed to improve the *quality* of medical care provided, just as Medicare would increase people's access to care. Then in 1966, legislation to provide federal grants to set up local agencies for "comprehensive health planning" (CHP) of all health services was another logical sequel to the 1965 laws for expanded economic support of health services.

While Medicare, and its companion legislation on Medicaid (general revenue assistance) for the poor of all age levels, doubtless helped many people, they both contributed to the spiraling of medical care costs in America. At the same time, they brought into sharp relief the inadequacies of the whole voluntary health insurance movement for millions of people who were still not covered, and also the far-from-complete scope of benefits for even those who had some hospitalization insurance. In 1969, the White House issued a statement saying: "This nation is faced with a breakdown in the delivery of health care unless immediate concerted action is taken by government and the private sector." Soon every journalist was speaking of the national "health care crisis" (American Assembly, 1970).

As a result, in 1970, hardly five years after the enactment of Medicare, the campaign for NHI legislation, which had been lost in the 1940s, was resumed again. Senator Edward Kennedy made the first move by introducing in August 1970 the Health Security Bill — a sweeping social insurance measure that would cover virtually the entire U.S. population and provide complete financial support (with no cost sharing) for a very comprehensive scope of health services (Committee for National Health Insurance, 1970).

NATIONAL HEALTH INSURANCE PROPOSALS

Within a few months of the Kennedy action, several additional health insurance bills were introduced in Congress. Soon, interest groups at almost every point on the political spectrum were sponsoring NHI bills — the insurance industry, the American Medical Association, the American Hospital Association, the labor movement, and others. By 1975 there were at least 20 bills before the U.S. Congress which would legislate some form of nationwide insurance for medical care (U.S. House of Representatives, 1976).

In this panoply of NHI bills, the details of population coverage, scope of benefits, mode of financing, methods of administration, and patterns of health care delivery were of a bewildering diversity. Moreover, with each session of Congress since 1970, several features of each bill have undergone modification. To attempt analysis of even the main provisions of all these proposed NHI bills would be of little value, but it is possible to classify them into five main types.

One type of NHI proposal clings to the principal of voluntary enrollment in the already established private health insurance plans, but would encourage greater enrollment through various forms of subsidy of the premium costs for low-income groups. The commercial insurance industry sponsors a bill of this type, providing for administration by state insurance commissioners, extensive cost sharing, and indemnity benefits in the customary manner of that industry.

A second NHI approach calls for *mandatory* enrollment by self-supporting people in existing insurance plans that meet certain standards. There are several variations on this theme, which resembles the original German social insurance laws launched by Bismarck in the 1880s (Sigerist, 1943). In some of these bills, indigent people would continue to be covered by a separate program, as prevails today; in others, they would become enrolled in the established voluntary plans, with the premiums paid by government. Because of the heavy drain on state revenues of current Medicaid legislation (in which costs are shared roughly 50-50 between federal and state governments), these bills would generally support costs for the needy entirely from federal revenues. This type of bill may encompass self-employed or only employed persons, allowing the self-employed to enroll voluntarily. There are various requirements on cost sharing, but the range of benefits offered in this NHI model tends to be broad.

A third NHI approach applies the Social Security principle of universal or nearly universal population coverage, but with limitation of benefits to very expensive medical services. These "catastrophic health insurance" bills assume that the vast majority of people are or would be covered by private insurance for ordinary medical, hospital, and related services. Only when expenses incurred exceed a certain threshold, such as $2,000 for doctor's care or hospitalization of over 60 days, would the NHI protection take over. At this point, there would typically be copayment of about 20 percent — presumably to control abuse. This approach appeals to many political leaders because it would help the dramatic hardship cases of serious and costly illness, while the costs to the Social Security fund would be relatively small.

The fourth NHI approach is that represented by the 1970 Health Security Bill — universal coverage under social insurance along with a comprehensive range of benefits. This model, originally backed by the organized labor movement, not only would be most far-reaching in its economic support of health services, but would also embody many incentives for modifying traditional patterns of medical care delivery in the United States. Learning an important lesson from the Medicare experience, it would set maximum levels on physician or dentist fees and impose ceilings on hospital costs through budget reviews and employment of prospective or global reimbursement. Moreover, it would offer inducements to both consumers and providers of health care to affiliate with programs which depart from conventional fee-for-service practices. The best-known of these are the Health Maintenance Organizations, to be discussed below. Other features of the Health Security Bill involve support for training needed health personnel, integration with local health planning, consumer participation in program administration, and an overall system of fund allocations that would promote equitable distribution of all health care resources throughout the nation (Committee for National Health Insurance, 1975).

This most comprehensive category of NHI bill has been criticized as being "too expensive" and inflationary. Such criticism, however, calls for a basic explanation about the nature of health care costs. Health expenditures are derived from both public and private sources. It is the sum of these two, in *both* sectors, that accounts for the billions ($163 billion in 1977) spent for health purposes. To examine spending in the public sector alone is very misleading. In general, public financing of health services is not supplemental; it *replaces* spending in the private sector. Moreover, public spending is usually associated with various controls that can promote prudent economies. Thus, although broad legislation, such as the Health Security Bill, would involve greater public sector expenditures than the other bills, the associated private spending would undoubtedly be reduced, so that the *total* outlay would probably be less than under narrower NHI legislation. It is relevant that in 1977 the United States population spent nearly 9 percent of its gross national product (GNP) on health, without an NHI program; this is much more proportionately than the expenditures of most countries that have such programs (U.S. National Center for Health Statistics, 1978).

Finally, the fifty type of proposal for national social financing of health care is not really insurance, but an approach using general revenue support. This is represented in a bill introduced by Representative Dellums for a "national health service," under which the entire system of health care in the nation would be radically changed (Dellums, 1974). All physicians and other health personnel would become employed by government on salaries and would work in public facilities. Ambulatory care would be provided at health centers, staffed by teams of health personnel, serving the surrounding population. Citizens' councils would be in charge of administration in every local community. Preventive and treatment services would be completely integrated and the scope of both would be comprehensive. While quite unrealistic politically, the introduction of this bill may possibly have been intended to show, by contrast, that even the most far-reaching of the NHI bills are relatively conservative in their acceptance of the basic private practice assumptions of the U.S. health care system. At best, the Dellums proposal has offered a rallying point for critics of the American health care system and perhaps a statement of ultimate goals toward which it might evolve. In the main arena of NHI political debate, however, it has attracted little support.

THE CARTER ADMINISTRATION AND NHI

When a new federal administration was elected in 1976, one might have thought that none of the NHI legislative movement just described had occurred. The Department of Health, Education, and Welfare (DHEW) set to work designing still another NHI bill. After months of planning, four "options" were produced: (1) a "Consumer-Choice Health Plan," (2) a "Target Plan," (3) "Publicly Guaranteed Health Protection," and (4) a "Quasi-Public Corporation" (American Public Health Association, 1978). These policy statements embodied a range of NHI philosophies, although none was so far-reaching as the Kennedy-Corman Health Security Bill. Only the fourth option would offer comprehensive services to the total population, but it would operate under a special nongovernmental authority— presumably with the intention of separating its costs from the official federal budget.

Evidently none of these approaches satisfied President Carter. In April 1978 Senator Kennedy along with the nation's labor leadership came forward with a major modification of the Health Security Bill in an attempt to win White House support (Kennedy, 1978). The compromise proposal would offer essentially the same scope of coverage and benefits as the original bill, but would do this through requiring everyone to join private health insurance plans that offered such benefits. Apparently even this crucial change did not meet the President's specifications, and instead the White House issued a roster of "ten principles" that should be embodied in any NHI legislation (Principles of Carter Health Plan, 1978). Some of these called for the lofty goals of universal coverage and comprehensive benefits, but others concerning implementation specified "no additional federal spending until fiscal year 1982–83," and required that the private insurance industry should have a "significant role" in the operation of the program. Perhaps most important was a requirement that the program be introduced in "phases," but that the implementation of each new phase would depend on the economic experience of the prior phase. Thus, in effect, a rise in costs under the first phase could be grounds for preceeding no farther toward the ultimate goals.

To many who had taken seriously the campaign pledges of the Democratic Party in the 1976 election, the Carter NHI "principles" were regarded as a great retreat. The problem of national *expenditures* for health service was given preeminence over the health needs of the population and everything else. Yet, with one exception, nothing was being done to modify the system of American medical care, which included so many incentives toward maximizing costs.

The exception was the heightened attention given to promoting the expansion of certain local health insurance programs, which do, indeed, offer incentives to economy. It was, in fact, under the previous Republican administration that the Health Maintenance Organization Act had been legislated in late 1973 (U.S. Social Security Administration, 1974). As noted earlier, consumer-sponsored health insurance plans had for decades been furnishing relatively comprehensive health services through teams of personnel organized in group clinics. Since doctors in these clinics were usually paid by salary, rather than fee-for-service, they had no financial incentive to hospitalize patients or prescribe costly diagnostic tests or treatments that were not fully justified; prudent use of hospitals and other secondary services, in fact, could yield savings which could mean higher earnings for the doctor and lower premiums for the plan member (Gumbiner, 1975). It should aso be noted that HMOs, unlike the major types of health insurance program, often provided medical social work services outside of hospitals.

In spite of the demonstrated economies of these plans (often called "health cooperatives" or "prepaid group practice plans"), without sacrifice of health care quality, their rate of growth was slow (Roemer and Shonick, 1973). Not only were they typically opposed by most private doctors, but — with a few exceptions — they did not attract many members, for whom the idea meant a deviation from traditional patterns of getting medical care. Then in February 1971, in a "National Health Strategy" message, President Nixon issued a strong advocacy of this modified pattern of health insurance, giving it a new name: the Health Maintenance Organization or HMO (Nixon, 1971). After extended discussion, a law was enacted in 1973 to put federal support in back of HMO growth, through subsidies for launching new ones and other provisions that would help to expand enrollment in all existent HMOs (Dorsey, 1975).

Soon after enactment of the HMO law, however, opposition from the private medical profession discouraged the Nixon Administration from serious implementation of the program. The funds for subsidies were greatly reduced from the amount authorized by Congress, and the general promotional activities became halfhearted and were obstructed by bureaucratic complexities (Strumpf, Seubold, and Arrill, 1978). In 1977, under the Carter Administration, federal management of the implementation of the HMO law was reorganized and simplified. Greater subsidy funds were appropriated, and the rate of HMO expansion soon accelerated.

Aside from these HMO initiatives, federal action in the health insurance field was meager toward the end of the 1970s. The priority political issues concerned the general energy crisis, unemployment, foreign affairs, and the control of inflation. As part of the latter, attempts were made to limit the escalation of hospital costs (Shabecoff, 1978). In 1979, the prospects for national health insurance of even modest scope generally appeared less bright at the federal level than they had been five years before. In late 1980, with the election of a much more conservative federal administration — committed to reduced social programs and expanded military expenditures — the prospects for any specific NHI legislation in the near future grew even dimmer.

STATE HEALTH INSURANCE ACTIONS

In this atmosphere, it is not surprising that a number of state governments took action to develop health insurance programs on their own. Before describing the state laws of the 1970s, it may be recalled that (aside from workmen's compensation) general health insurance proposals had been made at the state level many years before.

The bills, which would have covered mainly low-income workers and which were introduced in about a dozen state legislatures between 1915 and

1920, have been mentioned earlier. In California, a flurry of state health insurance activity occurred again in the mid-1930s and early 1940s (Sasuly and Roemer, 1966). It was probably the rapid growth of voluntary health insurance programs throughout the country that, more than anything else, accounts for the general lack of further state-level initiatives on health insurance during the 1950s and 1960s. The only related legislation enacted in these years were amendments to state laws regulating general private insurance, which granted special conditions for the operation of nonprofit voluntary health insurance plans (Eilers, 1963).

Another type of state legislation concerning sickness disability, but not medical care, was enacted in the 1940s (Sinai, 1949). Rhode Island in 1943 amended its state Unemployment Compensation Act to pay cash benefits for inability to work due to sickness. Soon after, in 1946, California also enacted a state Temporary Disability Insurance (TDI) law, followed by New Jersey, New York, and then Hawaii and Alaska. A noteworthy amendment to the California TDI law was made in the 1950s, providing that part of the costs of hospitalization of covered workers would be payable for 20 days. In a sense, this was the first venture of a state government into any form of social insurance to finance a segment of general health care for its working population (State of California, 1963).

The state health insurance measures of the 1970s were quite different. In 1974, the state of Maine established a "catastrophic medical expense fund" (financed in part from a tax on cigarettes) to pay for costly medical services required by a state resident not already protectd by some federal program (such as Medicare or Medicaid) (*Perspective,* 1976). To qualify for this "catastrophic insurance," the person must meet three conditions; he must incur medical bills that exceed (a) $1,000, (b) 20 percent of annual income before taxes, and (c) 10 percent of net worth (in cashable assets) over $20,000. It is evident that these restrictions must mean that only a small number of severe hardship cases are helped by the Maine program, but in time it may possibly be broadened.

Connecticut enacted a law that took effect in 1976, which does not mandate coverage of the entire state population, but which requires that all insurance carriers in the state must *offer* insurance protection for a wide range of medical and related services (*Perspective,* 1976). While permitting various deductibles and copayments linked to these benefits, this is the first state law requiring insurance carriers in the state to sell policies paying for specified ranges of comprehensive health care.

Minnesota, after several years of discussion, enacted also in 1976 a state health insurance law that includes features similar to the statutes of both Maine and Connecticut (Frederickson, 1977). It requires all insurance companies in the state to offer health insurance protection, with a minimum range of benefits, to state residents. At the same time, all employers are required to make health insurance available to all their employees. In addition, a state government "catastrophic health expense protection" fund is established to pay for care beyond specified thresholds (which vary with family income, averaging about 50 percent). To control costs, the State Insurance Commissioner is authorized to regulate insurance premiums, and also to establish a hospital rate review system.

In 1977, Rhode Island likewise enacted a Catastrophic Health Insurance Plan, which protects all state residents, to an extent varying with how comprehensively they are insured for basic hospital and medical services through an approved voluntary plan (Keeler, 1977). Thus, if an individual is already insured by a "fully qualified plan," the catastrophic expense protection takes over after personal expenditures of $500 or 10 percent of income, whichever is greater. There are six levels of entitlement, the lowest being for persons lacking any voluntary health insurance coverage, for whom the deductible threshold is $5,000 or 50 percent of income. An unusual feature of the Rhode Island legislation is its administration principally by the State Department of Health.

In 1978, two more states — New York and Alaska — enacted statutes for catastrophic health expense protection. Both laws, however, are dependent on low-income status and very high medical expenses, so that their impact will probably be quite limited (American Medical Association, 1979).

Undoubtedly the broadest health insurance legislation enacted by any state so far is that of Hawaii. Effective in 1975, this law requires that all employers pay at least half the cost of private health insurance, with minimum benefits, for every employee (Hawaii State Health Planning and Development Agency, 1978). The required benefits include overall physician's care (ambulatory as well as inpatient), hospitalization, diagnostic tests, and some other services. Provision of drugs, eyeglasses, and dental care is not required but encouraged. Since nearly all local labor-management contracts include dependents in health insurance "fringe benefits," as well as the primary worker, it is estimated that nearly 100 percent of the Hawaiian population is covered. The largest insurance carrier is the plan sponsored by the private physicians, the Hawaii Medical Service Association (HMSA), which offers much wider benefits than the average Blue Shield plan on the U.S. mainland. In spite of the exceptionally broad benefits, HMSA has substantial copayment requirements — 25 percent — on all services, including hospital care. This may help to explain a remarkably low rate of hospital utilization by the entire island population — about as low under the HMSA program as under the Kaiser Health Plan, the principal HMO in Hawaii (Segal, 1978).

Beyond these seven state health insurance laws, which doubtless emerged from the general atmosphere of NHI debate in the 1970s, several other states, including California, have been discussing the idea. With the example just north of the U.S. border in Canada — where health insurance laws were started in the provinces and then stimulated action at the national level (Andreopoulos, 1975) — health leaders in many states have naturally begun to think along similar lines. Social insurance at the state level, of course, is inevitably constrained by the resources available within each state, and can do nothing to redistribute the whole nation's resources in relation to health needs. Yet the very initiative taken by states — especially when it demonstrates the breadth of scope shown in the Hawaiian law —

may have the effect of hastening national action. It is relevant that almost all the new state laws stipulate that, should a federal NHI program of broader scope became enacted, the state law would be repealed.

TRENDS AND COMMENTARY

From this review of the development of health insurance — voluntary and statutory, national and state — in the United States, what general conclusions may be drawn? It may be helpful to summarize these briefly in observations and forecasts:

1. The general idea of insurance for medical care in America arose among groups of wage-earning workers, as it had arisen previously in Europe, on a voluntary basis.

2. In the strong free-enterprise setting of the New World, however, substantial growth of the health insurance idea came with the sponsorship of programs by providers of care (hospitals and doctors) and commercial middlemen (insurance companies). This sponsorship led to a major emphasis on insurance for high-cost services related to hospitalization.

3. Pressure for a broader scope of services, to include ambulatory care and preventive services, came from consumer groups. These groups, often in collaboration with their employers, organized health insurance plans providing comprehensive prepaid services through group practice clinics. The demonstrated advantages of the latter plans stimulated the larger health insurance programs, under provider or commercial sponsorship, to broaden their scope of benefits.

4. Action by government — except for an isolated early federal program for merchant seamen — was undertaken first in 1910 at the state level. As in nineteenth-century Europe, it was directed initially to compensation for work-connected injuries. An effort to broaden state social insurance to encompass general medical care for workers was soon also launched in many states, but failed.

5. The first national governmental proposal for medical care insurance came with the Great Depression as a sequel to the Social Security Act of 1935. It would also have depended on state actions, encouraged through federal grants-in-aid, but was thwarted by the outbreak of World War II in 1939.

6. As part of postwar planning, the first public proposals for truly *national* health insurance were made in 1943. Although they were not successful, a decade of debate on NHI stimulated robust expansion of voluntary health insurance, particularly among working groups, and often with employer contributions.

7. A major weakness in voluntary health insurance protection was coverage of aged persons, following retirement when medical needs usually increased. This presented a gap which national public insurance could fill, through enactment in 1965 of Medicare for the aged under the Social Security system.

8. Because of weak regulatory controls in Medicare (and its companion Medicaid legislation for the poor), medical care expenditures rose abruptly,

and the access of low- and middle-income groups to health service seemed to worsen. These problems soon generated a renewed campaign for national health insurance to cover *all* population groups.

9. With a wide range of proposals put forward by different interest groups, there was renewed NHI debate throughout the early 1970s. The movement lacked unity, however, and other political issues took precedence, so that by the end of the 1970s no NHI legislation seemed likely to be enacted.

10. Frustrated by the stalemate at the national level, several state governments finally enacted state health insurance programs of limited scope, on their own. The most comprehensive law took effect in the state of Hawaii in 1975, applying the model of mandatory enrollment of all employees in existent private health insurance plans of approved (relatively broad) benefit scope.

11. Meanwhile, the issues of rising health care costs and concern for quality, associated with both voluntary insurance and Medicare, stimulated various corrective actions. Most important was a renewed movement to promote "prepaid group practice" health plans (pioneered decades before by consumer bodies), under the new label of "Health Maintenance Organizations" or HMOs. National legislation in 1973 provided federal subsidies to facilitate the expansion of HMOs.

12. Beyond the HMO movement, health insurance led to other social actions to modify the traditional "laissez-faire" patterns of American health service. The Regional Medical Programs movement, PSROs, local "second surgical opinion" programs, state certificate-of-need requirements for hospital construction, and comprehensive health planning legislation in 1966 and again in 1974 (Rosenfeld and Rosenfeld, 1975), were all indirect outgrowths of the heightened utilization of services brought about by extension of both voluntary and social insurance for health care.

13. Trends over the last century in the United States and other industrialized nations point to the eventual enactment of some form of national health insurance covering all or nearly all of the U.S. population. The political forces at play suggest that such legislation will initially be built upon the infrastructure of voluntary health insurance programs that have evolved and gained strength over the last 50 years.

14. The election in 1981 of a changed and very conservative federal administration reduced greatly the prospects of any specific national health insurance legislation in the near future. The new government's determination to expand military expenditures and reduce the support of nearly all social programs emphasized once again the dependence of NHI actions on prevailing political forces.

15. The limitations and inadequacies of the characteristic American incremental approach to meeting the population's health service needs through health insurance will probably lead to gradual extension of voluntary plan coverage and benefits. In America, as elsewhere, social problems tend to generate their own reforms. In time, health insurance will be recognized for what it has always been—a means to an end, a socioeconomic device to meet health care needs. As this occurs, we will

evolve toward a more rational and effective system of providing health services (Roemer, 1973).

REFERENCES

American Assembly. 1970. *The health of Americans.* New York: Columbia University.

American Medical Association. 1979. Catastrophic health insurance plans. In *State health legislation report* 7:4.

American Public Health Association. May 1978. National health insurance. *Washington News Letter.*

Andreopoulos, S., ed. 1975. *National health insurance: can we learn from Canada?* New York: Wiley.

Beveridge, W. 1942. *Social insurance and allied services.* New York: Macmillan.

Committee for National Health Insurance. July 1970. *Health security program.* Washington, D.C.

──────. January 1975. *Health security program.* Washington, D.C.

Corning, P. A. 1969. *The evolution of medicare: from idea to law.* Washington, D.C.: Social Security Administration.

Dellums, W. 1974. Health rights and community services. *Congressional Record* 120.

Dickerson, O. D. 1963. *Health insurance.* Homewood, Ill.: Irwin.

Dorsey, J. L. 1975. The Health Maintenance Organization Act of 1973 and prepaid group practice plans. *Medical Care* 13:1-9.

Eilers, R. D. 1963. *Regulation of Blue Cross and Blue Shield plans.* Homewood, Ill.: Irwin.

Falk, I. S. 1951. Health services, medical care insurance, and Social Security. *Annals of the American Academy of Political and Social Science* 273:114-121.

Feingold, E. 1966. *Medicare: policies and politics.* San Francisco: Chandler.

Follman, J. F. 1963. *Medical care and health insurance.* Homewood, Ill.: Irwin.

Frederickson, L. R. 1977. The Minnesota Catastrophic Health Expense Protection Act of 1976. In J. Braverman, ed., *State health insurance plans: is anybody listening?* Washington, D.C.: Georgetown University.

Frankel, L. K., and Dawson, M. M. 1911. *Workingmen's insurance in Europe.* New York: Russell Sage.

Goldmann, F. 1945. *Public medical care: principles and problems.* New York: Columbia University.

──────. 1948. *Voluntary medical care insurance.* New York: Columbia University.

Gumbiner, R. 1975. *The Health Maintenance Organization: putting it all together.* St. Louis: Mosby.

Harris, R. 1966. *A sacred trust.* New York: New American Library.

Hawaii State Health Planning and Development Agency. 1978. *State health plan, 1978.* Honolulu.

Health Insurance Institute. 1978. *Source book of health insurance data 1977-78.* Washington.

Keeler, B. E. 1977. The administrative organization of the Rhode Island catastrophic health insurance plan. In J. Braverman, ed., *State health insurance plans: is anybody listening?* Washington, D.C.: Georgetown University.

Kennedy, E. 1978. New national health insurance program. *Congressional Record — Senate,* S16813-S16817.

MacColl, W. A. 1966. *Group practice and prepayment of medical care.* Washington: Public Affairs.

Millis, R. A., and Montgomery, R. E. 1938. *Labor's risks and social insurance.* New York: McGraw-Hill.

Mustard, H. S. 1945. *Government in public health.* New York: Commonwealth Fund.

Myers, R. J. 1970. *Medicare.* Bryn Mawr, Pa.: McCahan Foundation.

Nixon, R. M. 1971. *Message from the President of the United States relative to building a national health strategy.* Washington: U.S. Government Printing Office.

Perspective. 1976. States mandating health insurance benefits. P. 29.

Pierce, W. 1932. *The purchase of medical care through fixed periodic payment.* New York: National Bureau of Economic Research.

Principles of Carter health plan. 30 July 1978. *New York Times.*

Reed, L. S.; Henderson, A. H.; and Hanft, R. H. 1966. *Independent health insurance plans in the United States, 1965 survey.* Washington, D.C.: Social Security Administration.

Roemer, M. I. 1973. An ideal health care system for America. In A. L. Strauss, ed., *Where medicine fails.* New Brunswick, N.J.: Trans-Action.

—————. 1975. The expanding scope of government regulation of health care delivery. *University of Toledo Law Review* 6:591–616.

Roemer, M. I., and Shonick, W. 1973. HMO performance: the recent evidence. *Milbank Memorial Fund Quarterly* 51:271–317.

Rosenfeld, L. S., and Rosenfeld, I. 1975. National health planning in the United States: prospects and portents. *International Journal of Health Services* 5:441–53.

Sasuly, R., and Roemer, M. I. 1966. Health insurance plans: a conceptualization from the California scene. *Journal of Health and Human Behavior* 7:36–44.

Schottland, C. E. 1963. *The Social Security program of the United States.* New York: Appleton-Century-Crofts.

Segal, M. E. October 1978. *Evaluation of impact of Hawaii's mandatory health insurance law.* New York.

Shabecoff, P. 30 July 1978. President outlines his plan on health: focus on economics. *New York Times.*

Sigerist, H. E. 1943. From Bismarck to Beveridge: developments and trends in Social Security legislation. *Bulletin of the History of Medicine* 8:365–88.

Sinai, N. 1949. *For the disabled sick: disability compensation.* Ann Arbor: University of Michigan School of Public Health.

Skolnik, A. M., and Price, D. W. 1970. Another look at workmen's compensation. *Social Security Bulletin* 33:3–25.

Somers, R. M., and Somers, A. R. 1954. *Workmen's compensation: prevention, insurance, and rehabilitation of occupational disability.* New York: Wiley.

—————. 1961. *Doctors, patients, and health insurance.* Washington, D.C.: Brookings Institution.

State of California. 1963. Additional benefits. In *Unemployment insurance code,* Sacramento. P. 136.

States mandating health insurance benefits. 1976. (Anonymous) *Perspective,* p. 29.

Straus, R. 1950. *Medical care for seamen: the origin of public medical service in the United States.* New Haven: Yale University.

Strumpf, G. B.; Seubold, F. H.; and Arrill, M. B. 1978. Health Maintenance Organizations, 1971–1977: issues and answers. *Journal of Community Health* 4:33–54.

U.S. General Accounting Office (Report to the Congress). August 1972. *More needs to be done to assure that physicians' services — paid for the Medicare Hnd Medicaid — are necessary.* Washington, D.C.

U.S. House of Representatives, Subcommittee on Health of the Committee on Ways and Means. August 1976. *National health insurance resource book* (rev. ed.). Washington, D.C.

U.S. National Center for Health Statistics. December 1978. *Health: United States, 1978.* Washington, D.C.

U.S. Social Security Administration. 12 March 1974. *Health Maintenance Organization Act of 1973.* Research and statistics note no. 5. Washington, D.C.

12

FUTURE DIRECTIONS IN
HEALTH POLICY

Alfred Katz

INTRODUCTION

What future do we mean? 1984? 2000? Or the remote, barely-to-be glimpsed vistas of 2080?

Clearly, it is necessary first of all to establish a temporal boundary in any discussion of future directions in health policy. To this writer, the year 2000 — which would mark but the coming of age of a single generation of the contemporary newborn — sets an upper limit for feasible predictions. On the other and, the Orwellian nightmare year, 1984, is almost upon us; its near arrival will probably signal merely a heightening of present trends, not a fundamental departure from them.

In discussing future directions, then, let it be clear that we are considering possibilities and probabilities for only the coming two decades.

What forces will shape and what directions are probable in health policy in that proximate period?

Many contributions to this volume imply the salience for health policy of three major influences: the economy, environmental developments, and finally, human or public awareness. Policymaking always involves choices, based on available options for which this triad of factors sets the limits. Barring apocalyptic or catastrophic changes — a massive nuclear accident or the occurrence of an "unthinkable" nuclear war — broad economic, environmental, and psychological factors thus will determine what choices of health policies will be made in the next decade. But underlying all three factors are *political* events and political decisions, which have always shaped, and will continue to shape, policies about the human services. "Political" factors are not, of course, abstract, haphazard, or merely quadrennial electoral occurrences; they represent the continuous interplay of special interests — economic and professional, as well as popular, as filtered and expressed through the country's political structure and processes.

Also, basic to the kinds of policies that emerge from these broad forces and political processes are ideological considerations, such as the underlying concepts of the nature of health and disease. This writer believes that it is necessary to view health policy as public policy that affects *health* and not just health services. An understanding of "health" requires a concept of the nature of contemporary health problems that goes beyond conventional statistics of disease incidence and prevalence; that shows the complex inter-relationships between "causes," or sources of ill health, and "effects," as seen in both physical and psychological manifestations. Varying types and degrees of illness responses occur in different populations in the modern world, and these differential responses should be viewed as reflexive to such variables as environments, socioeconomic status, genetic endowment, and patterns of social relations and personal behavior. Thus, "health" should be viewed as a unitary and indivisible concept that reflects the response of a particular individual or population to its physical and social environment, in terms of both biological nature and developmental experiences.

Such an ecological and developmental perspective has not been central to the thinking of the dominant section of the medical profession, which has greatly influenced the formulation of both health policy and services, and of medical education in the United States. Rather, *therapeutic, disease-oriented treatment services for individuals* have been the major emphasis in U.S. health care and medical education in the seven decades since the Flexner Report, and is still the prevailing emphasis today.

This disease/treatment orientation of the U.S. health delivery system, which underplays or ignores the socioenvironmental, mass and preventive aspects of health, not only has helped to create the cost and access problems described in other chapters in this volume, but is inappropriate and very poorly adapted to the contemporary predominance of chronic disease mor-bidity/mortality in the modern world. As much as any other factor, this narrow concept of what constitutes and influences health has stimulated the wide and growing dissatisfactions with current medical care and created various consumer countermovements for remediation and change. Some of these countermovements go beyond cost containment, the redistribution of health care resources, and the improvement and equalization of access: they substitute for the prevailing provider and professional view of health care as primarily a matter of disease diagnosis and treatment, a wider con-cern, often termed "holistic," for all the factors — ecological, socioeconomic, biophysical, and interpersonal — that bring about human distress, and con-duce to ill health.

The alternative, contrasting concept of "health," being advanced here, which will permeate the present discussion of health policy, draws upon and is grounded in a combination of recent clinical, epidemiological, and social science findings, far too extensive to summarize. They can be illustrated, however, by some generalizations made by a leading epidemiologist, the late John Cassel, after a comprehensive analysis of many major studies of the last 20 years. In one of his last papers, which summarizes beliefs he had come to from his own research and his extensive knowledge of the work of others, Cassel wrote:

A remarkably similar set of social circumstances characterizes people who develop tuberculosis and schizophrenia, become alcoholics, are victims of multiple ac-cidents, or commit suicide. Common to all these people is a marginal status in soci-ety. They are individuals who for a variety of reasons (e.g., ethnic minorities re-jected by the dominant majority in their neighborhood; high sustained rates of residential and occupational mobility; broken homes or isolated living circumstances) have been deprived of meaningful social contact. (Cassel, 1976, p. 110)

His analysis goes on:

The existing data have led me to believe that we should no longer treat psychosocial processes as unidimensional stressors or non-stressors, but rather as two-dimensional, one category being stressors, and other being protective or beneficial. . . . The property common to these processes is the strength of the social supports provided by the primary groups of most importance to the individual. (Cassel, 1976, pp. 111, 112)

Discussing the implications for prevention that flow from his detailed analysis of clinical and epidemiological findings, Cassel indicates that the latter point to an essentially environmental strategy:

Disease, with rare exceptions, has not been prevented by finding and treating sick individuals, but by modifying those environmental factors which facilitate its occurrence. (Cassel, 1976, p. 113)

He concludes his review recommendations that embody the wide use of a self-help approach:

With advancing knowledge, it is perhaps not too far-reaching to imagine a preventive health service in which professionals are involved lately in the diagnostic aspects — identifying families and groups at high risk by virtue of their lack of fit with their social milieu and determining the particular nature and form of the social supports that can and should be strengthened if such people are to be protected from disease outcomes. The intervention actions then could well be undertaken by non-professionals, provided that adequate guidance and specific direction were given. (Cassel, 1976, p. 121)

Prevention is thus not simply a matter of finding the already ill and preventing their further disability. It is likewise not just a matter of giving people didactic instruction about personal health habits, the right foods to eat, exercise, sleep, and so on; nor is it simply a matter of immunizations, multiphasic screening, or periodic health examinations by health professionals.

Environmental and sociopsychological factors in the causation of ill health and in resisting and overcoming it must be taken into account. Illness seems to vary in populations in relation to environmental hazards, social support and social interactions, just as much as in relation to idiosyncratic personal behavior like smoking, or such conditions as obesity. Taking this view further, a person's idea of self, of being in control of his/her life and the factors that affect it, correlates highly with being vulnerable or at risk. A positive self-image, plus the resources necessary to cope with the environment and its pressures, is associated with resistance to illness and disability. The lack of such resources, and the resultant inability to cope with life pressures, increase the risk and incidence of ill health as evidenced in much data about needy and deprived populations — the poor, the elderly, racial minorities, etc. Thus persons and populations who are in relatively weak and powerless social positions are at the greatest risk of falling ill and have the poorest prognosis for recovery and rehabilitation when they do so.

The implications of this view of health for future policy planning seem clear and inescapable.

The view of the etiology of health problems herein advanced has major consequences for health policy, since it suggests that the promotion and maintenance of health, the prevention and diminution of disease in *populations* cannot be achieved and improved merely through the provision of more of what we have, but through better-distributed and more adequately financed health services by existing institutions and professional health workers. This view of health implies fundamental *conceptual* revisions that not only will alter the nature of primary health care services, but will shift the balance of primary responsibility for health maintenance from professionals to lay persons, from technical health-caring institutions such as hospitals and private physicians, to more natural institutions, such as community centers, schools, work places and families. This view also requires major attention to the regulation of environmental hazards and pathogens; to the inculcation of health-promoting attitudes, perceptions, and behavior among the population, starting in early childhood, through the use of effective health education methods and media (in contrast, and as counter to, the bombardment of antihealth media messages by commercial interests). Such an emphasis on prevention, health promotion and the regulation of the environment would necessarily involve new forms of cooperation and health involvement by many kinds of community organizations, and thus requires the improvement or change of present mechanisms for formulating health policies.

SCENARIOS FOR THE FUTURE

It is common for "futures" to outline some varying but plausible projections of economic, political, and technological development, and to discuss some concrete possible changes in the light of these "scenarios." Let us attempt to do this by postulating two contrasting scenarios of social development in the next two decades and considering the kinds of health policy that would characterize each. The two scenarios might be described as a "traditionalist" and a nontraditionalist or "transformational" one. They would highlight differences between the traditional values of a social system based on personal achievement, individualism, and material acquisitions, and the contrasting view that the values that had carried the United States through its first 200 years were no longer viable, and need to be altered by socioeconomic arrangements and a value structure that emphasize collectivism, communalism, and shared responsibility.

For traditionalists, actions based on the economic principle of self-interest are seen as the chief means of distributing wealth and of raising the standard of living, through the "trickle-down" theory. This view goes hand in hand with the use of technical expertise, with rational, scientifically based decision making by the elite—the possessors of wealth, power, and education and knowledge. "Bigness," technology, and centralization arc seen as cardinal virtues in government, cities, industry, and science—and excesses of bureaucracy, waste, corruption, and depersonalization can be tolerated as incidental excrescences that do not significantly detract from the system's overall function virtues.

Ever-increasing consumption based on rising material expectations and standards is the chief social goal; and success toward it is obtained by a special kind of planning process, the application of rational social engineering, based on the knowledge accumulated by experts.

Such a broad philosophical approach would represent little change in the closing two decades of the century from the prevailing present values and patterns of socioeconomic life in the United States. Based on what we see today, it is probable that energy shortages and inflationary trends would continue over this period, and perhaps worsen and intensify the difficulties and discontents of many sections of the population—especially wage workers, pensioners, and others dependent on more or less fixed incomes, that is, consumers in general. The traditionalists, however, would confidently expect that with minor adjustments, the system would continue to muddle through, despite unemployment, chronically insufficient energy supplies, and perhaps food shortages. The hope for solutions of these problems would rest on the promise of technological breakthrough, rather than on basic social change and philosophic reorientation.

The planning of health services, under this traditionalist scenario, would embody similar views and values. By the closing years of the twentieth century, no doubt a "comprehensive," highly regulated federally organized health insurance plan will be in operation, replacing the earlier-legislated, partial insurance against the risks of "catastrophic" illness. "Fee-for-service" medical care might even be controlled by a federally regulated price schedule, chiefly addressed to cost containment.

It can be envisioned that under such a system much primary care would be rendered at community clinics, stocked by diagnostic instruments feeding into computers, and managed largely by paraprofessionals. Hospitals would continue to employ the most highly trained health professionals in all kinds of specialities, and would continue to be centers for the development and application of complex technology. Medical "breakthroughs" in the form of surgical innovations or dramatically effective specific drug treatments would be the chief goal of research. The extension of life and its prolongation by every technical means would be considered the prime goals of health care.

In the mental health area, while personal counseling by professionals would be recognized and provided, major research emphasis would be on the search for physiological, surgical, and chemical treatments that would restore or bring about "normal" psychological functioning.

Such a highly technical health system would be based on the premise that responsibility for good health lies not on the individual, but on health providers themselves. Technical innovations, to "cure" disease, or at least to allay its effects, would be the chief goals of research, and their applications the chief methodology of health care. Prescribing drugs for every ailment—no matter how generalized and unspecific—would be a major modality in care. Humanizing provider-patient contacts, involving the patient and family in self-care, whether for treatment or prevention, would be regarded as irrelevant or unnecessary in the face of biotechnical advances. In the mental health area, even depression and anxiety — to be expected as increasingly common reactions to a depersonalizing and stressful social environment — would be thought to be conditions best treated by chemical or surgical means.

What would be the socioeconomic effects on health if these probable aspects of the traditionalist scenario came to fruition?

While forecasting is always hazardous, it seems likely that, with the continuation and expansion of a delivery system centered on the hospital, high technology, and the specialist corps necessary to administer it, the economic costs of illness would continue to rise steeply, despite governmental gestures to regulate and contain them. While the expansion of a delivery system financed by federal health insurance could be expected to bring about some improvements in coverage, and in beneficial treatments for some specific illnesses, these advantages might be outweighed by continued and perhaps heightened environmental pollution, by high rates of occupationally connected illness, and by the wide use of both drugs and foods having health-damaging effects.

Increasing amounts of chronic disease and disability, resulting from correctable but uncorrected environmental and occupational hazards, would unquestionably push up the nation's total medical care bill.

As the population increasingly ages, the failure to prevent some of the major causes of morbidity — cardiovascular, respiratory and neoplastic diseases in particular — would result in a greater number of persons needing secondary and institutional care, and the ability to reverse unhealthful life patterns that generate illness would be diminished.

A TRANSFORMED SOCIETY

In contrast with this traditionalist scenario, which may be seen as a logical extension of trends already strongly apparent by 1980, a "transformationist" scenario would depict the reversal of many current tendencies through reevaluation of a number of basic American values. The redefinition of what constitutes the good life would also lead to a major reorientation in health care philosophy and structures.

We cannot clearly depict the economic and political levers that would spark such a transformation; for purposes of this scenario, they must be taken for granted.

Whatever the underlying social dynamics, however, it is probable that continued energy and economic crises would combine to bring about a deep and prolonged economic depression, during which government expenditures on health and welfare, as well as the average standard of living, would decline, the consumption of material goods by the population would be reduced, and the economic goals of a constantly rising level of consumption and personal acquisitions would be gradually replaced. A "small is beautiful" philosophy would emerge, emphasizing localism over centralism, collective over individual actions to solve social problems, simplicity over "high" technology, and self-help and mutual aid through family and friends over the receipt of services from professional providers and experts.

For the health field, these value changes would bring about an altered philosophy of care, a different method of policymaking, new forms of professional training, roles and deployment, revised priorities in research, and major alterations in delivery structures.

An altered philosophy of care would regard "health" as the product of fulfilled human potentials in relation to the physical, social, and interpersonal environment in which people live. It would emphasize the regulation and control of pathogens — physical, social, and "life-style" — that increase vulnerability to disease. It would regard the maintenance and promotion of health as the joint responsibility of the state and its institutions, the health professionals, and the public — individuals, families, and other small groups that influence behavior.

The state would have a strong role in the regulation of harmful environmental conditions, including the advertising of health-damaging products by commercial interests; in providing for technically competent secondary and extended care; in stimulating health eduction and clinical and basic research. Community organizations, on a neighborhood level, would have a large responsibility for the development of primary care delivery through structures that would vary with local conditions but would assure accessibility, equal treatment without reference to ability to pay, and linkages with institutions concerned with employment, housing, food supplies, and education.

The training of health professionals would be less disease- and more prevention-oriented than at present. More generalists and fewer specialists would be trained, and there would be a wide acceptance and use of lesser-trained professionals for primary care functions — nurse practitioners, physicians' assistants, nurse midwives, and the like, with a corresponding legitimation and widening of their roles in delivery systems.

"Self-care" performed by the individual, his family, or other significant persons with whom he interacts, such as memers of self-help or mutual aid groups, would be considered important ingredients in first-line health maintenance, assessment, and treatment. Health professionals, including physicians, nurses and others, would take on guiding and educational roles with respect to such self-care and self-help activities. Government would subsidize local-community-based lay groups that had demonstrated the ability to contribute to the health and welfare of their members through mutual aid methods — counseling, resource provision, advocacy, and linkage.

In this scenario, health policy formulation would necessarily involve a major role for those affected by the policies — the general public, consumers, and indigenous community groups. Such involvement would far transcend the present "tokenism" of the formal representation of a few minority, consumer, and labor representatives on policy bodies in the main dominated by professional, commercial, and bureaucratic interests.

It is worth noting that the alterations envisaged in the transformationist scenario resemble many of the recommendations advanced by Lalonde in his seminal 1974 essay "A New Perspective on the Health of Canadians" (Lalonde, 1974). This important document has large implications for social policy and health planning in the United States and should be studied by every health professional, since it outlines a comprehensive approach to current health problems that is multifaceted, pertinent to U.S. problems, and achievable. Lalonde analyzes the chief health problems of the Canadian population, which in terms of its morbidity and mortality and its demographic structure is rather close to that of the United States (with the exception that there are not as many populations of sizable and under-privileged ethnic minorities in Canada as in the United States.

After laying out the major contemporary health problems, Lalonde proposes several strategies to reduce mental and physical health hazard. For the present purpose, the most important are, first, a health promotion strategy "aimed at informing, influencing and assisting both individuals and organizations so that they will accept more responsibility and be more active in matters affecting mental and physical health"; second, a regulatory strategy "aimed at using federal regulatory powers to reduce hazards to mental and physical health"; third, a research strategy designed "to help, discover and apply knowledge needed to solve mental and physical health problems." As part of each of these strategies, he recommends extension of support of programs for persons with special needs, enlistment of the support of women's and other community movements to bring about greater interest in self-care and health-promoting activities, helping to develop community facilities and supports for those at high risk. These recommendations are joined with those under the regulatory strategy which are designed to reduce or eliminate the advertising and the dissemination of physically harmful products such as food additives. The whole approach is a multiple one, joining considerations of greater access to and better distribution of health care, with preventive strategies for self-care, self-help, and environmental action.

THE ROLE OF GOVERNMENT

Health Policy formulations would vary significantly under these two projections of the future, but it is clear that a major role for the federal government would continue in each.

The traditionalist scenario envisages the probable expansion of the current level of federal expenditures on health through passage of either a series, or of a comprehensive, federally organized health insurance program. The federal share of national health expenditures is now about 40 percent of the some $170 billion, or almost 9 percent of the GNP, spent annually on health in the United States (*Health, United States,* 1978). About 70 percent of federal dollars are spent to provide personal health services, and whatever variant of national health insurance is legislated, those costs will rise both absolutely and in relation to overall health expenditures.

It can be expected that if present trends continue, by the year 2000 some 90 percent of federal health spending would go for the delivery of personal health services, the remainder being divided among biomedical research, professional education, and environmental controls. Allotments for *prevention* would continue to be relatively minor, although support for life-style-oriented health education, directed toward changing peoples' habits, would probably expand somewhat. State and local departments of public health, which today devote a major share of their expenditures to personal health services, would, with federal subsidies, continue similar patterns of spending (*Health, United States,* 1978).

The largest component of public expenditure, hospital care, would continue to claim and receive most of the federal health budget; all the present trends in the traditionalist scenario toward costly, high-energy and capital-intensive technology would continue and intensify. The numbers of hospital employees needed to administer and use the new technologies would continue to expand, so that the inflation of daily hospital bed costs would continue to mount, despite attempts at cost-containment measures.

In the traditionalist projection for the next 20 years, the influence of special interests — providers, health professionals, third parties such as insurance companies, and commercial interests such as drug and medical equipment manufacturers — would obviously not diminish in the formulation of health policy. The lobbying of such groups in Congress would continue to influence legislation, both conceptually and in implementation, so that federally financed hospital and ambulatory care programs would continue to embody provisions and practices that would guarantee the profits of these interest groups. Such present policies as paying hospitals on the basis of their actual costs for providing the kind of care they deem necessary or compensating physicians at "usual" or "customary" fees for services rendered could hardly be expected to change.

Federal policy would also, no doubt, continue to support increases in the supply of health professionals through the funding of medical, nursing, and allied health education programs. Present trends toward specialization — with almost 85 percent of U.S. physicians being or becoming specialists — would be continued (*Health, United States,* 1978). Primary care or first-line medical contacts would continue to be underestimated in importance, and relegated to lesser trained professionals, paraprofessionals, and computers.

But the most significant present trend whose continuation can be projected under the traditionalist approach is the divorcement of health considerations from basic issues of environmental regulation. Federal health policy, with its major emphases on personal health care delivery systems and its habitual compromises between public and private vested interests, is simply not adequately geared for the remedial environmental actions necessary to cope with many major present sources and patterns of disease. Air and water pollution, road and occupational accidents, the presence of carcinogens and teratological agents as the result of techniques of agriculture and food processing, other environmental realities such as nuclear waste and fallout, and noise and crowding in cities have all been demonstrated to play roles in the etiologies of the chronic diseases that are the modal types of present morbidity. Yet the traditionalist scenario, carrying on present federal health policy, with its orientation toward disease rather than prevention, would not envisage more than the present minor percentage of federal health expenditures devoted to them.

Similarly, the health-damaging effects of economic developments such as unemployment and the inflation of food and fuel costs on all segments of the population, but especially on the poor, the aged, and others on fixed incomes would not be adequately recognized or dealt with under a philosophy and structure of health care that is oriented to the treatment of disease after it has occurred, rather than to altering environmental and living conditions that lead to its occurrence. The long-range consequences of exposure to environments with either specific or general pathogens, whether physiological or mental, without remedial actions have not been fully studied, but these factors must increasingly be viewed as health hazards at least as damaging and potentially lethal as bacteria or viruses.

ARE THERE FEASIBLE ALTERNATIVES TO PRESENT HEALTH POLICYMAKING?

As is well known, other countries exceed the United States in various important indicators of the health of the population: longevity and life expectancy, infant mortality, and ajusted death rates (Silver, 1978). These conditions persist despite the many technological triumphs of U.S. medicine, and there is little ground for the belief that even the institution of universal health insurance coverage will bring about significant changes in them.

Many contributions to this volume indicate that U.S. health policy over the past 30 years has not achieved its purpose of substantially improving the health status of all sections of the population and ensuring an environment in which healthful living can take place. McKeown (1965), Illich (1976), and many U.S. writers have shown that the undeniable nineteenth- and twentieth-century increases in general health and longevity are attributable more to improvements in living standards, especially in nutrition, and to some environmental control measures than to the wider contemporary availability and use of curative personal health services. As our analysis suggests, the mere expansion of health resources, financing, and the supply of health professionals in the absence of massive and powerful measures directed toward control of the environmental and social hazards will lead to more, not less, chronic disease, human disability, distress, and unproductiveness.

This situation, which reflects the major influence on health problems of environment, economics, and technology, has been brought about by policymaking processes and provider attitudes that heighten the political influence of special interest groups, including, unfortunately health care providers and professionals. The philosophic justification for these policies is summed up in some outworn political and economic axioms such as "free enterprise," "states' rights," and "minimal governmental interference" and, in the professional sphere, by such shibboleths or catchwords as "free choice of physician," the "doctor-patient relationship," and "the doctor knows best."

In the political sphere, U.S. health policy has been largely formulated by Congress, which is responsive to many special interests, despite some legislative provisions to regulate lobbying. Congress usually draws on the technical knowledge and data supplied by carefully selected health professionals, and long-range planning, when it occurs, emphasizes the use of "experts" whose political views are acceptable, whether or not their knowledge of the problem is sufficient. The 25-year history of governmental inattention to or even supression of dissenting or unpopular views of nuclear hazards, as witnessed in the 1979 Three-Mile Island nuclear accident and the many suits brought by Love Canal, Utah, Nevada, and Ohio residents because of the failure to protect them against hazardous nuclear and chemical wastes, sufficiently reveals the dangers of this style of health-related policymaking.

Can this style be reversed to provide more choices and more preventive, health-promoting approaches, as briefly sketched in the transformationist scenario? Can consumers, local community interest groups—labor, families, minorities, lay people — summon sufficient energy and political influence to counter the pervasive lobbying of vested interest groups, the self-serving, self-perpetuating inclinations of many health providers and professionals, the access to the media and the extraordinary political influence of commercial vendors of health-damaging products?

At first blush, the experience of the past would not give much ground for optimism for an early change in health philosophy and health policies in the influential seats of power in the United States. But a closer look indicates that a number of important reforms have indeed been legislated in answer, especially, to public concern for broader planning and consumer resistances to dysfunctional health policies. Recent legislation has provided for establishment of the Occupational Safety and Health Administration, the Office of Technology Assessment, a large number of Health Systems Agencies, and a National Consumer Interest Unit in the federal government. These reforms were excellent in intent, and, in addition to their programmatic aspects, provided for the heightening of public participation in policymaking. But the unequal power of the public and consumers vis-à-vis the oft-combined forces of providers, health professionals, and commercial interests has, as in the case of many HSAs, so watered down their implementation as to render them either ineffective or counterproductive to their original aims.

Failing the emergence of some strong national coalition of popular counterforces, probably the most hopeful arena for action to bring about policy changes is the local community, and the neighborhoods within it.

In an important article on "macro" planning in a tightening economy, Rothman quotes Wireman's assessment of both governmental and citizen grass-roots activity:

Despite a weakening of citizen input in many programs, new legislation in the mid-1970s strengthened the citizen's role in some instances; therefore, the situation remained mixed. Changes in Title XX of the Social Security Act mandated a period of public review before state plans for a variety of social service programs could be adopted. A majority of the members of health planning agencies must now be consumers. Almost nine hundred community action agencies still exist, providing employment, community organization, and social services. Some citizens continue to be active in decentralized city halls and neighborhod service centers. Others participate in consumer cooperatives or community development corporations in an attempt to make their neighborhoods more self-sufficient economically. Many citizens have turned to mass consumer education or political activities. (Rothman, 1979, p. 277)

This situation is further developed by Perlman, who states:

The seventies are spawning a plethora of grass-roots associations involving local people mobilized on their own behalf around concrete issues of importance in their communities. . . . Evidence thus far shows that not only have the groups been growing rapidly but also that participant turnover in the groups has been relatively low. . . . Given the widespread disillusionment with existing institutions . . . a tremendous surge of neighborhood vitality in the United States has expressed itself through grass-roots associations. (Perlman, 1976, p. 4, 19)

Subsequent health policy directions and recommendations to Congress of the Reagan Administration involve a major philosophical shift that calls for massive rollbacks of federal financing of personal health care services, of many other programs such as food stamps and school lunches that contribute to well-being, of programs to regulate environmental and occupational health hazards, of social-behavioral research, of health professional training, and so on. As of this writing, most of these proposals have not yet been effectuated by congressional action, but their general thrust will clearly be implemented.

This change was not anticipated by either of the future scenarios sketched above, and it is necessary briefly to consider implications for each of the latter. At first blush, the changes seem to contradict the premises of the "traditionalist" projection by reducing government responsibility for financing and standard setting in health and emphasizing the role of the private sector in a "free" market economy. But it is clear that stress on market operations in the health care field will only underline the trends to high technology and high expense in health care, consequently limited access, and the reduction of resources devoted to preventive and holistic care. Present trends toward depersonalization of health care will be accentuated, at least in the short run. Of course, every action produces a reaction, and in the longer run, one can expect a widespread consumer resistance to these cutbacks and their consequences, just as other elements of the Reagan program, once their consequences are known, will also provoke an organized opposition.

Some elements of the new turn in health policy might seem to be compatible with some aspects of the "transformationist" scenario, such as the emphasis on decentralization and localism. For economic reasons, the movement for self-care and self-help in health may be heightened — people who lack resources to buy medical care may be more inclined to learn how to look after themselves. But despite these benefits, the thrust of the all-round reductions proposed would inevitably add to, rather than diminish, the burden of human misery, stress, and disease, especially among those least able to cope with environmental rigors and economic deprivations.

All other considerations and controversies apart, resistance to these Draconian measures seems to be essential to preserve the possibility of an enlightened national health policy.

REFERENCES

Cassel, J. 1976 The contribution of the environment to host resistance. *American Journal of Epidemiology* 104:107–23.

Health, United States, 1978. 1978. Rockville, Md.: Department of Health, Education and Welfare, Health Resources Administration.

Illich, I. 1976. *Medical nemesis.* New York: Pantheon.

Lalonde, M. 1974. *A new perspective on the health of Canadians.* Ottawa: Health and Welfare Directorate.

McKeown, T. 1965. Reasons for the decline in medical mortality. In *Medicine in Modern Society.* London: Allen and Irwin.

Perlman, J. 1976. Grass-rooting the system. *Social Policy* 7:4–19.

Rothman, J. 1979. Macro social work in a tightening economy. *Social Work* 24:274–81.

Silver, G. A. 1978. *Child health, America's future.* Germantown, Md.: Aspen Systems.

PART THREE:
Summary and Conclusion

13

SOCIAL WORK AND HEALTH CARE POLICY REVISITED

Doman Lum

Current health care policy issues require continual updating and reframing during the decade of the 1980s. This volume has sought to present health policy problem themes as they are expressed in legislation and programs. The perimeters of health policy were drawn around definition, problem areas, social values, task roles, and policymaking process. Health policy trends, legislative programs, and treatment services provided more detail on historical background, current analysis, and future directions for action.

Part Three, "Summary and Conclusions," integrates the various themes of this anthology so that the reader has an interpretation of policy perspectives. It begins with a probable projection of health policy for the rest of this decade. This scenario is based on an appraisal of present legislation and program trends as well as efforts of health care authors who have peered into the future. Given the plausibility of these events, the major question is: What will be the policy problem issues, policymaking agendas, and task roles? Insights and recommendations of our eleven health policy contributors focus on various facets of this probe. It is hoped that, as social workers and other readers reflect on these following sections, program strategy may be formulated on health policy at the local, state, and federal levels.

HEALTH CARE POLICY IN THE 1980S

With the emergence of the Reagan Administration, a conservative political climate has affected public policy during the first half of the 1980s. Prior to this, two opposing policy philosophies in health care were clearly distinguished: reprivatization and public participation. Blendon explained that private proprietary and voluntary management were seen as inherently superior to public sector management. The interests of patients would be best served if local government were not in the "business" of operating hospitals or health clinics. Accordingly, the reprivatization approach recommended the replacement of public-supported hospitals with the voucher purchase of individual health care services from private providers. On the other side, those who held to public participation of health care believed that the performances of the private market and nongovernment institutional providers were clearly discredited by the cost-escalation crisis in health care. Public-sponsored health care services offered greater political accountability and responsiveness than voluntary hospitals and private physicians. While there were financial and administrative short-comings of public programs and institutions, government funding and control of health care were vital for the public interest (Blendon, 1981).

The public-participation philosophy has prevailed during the last decade and a half since Medicaid and Medicare. Its tenets have been the foundation for government-sponsored comprehensive health care insurance and for legislative incentives and regulations. However, with changing economic, political, and fiscal trends, health care policy in the 1980s is destined for major shifts and revisions.

The emphasis on deregulation of the health care industry has become a reality in the form of federal budget cuts in the Reagan Administration. However, Mechanic believes that, apart from a budget cut, the regulatory approach to controlling cost is questionable. Utilization review, certificate of need, modification of losses for reimbursement, review of eligibility criteria, and similar measures have probably produced marginal net savings. At the same time, Mechanic asserts that American physicians are more highly monitored and regulated than doctors in many other countries. When compared with their English counterparts, they are more burdened with detailed rules and guidelines relating to their modes of practice and clinical work (Mechanic, 1981).

As a first order of business, the Reagan Administration has taken an early stance against regulation and has sought to virtually eliminate the role of Health Systems Agencies as a prime example of a health care regulator.

While there has been no formal unveiling of a comprehensive Reagan Administration health policy plan, the National Health Care Reform Act of 1980 (H.R. 7527 sponsored by Stockman and Gephardt) is a working document for marketplace competition and consumer choice and responsibility. Its major underpinning is a deregulated health care industry operating through marketplace incentives. Much of the theory behind this legislation has been influenced by Enthoven's Consumer-Choice Health Plan (Enthoven, 1978). Citing inflation and inequity, the lack of competition and choice, and the ineffectiveness of regulations, Enthoven proposed an organized health system based on consumer choice and competition among qualified health plans. The Consumer-Choice Health Plan was earlier detailed in an extensive memorandum to the then Secretary of Health, Education, and Welfare, Joseph A. Califano (Enthoven, 1977). The Carter Administration considered the Enthoven memo but did not incorporate it as a part of its phased-in National Health Insurance Plan.

The Stockman-Gephardt bill is a serious step toward implementing the Enthoven approach. The legislation is based on the belief that marketplace dynamics would decide the share of the GNP devoted to health care, appropriate bed/population ratios, types of delivery systems best serving health care needs, viability and cost-effectiveness of new technologies, and appropriate rates of utilization. It would remove government regulations on Medicaid, Medicare, and health planning as well as state rate review and certificate-of-need laws. In its place, individuals would determine the level of health insurance purchased. Employees would use employer's financial health contributions for the plan of their choice. Persons would pay the difference for a more costly plan than the employer's contribution. However, employees could pocket up to $500 (rebate-tax free) if they selected a more economical plan. Medicare and Medicaid would be converted to a similar system of financial contributions. There would be a catastrophic illness clause. Plans would be required to include coverage beyond $2900 creating a private market safety net. In order to market consumers, general contractors would help them make suitable benefit choices, be responsible for setting up and collecting premiums, and offer various benefit packages.

There are three basic assumptions in this legislative proposal. First, competition would drive insurers and providers toward cost controls, utilization patterns, and marketable premiums. Second, profit would be the determinant for making cost-effective decisions in terms of private and voluntary control mechanisms. Third, the marketplace system would be more efficient and rationally organized than a government-organized national health program (Lesparre, 1980).

The debate over a marketplace competition approach to national health care has emerged during the past five years. Will consumers (individuals/families and employers) be motivated and able to seriously *shop around* for more cost-beneficial arrangements to the point of forcing competition among insurers/providers? Will insurers/providers respond to this "shopping around" by designing new or cheaper arrangements that are cost-beneficial enough to satisfy the social demand for "affordable" health care? (Observations on Alain Enthoven's Consumer Choice Health Plan, 1977). Mechanic also has misgivings about the problem of uncertain assumptions — namely, consumers making informed economic choices, large providers competing with economical and efficient plans, and providers using institutional powers to effectively constrain physician decision making. Moreover, he has reservations about the problem of radical restructuring of existing institution arrangements and practice patterns as well as the problem of momentum necessary to implement such change (Mechanic, 1981). Drake asks questions around deregulation, the first step toward a marketplace competition approach. Will free-market controls really be given a full test by the elimination of economic regulation in the health care industry? If the industry is deregulated, will free-market controls work to lessen the nation's allocation of resources for health care services (Drake, 1981)?

At the outset, the initial issue for the Reagan Administration may be to what extent the health care industry should be regulated if federal health expenditures continue to rise and threaten the goal of a balanced budget. However, let us grant that a deregulation balance is achieved. If the direction of the Reagan Administration is toward a marketplace competition health policy, there may be intermediate steps to test the potential of the private sector. The federal government could establish budget cost ceilings for health care entitlement programs such as Medicaid and Medicare. In a deregulated system, there would be minimal program guidelines and an annual contract negotiation with the private sector over health care services to the poor and elderly. Negotiated medical plans would then devise their own internal efficiency controls to meet funding budgets (Mechanic, 1981). Over a short-run period, the Reagan Administration could project the likelihood of whether full-scale marketplace competition would be feasible based on the response of private health plans to a deregulated system.

In any case, health care policy in this decade will undergo significant change. At the same time, there is a need for social workers to maintain a perspective on the necessary programs for public and social dimensions of health care. While social workers may be tempted to join the private health plans in search of reimbursement for contracted social services, the profession must be an advocate for substantive health care program content to poor, minority, and elderly target groups.

Two of the contributors to this volume, Hyman and Katz, articulate an action agenda for the 1980s. Hyman identifies the major policies for the decade: environmental protection, self-care, prevention, community support and social services, and incremental national health insurance. Katz offers a detailed plan for implementing a policy program emphasizing prevention, health promotion, and environmental regulation. He starts with the notion that health is the product of fulfilled human potential in relation to the physical, social, and interpersonal environment in which people live. The general public, consumers, and indigenous community groups would have major roles in health policy formulation. There would be community organization participation in developing primary care delivery and assuring accessibility, equal treatment, and linkages with life-sustaining institutions. Individuals, families and other interacting significant persons would perform self-care and self-help in health. The state would concentrate on regulating and controlling harmful environmental conditions. Bracht and Harrington also underscore the importance of environmental factors determining physical and mental health status and the improvement of environmental and social conditions.

Emerging from this discussion is the need for a social, environmental, and behavioral health policy that reorders budget priorities toward public health and environmental change, preventive health and life-style, and other nonmedical determinants of health. Whether one can reverse an accelerated health system consisting of a hospital network with high technology, specialist corporations, and rising health cost remains a question. Katz believes that rather than a national policy change of emphasis, community neighborhoods are best suited to initiate local government and citizen grass-roots efforts in prevention, self-help, and environmental health. No doubt, demonstration projects sponsored by county health departments and consumer health groups may be funded along these lines. Both Hyman and Katz anticipate an alternative to the health policy emphasis on traditional treatment programs. Programs of health maintenance and prevention and environmental health could surface as major priorities in this decade.

UNRESOLVED HEALTH POLICY ISSUES

Several authors have identified unresolved policy problems that affect legislative programs. The issues of medical manpower and government regulations are the subject of Davidson's treatment of reduced participation of physicians in Medicaid. Part of the problem is the varied array of regulatory policies on coverage limitations, benefit changes, eligibility requirements, and medical need determination. This variation is due to the fact that each state has elected to administer its own version of the Medicaid program. Crucial to the discussion on physician participation is the compensation mechanism for provider reimbursement. Davidson contends that funding reimbursement and regulatory policies interfere with the physician's ability to exercise professional judgment.

He suggests that Medicaid should mandate a required range of service coverage, lengthen the eligibility time, compensate physicians on par with their real costs, penalize states that fail to pay their bills, conduct selective accountability checks, and review the process for benefit changes. These recommendations move the program toward uniformity, equitability, and efficiency measures.

Related to Davidson's thrust on uniform regulations is Harrington's contention that Health Systems Agencies should expand their scope of authority. In this instance, the regulation issue focuses on power and control of health services and facilities. Provider critics would argue that the National Health Planning and Resources Development Act tends to overregulate the health industry. However, as a former director of a regional planning center, Harrington differs with this view. Rather, she proposes controls over health expenditures and reimbursements, authority to decertify or close unnecessary services and facilities, control over health service budget or rate setting, consolidation of organizational and operational functions, and even regulation of the number, distribution, and types of physicians.

While Harrington recognizes that intentional authority limitations have been imposed on health planning legislation, Health Systems Agencies are the sole vehicles to exercise national coordination in health service, facilities, manpower, and cost issues. The private health sector will not allow the degree of government regulation seen in George Orwell's *1984*. However, the question remains whether we have struck a balance between appropriate government intervention and free-enterprise market competition in health care.

Noble and Conley portray the issue of rising hospital cost against the reality of limited resources. They elaborate on a number of policy options to controlling medical cost. A primary policy alternative is to reduce the quantity of medical care. This would be achieved partially through preventive health techniques to curtail medical care demand and through reducing medical facility construction and the supply of physicians. A related approach is to curtail the price of medical care. Recommendations include a limit on annual expenditures per person per episode of illness or on annual hospital utilization. Still another alternative is to change the composition of medical services. Present cost-effectiveness measures are employing these policies: use of generic rather than brand-name drugs, less use of X-rays, use of nursing homes rather than inpatient care, limited hospital stays, and provision of home health care.

As alternative to a mandatory hospital ceiling rate solution, Noble and Conley advocate the use of cost-effective Health Maintenance Organizations, capitation payment of fixed fee, negotiated fee schedules between insurance funds and physicians, PSRO monitoring of inappropriate services, and more allocations to social services, which may reduce the need for medical care. In this last instance, they believe that nutrition, stress reduction, and community reentry are appropriate social service programs that maintain good health and social adjustment and reduce the need for hospital stays. A major policy thrust may be to reframe cost containment in terms of the preceding emphases. Health Maintenance Organizations generally incorporate a prepaid capitation fee and negotiate annually with their physicians on salary and rate schedule. In fact, there has been a significant increase of HMOs, which currently number over 250 throughout the United States. Furthermore, a preventive health component in social service programs may be useful to teach discharged patients proper nutrition, social readjustment, and health maintenance skills. From this perspective, cost containment is focused on ambulatory and community services rather than inpatient care.

In his treatment on national and state health insurance, Roemer touches on the issue of accessibility to individual health care for all Americans. Roemer assumes a pessimistic attitude as he analyzes the Carter Administration policy on national health insurance. It placed the problem of national expenditures for health services over the health needs of the population. It offered nothing to modify the existing medical care system, which has incentives toward maximizing costs. Roemer believes that the prospects for national health insurance legislation are dimmer with a conservative federal administration. In brief, the promise of access to comprehensive health care for all citizens has eluded us during the present period.

However, Roemer poses an alternative strategy for obtaining access: state health insurance. Numerous states have developed their own health insurance programs for their residents. Maine set up a catastrophic medical expense fund in 1974. Connecticut asked insurance carriers to sell policies for a range of comprehensive service care. Rhode Island (1977), New York (1978), and Alaska (1978) passed catastrophic health insurance. Roemer also reports that Hawaii has the broadest state health insurance legislation since it required employer-employee health insurance in 1975.

Certainly, as national health insurance legislation passage wanes in Congress, other states may enact legislation that offers comprehensive coverage for their populations.

POLICYMAKING AGENDAS

Our guest contributors have given us numerous suggestions on policymaking proposals which may become working agendas for health policymakers, legislators, and administrators.

Coulton suggests that Health Maintenance Organization policy addresses the issue of physician inducement and recruitment, particular performance efficiency and effectiveness models, uniform utilization standards, criteria for ancillary professionals, continuity of care, and economics of scale. Furthermore, she advocates HMO-Medicaid contracting with monitoring of data on utilization patterns.

Bracht pinpoints numerous policy needs for long-term care: the development of an explicit policy on long-term care for the chronically ill, infirm, and disabled; the systematization of intervention modes for long-term care; budget increases for Medicare and Medicaid programs in home health care and long-term care; and the involvement of Health Systems Agencies in effective and coordinated services for long-term patients and the chronically ill.

Hookey believes that health policy should articulate a national primary care delivery system that includes organizing primary human services. Drawing on European urban and rural primary health centers, Hookey presents us with alternatives to a medical model: holistic health centers, health care, life-style behavior changes.

Along these lines, Bracht observes that hypertension, lung cancer, drug abuse, heart disease, obesity, and industrial accidents fall under a common principle. They are examples of social diseases that have social causes amenable to social intervention. Policymakers, physicians, and health educators need to formulate prevention and treatment strategies to alter deleterious health habits that contribute to debilitating functioning. More research is also required to understand the relationships between life-style, diet, and environment and their contribution to illness patterns.

The Medicaid agenda calls for substantive policy revisions to curb the variation of program differences from state to state. Medicaid and Medicare require uniform policies and procedures in coverage, benefits, eligibility, provider reimbursement, and accountability. It seems appropriate for the Department of Health and Human Services to propose a merger of Medicaid and Medicare under the auspices of a single federal agency. With the consent of states and congressional passage of a revision bill, we may be able to cope with some of Davidson's recommendations.

Hospital-cost-containment legislation may be revised and reintroduced in the next session of Congress and in many state legislatures. Health policymakers are monitoring the net effect of voluntary hospital-cost-containment efforts. In the meantime, Noble, Conley, and Coulton urge us to support Health Maintenance Organizations that demonstrate cost-efficiency and cost-effectiveness outcomes on patients and operations. Hyman, Katz, and Hookey emphasize the need to develop substantive health prevention programs with self-help and self-care components. It is hoped that, in the coming years, health policymakers will include these proposals in cost-containment emphases.

A final policymaking issue is the need to revive the political momentum for a universal comprehensive national health insurance program. As indicated in previous sections of this book, the passage of national health insurance depends on the political and economic climate of the nation. We may perpetuate the present form of medical care delivery with a fee-for-service and third-party reimbursement policy. Medicaid and Medicare represent the full limits of expansion for the national health budget. We may need a crisis event comparable to the Depression and the social unrest of the 1960s which brought Social Security, Medicare, and Medicaid. We may be waiting for a charismatic Roosevelt or a politically skilled Johnson to facilitate the passage of an NHI law. Furthermore, national health insurance requires a vital economy to produce a sufficient budget surplus for a major program outlay. In short, the opportune conditions for national health insurance are not present during the early years of this decade as far as we can determine. The issue then becomes: Is the marketplace competition approach based on consumer choice of viable private health plans sufficient to create universal health care for all Americans? Health policy planners, political leaders, and economists may have new insights on this topic for us.

SOCIAL WORK TASK ROLES

This book on social work and health care policy would not be complete without a concluding note on the task roles of social workers. Virtually all contributors have mentioned the contribution of social work in health care from numerous program policy perspectives.

Bracht reminds the social work profession about the development of academic content and patient experience for the social work health professional. Social work health curriculum should focus on care and prevention, assessment of impairment to individual functioning, knowledge of natural support networks and self-help groups, and understanding of the interrelationships between life-style, diet, and environment on illness patterns.

Hyman and Hookey touch on the clinical role of the social worker in health care: improved discharge planning for patients, greater participation in diagnosis and treatment of patients, team members and leaders in primary health settings, and systematic visitation of clients in community institutional and residential settings.

Harrington, Hookey, Bracht, and Hyman bring varying emphases on advocacy roles for social workers in health care. Hyman stresses advocacy for joint decision making between the client and physician on treatment. Harrington believes that Health Systems Agencies provide consumers with opportunities to advocate health reform. Social workers can become active participants in health planning subcommittee groups. Hookey underscores the need for more professional advocacy to promote social work's participation and role in primary health care. Bracht alerts social workers to argue against second-class care for the chronically ill, which results in unnecessary physical and mental deterioration. Nursing home and board-and-care facilities are particular advocacy targets for improved programs and environmental conditions.

Related to these direct service roles is the need for relevant social work research in health care. Bracht suggests research goals measuring the capacity for or impediments to social functioning. He has in mind such client factors as family and marital status, institutional adjustment, and self-health appraisals. Likewise, there are related care system areas such as absences or gaps in service, the effects of unnecessary institutionalizations based on income deficiencies, and the adequacy of subsidized housing.

Above all, Hyman and Katz point social workers to preventive programs in social action, client behavior, and environmental change. Their emphases on shaping life-style and health through self-care and self-help education are principal areas for social work. What is the particular social content in preventive and environmental health that can be developed by social workers? What are specific community organizing efforts in health legislative advocacy as it pertains to social and health environmental problems?

As social workers consider their roles for health care in the 1980s, there may emerge a specific problem issue that becomes a rallying point for many participants. Our purpose has been to set forth many agenda items for reflection and action. It is our belief that social workers and other professionals have a stake in health care policy as professional providers and consumer recipients.

All contributors to this anthology have presented a cross section of current health policy issues and legislative programs affecting the American public. As social change agents in policy discussion, program planning, and legislative action groups use this book as a reference, it is our hope that there will be understanding of health issues, articulation of far-reaching policy proposals, and improved health for Americans in the coming years.

CONCLUSION

Based on these integrated health policy themes, the decade of the 1980s reveals a change process in health care policy and delivery. Among the dominant trends are the following priorities:

growth of family medicine with an emphasis on primary care and programs of disease prevention, health maintenance, and self-care health education.

budget increases and policy program refinement in long-term care for the chronically ill and disabled in nursing homes and care institutions.

improved coordination and cooperation between hospital inpatient programs and social services around community-based prevention and community reentry.

expansion of programs promoting life-style practices contributing to health and environmental protection of water, air, and community habitat.

massive public health education that focuses on personal responsibility

for health maintenance, self-checkups, and periodic physician contact.
control of rising medical cost through voluntary or mandatory hospital
   rate limits, Health Maintenance Organizations, or government guidelines or through a marketplace competitive approach in the private
   health sector.
varied health care manpower available to medically underserved areas
   through prescribed intern and residency rotation programs, a mandatory service period of health personnel in lieu of military service, and
   a strong voluntary medical and allied health corps.
mobilization and creation of national health consumer groups that have
   credibility and power to influence state legislatures and Congress on
   consumer-related health issues.
political consensus and economic trends favorable to passage and launching of a national health program in the mid- or late 1980s.

As social workers in health care interact with other health providers,
legislators on health and welfare committees, and community consumer
groups, these agendas are bound to recur in meetings. Social workers are in
unique positions as they assume the role of front-line staff to clients with
eligibility and service needs, policy committee workers in medical centers,
legislative researchers, program planners, and concerned citizens for high-
quality health care. Social perspectives on health care are crucial for the
development of these priority programs. Certainly, health care social
workers will be asked to take public policy positions that articulate program
recommendations.

We are confident that this volume on social work and health care policy
will be a major resource for social workers in policy and planning tasks.

REFERENCES

Blendon, R. J. 1981. The prospects for state and local governments playing a
   broader role in health care in the 1980s. *American Journal of Public Health* 71:9–14.
Cunningham, R. M., Jr. 1980. Competition and regulation: we need them both.
   Hospitals 51:63–64.
Drake, D. F. 1981. The struggle over health care controls continues. *Hospitals*
   55:159–64.
Enthoven, A. C. September 22, 1977. Memorandum for the Honorable Joseph A.
   Califano, Secretary of Health, Education, and Welfare. Subject: National
   Health Insurance (NHI).
_____ . 1978. Consumer-choice health plan: parts one and two. *New England
   Journal of Medicine* 298:650–58, 709–20.
_____ . 1980. Does anyone want competition? the politics of NHI. In C. M.
   Lindsay, ed., *New directions in public health care: a prescription for the 1980s.* San
   Francisco: Institute for Contemporary Studies.
Lesparre, M. 1980. Stockman sees competition plan as only way to go. *Hospitals*
   54:58–61.
Mechanic, D. 1981. Some dilemmas in health care policy. *Milbank Memorial Fund
   Quarterly* 59:1–15.
Observations on Alain Enthoven's Consumer Choice Health Plan, unpublished
   August 23, 1977 memo, unknown author.

INDEX

THE CONTRIBUTORS

NEIL F. BRACHT, M.A., M.P.H., is Professor and Director of the University of Minnesota, School of Social Work. His professional experience has been as a clinician, health planner and consultant, medical school administrator, and social work educator. Professor Bracht is a consulting editor for *Social Work,* a member of the editorial board of *Social Work in Health Care,* and author of numerous articles. His book *Social Work in Health Care: A Guide to Professional Practice* was published by Haworth Press in 1978.

CLAUDIA J. COULTON, M.S.W., Ph.D., is Assistant Professor at the School of Applied Social Sciences, Case Western Reserve University. She has been in public welfare medical assistance programming and hospital research. Author of several articles, she has also written a monograph, *Social Work Quality Assurance Programs: A Comparative Analysis.* Coulton is presently a task force chairperson for the Society of Hospital Social Work Directors, American Hospital Association.

RONALD W. CONLEY, Ph.D., is Special Assistant to the Deputy Assistant Secretary for Social Services Planning at the Department of Health and Human Services, Washington, D.C. He has worked in federal government and written numerous books and articles on mental retardation, mental illness, and Workers' Compensation, and is an Adjunct Professor affiliated with the University of San Francisco and the University of Maryland.

STEPHEN M. DAVIDSON, Ph.D., is Associate Professor, Kellogg Graduate School of Management, Northwestern University. He was formerly on the faculty of the University of Chicago, School of Social Service Administration, where he taught public policy related to health care. In addition to Medicaid, he has written about emergency services, the utilization of hospital services, national health insurance and the elderly, and other issues. He is the author of a study of the Illinois Medicaid program and is principal investigator of a 13-state study of physician participation in Medicaid.

CHARLENE HARRINGTON, Ph.D., is on the faculty of the University of California, San Francisco, where she works with the Schools of Medicine and Nursing in the Aging Policy Center and Health Policy Center. She is a former director of the Golden Empire Health Systems Agency in Sacramento, California, has served as Deputy Director and Special Assistant to the Director of the California State Department of Health for licensing and certification of health facilities, and has conducted research in medical sociology and health education. She has practiced and taught clinical nursing in the field of public health and has written in the area of health care and medical ideology.

PETER HOOKEY, Ph.D., is Project Director, Association of Concerned Christians for Emerging Social Services (ACCESS), Jenkintown, Pennsylvania, and was formerly Assistant Professor at the School of Social Work, University of Illinois at Urbana-Champaign. He has presented papers on various aspects of social work in primary health care at several international health care conferences. Since 1976 he has concentrated on cross-national study of interprofessional cooperation in primary care settings.

HERBERT H. HYMAN, Ph.D., is Professor of Social and Health Planning, Hunter College of the City University of New York. He has written three books on health planning, health regulations, and health planning methods and has been a consultant to various city, state, and regional health and mental health programs. He is currently developing a model plan for an urban consumer health information center and is on the National Staff College of the National Institute of Mental Health.

ALFRED KATZ, D.S.W., is Professor of Public Health and Social Welfare, University of California, Los Angeles. Long active in the relationship between social work and public health, he has presented numerous papers and written widely in both fields. His primary interest has been in the area of self-help for health care patients. Dr. Katz teaches courses in the School of Public Health, integrating social work and public health, and has made contributions in international health care delivery.

DOMAN LUM, Ph.D., Th.D., is Professor of Social Work, California State University, Sacramento. He has written numerous articles on Health Maintenance Organizations, ethnic minorities, suicide prevention, lay counseling, and religion and mental health. He is also the author of *Responding to Suicidal Crisis* (Eerdmans). Lum teaches social work practice, health care delivery, health policy, and crisis theory and intervention. He has also held positions in alcohol rehabilitation, mental health, corrections, and marriage and family relations.

JOHN H. NOBLE, JR., Ph.D., is Assistant Commissioner for Policy and Research Development, Department of Mental Health and Mental Retardation, Commonwealth of Virginia in Richmond, Virginia. He was former Senior Program Analyst and Special Assistant to the Deputy Assistant Secretary for Planning and Budget, United States Department of Education, Washington, D.C. He has held a similar post with the Department of Health and Human Services and is familiar with major policy related to social services and human development. A member of the editorial board of *Evaluation Quarterly* and *Journal of Social Services Research*, he has written numerous publications in disability and long-term care, vocational rehabilitation, emergency medical services, psychiatric social work and mental health, and related areas. His professional background includes university teaching, social casework services, research and system analysis consultation, and program evaluation.

MILTON I. ROEMER, M.D., M.P.H., is Professor of Public Health at the University of California, Los Angeles. He has held county, state, federal, and international health positions. As a consultant to international agencies, Roemer has studied health care organization in 50 countries and has written 18 books and more than 300 articles on social aspects of medicine. He was the 1977 recipient of the American Public Health Association International Award for excellence in Promoting and Protecting the Health of People.